NEIL ROBINSON

Author: Neil Robinson

Cover design: McKie Associates 01604 497577
Cover photography: Tracey Sherwood
Cover model: Caleb Foster
Editor: Mark Webb

ISBN 1-899820-05-1

Published by Paragon Publishing, F9 Moulton
Park Business Centre, Redhouse Road,
Northampton, NN3 6AQ.

Tel: 01604 497549. Fax: 01604 497762.
Want to buy books about beer on the Internet?
Email: paragon@mcmail.com

© 2000 Paragon Publishing, Rothersthorpe

text © 2000 Neil Robinson

Printed by Interprint, Malta

CONTENTS

INTRODUCTION

My brother, my friends and my colleagues tell me I have an encyclopaedic knowledge of beer. Sometimes they kindly point this out by way of what I trust is admiration; sometimes they wearily mention it when I have unsuccessfully sought to wow them with a piece of hop-encrusted trivia – the original gravity of Pilsner Urquell, the units of bitterness in Orval, or something else in which they have not the slightest interest.

Perhaps these unfortunate and long-suffering souls are merely conspirators in a desperate scheme to shut me up and redirect my outpourings to a wider audience – or indeed to any audience except themselves – but they also tell me I should write a book. As a journalist who spends his days editing thousands of words' worth of copy, I'm surely qualified to write something; since that copy usually revolves around murder, robbery, car-crashes and assorted other instances of general mayhem, however, I had to wonder whether a topic as pleasant as beer was really suitable for my attention.

In the end – after a good few seconds' deep thought – I decided it was. Beer is suitable for the very reason that I *am* a chap whose working hours have bugger all to do with it. I'm not in the licensed trade; I don't possess millions of pounds for the purpose of travelling the globe in search of frothy ones; I'm not sent scores of gratis samples by breweries; I'm unlikely to share a Michelob with the chairman of Anheuser-Busch (thank God). I'm just a bloke who happens to care about the subject; who has only decent pubs, a smattering of superior off-licences and the occasional imaginative supermarket at his disposal; and who manages to snatch the odd weekend break in Belgium. I am, if you like, an average sort looking for an above-average drop; and it's in precisely that role that I might just be of some use.

5

There's no sense in my penning a magnificent treatise on the world's classic beer-styles: that has been done elsewhere by people far better equipped for the task, and I owe much of what I've learned to them. Similarly, there's no merit in my painstakingly detailing all the worthy brews/bars/boozers in any given country: such issues have also been covered by others, and I owe much of what I've learned to them, too. Explaining the brewing process would be a waste of time: I don't make the stuff – I drink it. And I'm not in the habit of reflecting upon a drink's qualities in terms of tarmac, pencil-boxes, railway sleepers, footwear or soil – I've never eaten any of them and thus feel unable make such grand comparisons – so don't expect a feast of tasting notes on the wild side of ludicrous.

What I am most usefully able to do is provide proof of how someone who loves beer and everything associated with it – the pubs, the breweries, the cafés, the company – can seek out its finest and most interesting elements (and sometimes, purely in the course of experimentation, the not-so-fine and the not-so-interesting) with the limited means available. This book, recording 12 months of my humble beer-hunting efforts, will hopefully show that a mildly teeth-grating crawl to the shops every now and then, a modicum of legwork and a modest sense of adventure can liberate anyone from the horrors of a lifetime's devotion to Carling Black Label or Whitbread-brewed Budweiser (the likes of which, I must stress at this early stage, we can disdainfully dismiss here and now).

What they say is true: life *is* too short. I'm now hammering on the door of 30; let's say I contrive to stick around until the grand old age of 75. By my calculations, come the end of my innings I would have supped more than 17,500 different beers if I were to sample a new one every 24 hours for the rest of my days. Given that there are probably in excess of 4,000 breweries in the world, some of which offer but a single product and some of which boast a portfolio of 10 or more, it's mathematically arguable that I might just succeed in knocking the top off every frothy one known to man; but I suspect it's safe to assume that chasing such a dream, honourable though the mission undoubtedly is, would leave even the most determined devotee utterly penniless, pretty damned fat and quite possibly a jabbering wreck.

As in anything, the appreciation of beer is very much a case of doing the best you can. Jetting around in search of the perfect pint (or Krug, pul, bolleke, flute or whatever receptacle happens to fall into your grasp as you clock up the miles) would make for a rather agreeable existence, to say the least; but it is, alas, a pastime sadly beyond the scope of the grain-loving masses. I would dearly like to hop on to a plane to Bavaria every other weekend or trundle to the Ardennes at regular intervals to sip Chimay amid the monastery's ruins; but 99 times out of 100 I have to settle for a Weissbier from Sainsbury's or a wretched drive to a resourceful off-licence, because annoying little things – pesky concerns like work and money – almost invariably hamper my more grandiose strategies. Fair it ain't, but that's how it is.

Do such compromises have to render one's experiences any less rich? Well, the simple admission of a compromise is evidence enough that we're dealing with what could reluctantly be termed second-best. I can't pretend that a Schneiderweisse consumed in your own home is a legitimate match for a Schneiderweisse tasted in the brewery's restaurant; that a Westmalle Tripel which has survived the soul-destroying car-ride from a far-flung shop is as precious as a nine-year-old vintage at the Kulminator café in Antwerp; or even that a pint of Bass dispensed 50 or so miles outside Burton-on-Trent is as palatable as a pint served at the brewery's museum bar. When all is said and done, though, if the epitome is beyond your reach then you might as well grab the chance of the next best thing; and the next best thing is not the easy but heinous option of confining yourself to your favourite brand, your favourite style, your favourite hostelry or even the wares of your own country.

I've been making the extra effort for six or seven years. And it's worth it, as I hope I can demonstrate in the coming months and the following pages.

Finally, if you are genuinely set on widening your range of experience then I recommend you bear in mind

CRATE EXPECTATIONS

I once had a friend and colleague whose laid-back attitude was the substance of legend in our office. A New Zealander, he never planned a thing and was instead content to follow his spur-of-the-moment whims – many of them quite dramatic – and nonchalantly arrive at wherever they took him. When he felt my own approach to life was drifting into the realms of the predictable he was wont to warn: "Never get into a routine, Neil, mate." His haphazard but endearing stance was perhaps best exemplified when he suddenly announced he was quitting the drudgery of the Midlands and buggering off to South America, "maybe to check out a war-zone": he was, needless to say, never heard from again, but that's beside the point.

The point is that he was at least half-right: it doesn't do to fall into too much of a routine – definitely not where beer is concerned, anyway. By this I don't mean the aforementioned trap of eternally restricting yourself to one product or one pub: I mean the trap of being afraid to drink the "wrong" beer at the "wrong" time.

To present the matter at its simplest, it's obvious to even a layman that warming ales are better drunk during winter and refreshing lagers better drunk during summer. Fair enough. But to adhere to this truism with such zeal that not a single ale is sipped during summer or a single lager knocked back during winter is pure folly. If you're tempted by a bottle of Pils then you should have one, even if it's snowing and -10°C outside; and if you feel like polishing off a glass of barley wine then you should do so, even if you're smothered in Factor 15 and chomping on a choc-ice. It's ultimately worth remembering that whatever you fancy at any given juncture, however incongruous, is liable to taste considerably better than whatever you might otherwise force yourself to suffer in the spirit of perceived correctness.

There is also the question of availability, of course. Seeking to follow the beer calendar – with its Maibock, saison, Oktoberfestbier, Christmas ale etcetera – indicates noble dedication, but it also requires enormous helpings of luck. Seasonal specialities don't normally fall off the shelves of the average store, and the chances are you might struggle to lay your hands on them – in which case an approximation, if not something entirely different, will have to do the trick. There's no disgrace in straying from the accepted norm, particularly if circumstances leave you with little choice.

Taking the above into account, it's difficult to envisage how the year might shape up. I can't swear that any month's drinking will be dominated by an "appropriate" style; nor can I state with conviction that beer A, B or C will be off the menu during month X, Y or Z. Maybe that's all for the best, though: no-one wants a life utterly devoid of surprises. On the other hand, it's not beyond the bounds of realism to risk some general predictions about the next few months.

One thing I can forecast with reasonable confidence is that January will be lousy. Nothing in the beer calendar dictates this: it's simply that January, with all its inherent post-Yuletide malaise and financial woes, isn't greatly renowned for lending itself to the pursuit of anything pleasurable. There was a marvellous exception to the rule in '95, when I survived on a fabulous selection of leftover Chrimbo fare (most of it German); but no such haul was to be found at the tail-end of last year, so the start of this campaign threatens to be a trifle grim.

For reasons seemingly almost too ridiculous to relate, February could see a mad rush on ales. Since I don't own a fridge specifically set aside for the storage of top-fermented brews, my pantry has to act as a cellar; and during November, December, January and February the temperature therein is around 13°C, the mark ideal for storing such beers. Come March (and with it the milder weather) I have to fall back on the wretched and profoundly irritating procedure of slapping an ale in the fridge 20 minutes or so prior to serving it – hence my annual bid to make the most of the final weeks of winter. People who moan about cold snaps obviously aren't beer buffs.

It will be very much a mixed-bag affair thereafter, with two conceivable highlights in the opening third of the year:

(1) The year's inaugural jaunt to Belgium should have been enjoyed by the end of March at the latest. My travelling companion for such an excursion is traditionally either my Bro' or my dear mucker and erstwhile workmate Eugene; the latter, who must take the credit for introducing me not to the delights of Belgium's beers but to the delights of the nation itself, will soon be off to Hong Kong for a lengthy spell and will no doubt be keen to avail himself of some classics before departing for a land where Heineken is deemed dangerously exotic.

(2) My Bro' expects to make a rare trip to blighty in March or April. He currently works in New Zealand (no sightings of my aforementioned mate, unfortunately) but is due to be shifted to Singapore – a cruel fate for a man whose appreciation of the hop has risen by several hundred per cent in the past couple of years. It's my most fervent wish that his paymaster, Rolls-Royce, accords him a posting in Antwerp, but he assures me – most glumly – that this is less than likely.

Treks abroad or get-togethers with my Bro' are sheer bliss for me, incidentally, for they represent the only contexts in which I will allow myself to exceed my self-imposed weekly intake limit. Exactly what that limit is I'm not prepared to reveal; but rest assured that it habitually demands Vulcan-like willpower and those who do know it are astonished by its miserly lowness. Theories as to why I abide by it include that I want to stay fit (in days of teenage abandon – i.e. much Marston's Owd Rodger – I was pathetically out of condition), that I am a Scrooge (not so) and that I am mad/sad (debatable). Now I have a new and supremely understandable reason for not going OTT: I won't have to write so much.

Save for the happy news that Henny, my Kölsch-loving German uncle, is popping across the water for a weekend in May

– a situation which should ensure record British sales of Früh – what happens after April is, to be frank, anyone's guess; besides, my New Zealand friend, wherever he is, would bristle at the thought of my planning so far ahead. In the absence of certainties, then, I can only hope for sporadic voyages to mainland Europe, for sufficient reliability from my MG to facilitate roof-down journeys to the likes of the Falkland Arms in Great Tew, Oxfordshire, and for as many outstanding frothy ones as possible. Surely that's not too much to ask?

Oh, sorry about the "Crate expectations" line, by the way. The curse of a career in journalism, I'm afraid.

THE BEERS TO BEAT

Even where excellence is concerned, there are levels above levels. This is widely recognized in almost every area of life, from the Rolex Daytona to the Lotus Elise to Michael Jordan. Yet the cold facts strongly suggest that the levels of excellence in the beer world are escaping too many people's notice.

My Bro' was once engaged in a round of golf with three Rolls-Royce colleagues when the talk turned to the subject of drink and subsequently to that oft-asked *Desert Island Casks* question: what would be the one beer you would take with you if you faced splendid isolation on some lonely island? My Bro', fresh from his first-ever visit to Antwerp's Kulminator café, nominated 1991 Abbaye des Rocs; all three of his playing partners, meanwhile, chose Boddington's Bitter – the canned variety, no less. What a depressing indictment: all the beers in the world from which to choose, and three out of four people chose something out of a bloody tin.

There are a handful of brews by which I like to measure all-comers – and canned Boddington's, you'll be less than stunned to learn, is not among that select crop. It's intriguing to kick off the year with a top 10 in mind and then see which have fallen from grace and which ex-pretenders have superseded them 365 days down the line. The members of this elite chop and change more often than might be presumed, but here – in no order whatsoever – is how they stand now:

Abbaye des Rocs	Marston's Pedigree
De Kluis Benedict	Pilsner Urquell
Orval	De Kluis Hoegaarden Wit
Schneiderweisse	Timothy Taylor Landlord
Anchor Our Special Ale	Westmalle Tripel

The most interesting inclusions are Abbaye des Rocs, De Kluis Benedict and Anchor Our Special Ale, all of which earn a slot on the roll of honour not only because of their sheer magnificence but because of their rarity. For three years I could only find Abbaye des Rocs at Kulminator; indeed, my initial joy at locating it in a Leicester off-licence in June '96 was perversely but quickly dulled by the realization that the thrill of its scarcity had been lost. Production of De Kluis Benedict, for reasons I cannot imagine in my most gruesome nightmares, was discontinued in the early '90s, so Kulminator, whose cellar holds bottles of various vintages, is again the only source I know. Anchor Our Special Ale is an exquisite Christmas beer which is becoming increasingly tough to track down in Britain.

The other interesting entry is Westmalle Tripel, which had long lingered on the fringes of the top 10 until two momentous incidents in Belgium elevated it to the loftiest echelon. First my Bro' and I sipped some within sight of the Westmalle monastery itself; and then Dirk van Dijk, Kulminator's infamous owner and a man not renowned (unfairly, I say) for his gregarious nature, shared with us one of his six remaining nine-year-old bottles in a show of kindness which amazes us to this very day. Ample proof that memories of the events surrounding a drink can make it taste even better in years to come. (Maybe the golfers who so dismayed my Bro' had many fond recollections of canned Boddington's. Somehow I doubt it.)

The top-tenners tipped to lose their places are Pilsner Urquell and Hoegaarden: each has trundled downhill of late, with spiralling commercialization to blame in both sorry instances. Snapping at their heels are: from Belgium, Chimay White, Rochefort 10°, Westvleteren Dubbel and Van Eecke Watou's Witbier; from Britain, Burton Bridge Summer Ale and Samuel Smith's Old Brewery Bitter; from the Czech Republic, Budweiser Budvar; from the US, Anchor

Steam Beer; from Germany, Richmodis Kölsch, Andechs Doppelbock, St Georgen Bräu Kellerbier and Schlenkerla Rauchbier; and several others.

All of the above are virtually guaranteed to pass my lips in the next 52 weeks, so there's no value in wasting time by describing them here. For the purposes of grading their and others' eligibility to the top 10 when they do crop up, however, it's necessary to operate some form of scoring system – so here it is:

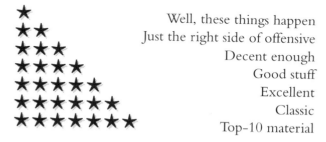

★	Well, these things happen
★★	Just the right side of offensive
★★★	Decent enough
★★★★	Good stuff
★★★★★	Excellent
★★★★★★	Classic
★★★★★★★	Top-10 material

If you want to get an instant idea of the difference between a "Well, these things happen" beer and a top-10 beer then I suggest you accord yourself a can of Skol and a bottle of Orval. And anyone who thinks the Skol is the top-10 beer is politely requested to stop reading now.

January 6

I told you January would be lousy. Only a recovering alcoholic would consider five bone-dry days an encouraging start to the year. I blame Christmas – and possibly the fact that I've just spent nearly £2,000 on a new computer, an act of outrageous lavishness which has left my wallet disturbingly light. Still, though I am resigned to a month of utter misery, I can't let myself become wholly abstinent.

Which brings us to the Burton Bridge, in my opinion both the finest pub and the finest brewery in Britain's brewing capital – and therefore an expedient venue for the commencement of my quest. I hesitate to use the phrase "dying breed", but there aren't many boozers like this left: a thoroughly unpretentious establishment where you can enjoy first-rate beer and actually hear yourself speak. During last month's alleged festivities one of the national newspaper reporters who deals with the press agency for which I work arrived at the office to take me to lunch, making it abundantly clear that his expense account was near-boundless and giving me the choice of eatery: I had no qualms about picking the Bridge, and my host was happy to admit that the welcoming atmosphere and the quality of the ale more than compensated for the pain of only being able to claim £5 in exes for a meal for two (bacon, egg, pie, chips and similarly honest fare).

My companion for tonight's visit was Guillo, another ex-colleague. We generally see each other but once a week – he's a married man, so his time is precious – and inevitably end up having a couple of frothy ones and filling our faces, a pastime of which no-one should be remotely ashamed. Guillo is no beer-hunter, but he admires a good British ale and has a soft spot for Staropramen, the increasingly popular Prague-brewed lager imported by Bass.

Of course, no-one in his or her right mind would shun the Bridge's extensive and uniformly impressive range of ales in favour of a lager; yet, to my acute embarrassment, I was once forced to do so some years ago – although the fault was not mine but that of the *Daily Star*. At the time the paper was sending a features writer the length and breadth of the country to investigate pubs for what turned out to be a rather half-hearted piece on the "best" in the land; and a hack from a local agency was required to meet her in every town/city she surveyed, so allowing her to compile details of how members of both sexes rated each hostelry.

I arranged to see her in the Bridge and was patiently nursing a half when she walked in and promptly took a dislike to the place, bizarrely branding it, on the strength of a man who was quietly reading his *Daily Telegraph*, "a Tories' pub"; then she produced a form which required us to fill in such monumentally futile minutiae as the price of a glass of wine, the price of a pint of lager and so on. Thus was I compelled to approach the bar in one of the premier real-ale pubs in the country and, toes curling with humiliation, ask for a half of UK-brewed Löwenbräu and a white wine. The landlord, to his credit, remained unmoved, but I was less than chuffed: after all, if the *Daily Star* is going to buy you a drink in the Bridge then it might as well be a proper one.

Thereafter the lady from the *Star* insisted we concentrate on "a different kind" of watering hole – i.e. anywhere with karaoke machines, freezing beer and a teeming multitude of kids and/or yobbos. Predictably enough, there was a slight disparity when it eventually came to totting up our respective marks for the evening's contenders: I gave the Bridge 20 out of 20 and everywhere else a single-figure score, while she accorded the Bridge next to nothing and everywhere else something in the high teens. The Bridge, needless to say, did not come to grace the pages of the *Star*.

No lager tonight, anyway. During the winter months it is advisable to make the most of the chocolatey **Burton Bridge Top Dog Stout**, which is only offered during the cold season. It might not sit snugly with the *Daily Star*, but it's a terrific match for a chat and a bag of pork scratchings on a bone-chilling January night.

A belated Happy New Year.

***

Burton Bridge Top Dog Stout (5 per cent ABV): ★★★★★

***

January 11

Another barren five days, with even my birthday – January 7 – failing to ease the drought. There was a time – perhaps eight or nine years ago – when I would have celebrated my birthday by getting rather hammered, probably on Pedigree or (God forbid) Owd Rodger; but those carefree days, alas, are gone.

Years ago I sought to begin a fresh tradition by marking the 7th with a bottle of the now-dead Samichlaus, from Switzerland's Hürlimann brewery. At somewhere between 14 and 15 per cent ABV, it was widely acknowledged as the world's strongest bottom-fermented beer (much to the chagrin of EKU, of Kulmbach, Germany, whose EKU 28 previously held that dubious distinction). Since it was brewed on just a single day each year – St Nicholas' Day – I thought it would make a perfect product to be *consumed* on just a single day each year. I was more than a little alarmed, however, to discover that after but one bottle I was, shall we say, a trifle the worse for wear: I know this to be true, for immediately after reverentially sipping a mere 275ml worth I found an episode of *Happy Days* absolutely hilarious – a hugely disturbing state of affairs.

Nowadays, then, January 7 has as much chance of being enhanced with a frothy one as any other date – which on current form is practically no chance, it seems. Still, though I am either willing or constrained to ignore it, someone wouldn't let it pass: sports editor NG, who knows his British beers and is also a passionate devotee of Budweiser Budvar, returned from the supermarket and plonked on to my desk a **Sainsbury's Hefe Weissbier** and a Sainsbury's Trappist Ale – most kind.

The latter will need a while to settle after being brutally bounced around the car during the ride home, but I polished off the Weissbier tonight while watching – such is my twisted sense of the appropriate – *Till Death Us Do Part*. There's no doubt that Alf Garnett liked a drink – during this episode he tried to persuade his two-day-old grandson to suckle on a hip-flask, opining that "he's got to get a taste for it some time" – but what he would have made of a British supermarket which sells German beer I don't know; and what he would have had to say about a British supermarket which actually requests a German brewery to produce something for its shelves doesn't bear thinking about. "Gawd, bloody marvellous, innit? Now they're bloody *asking* the Krauts to make the bloody stuff!"

Alf's view notwithstanding, Sainsbury's Hefe Weissbier is extremely pleasant. It definitely looks the part – turbid, orangey, sparkling and (a bit like Alf himself) topped with a huge, dense head; and it has all the fruity acidity and spiciness of the style. And, although very much a summer beer, it hits the bullseye on a wintry night – especially if served at a temperature of somewhere between 10°C and 13°C (it is an ale, after all, and the pantry is still doing an admirable job).

The package is spoiled a tad solely by the secrecy shrouding the brewer. The label on the front of the bottle provides only the ultra-vague disclosure that the beer is "brewed in Bavaria", while the one on the rear is daring enough to go further and mention the town of Hof. Where's the harm in going the whole hog? Maybe the brewery is worried about being stormed by Teutonic Alf Garnetts expressing their fury at energy being wasted on a beer for Englanders.

Incidentally, one thing I find essential to the enjoyment of any Weissbier – any beer at all, really – is the correct glass. Fortunately – or unfortunately where bills for kitchen cupboards are concerned – I own 20-odd Weissbier glasses among a collection of several hundred vessels from around the globe (I warned you that I have been criticized as mad/sad; but remember that in countries like Belgium and Germany every beer boasts its own glass). I used to have a colleague who had grown fond of Weissbier after encountering it in German bars during what I imagine were wholly abysmal holidays in the racier parts of Spain, and whenever he asked me what he should use at home for his favourite, Schneiderweisse, I would urge him either to invest in a suitable glass or employ a sizeable flower-vase; but somehow I doubt that he ever acted upon this honourable advice.

Sainsbury's Hefe Weissbier (4.9 per cent ABV): ★★★★

January 12

Come in, **Pilsner Urquell**, your time is up.

How can the beer which has spawned more imitators than any other in history be condemned? I don't know, to be honest; but there is no denying that Pilsner Urquell isn't quite what it was. The fact that 95 per cent of its pretenders still can't hold a candle to it is not necessarily germane to the argument: the truth remains that it is no longer the undisputed king of the style which so cheekily adopted its name.

The term Pilsner – a.k.a. Pilsener or Pils – would ideally apply uniquely to beers brewed in the Czech Republic town of Pilsen and not to any old loose and often virtually criminal interpretation of the original. Even Marston's once trotted out a fizzy golden fluid and branded it a Pilsner, which is nothing less than terrifying. But Pils has become the watchword for a lager in need of a marketing boost, and some of the products possessing the reprehensible gall to advertize themselves as such are, to be blunt, barely fit to subtract an L and add another S.

This is not to suggest for a second that Pilsner Urquell (literally, "the original Pilsner") is anything less than excellent – by its very nature it must rank as a classic – but I'm not convinced that it is as genuinely outstanding or as memorably complex as it was (certainly not by the time it has arrived in blighty, anyhow). Since I can't envisage a faith-restoring trip to Eastern Europe in the near future, I will have to accept that the problem exists and idly speculate that it can be traced to (1) the brewery's gradual replacement of its wooden fermentation and maturation tanks with steel versions and (2) the apparently inexorable move from 660ml to 330ml bottles (I recall Budweiser Budvar was adversely affected, albeit minutely, by a similar change).

I half-suspect that the bottle I had tonight was a bit too cold (my fridge is sometimes prone to wild mood-swings), which hardly helped its cause, but in my heart of hearts I must admit that on this day, January 12, Pilsner Urquell dropped out of the top 10. It could return within weeks, such is the outlandishly subjective way of things, but at present – sob – I can't see that happening. Tragic.

It can take consolation from the fact that it still has the measure of the hoppy **Staropramen**, which is to Prague what Urquell is to Pilsen. Staropramen is a quality beer, with a striking dry/bitter finish, yet it can't help but reveal its comparative lack of panache when sampled back-to-back with Urquell.

However, it is surely significant that, with the might of Bass at its rear, Staropramen already seems to have achieved

in Britain wider repute than Urquell, a beer which, even allowing for its recent slip, can stake a greater claim to meriting shelf-space at every supermarket in the country.
I am depressed now.

Pilsner Urquell
(4.4 per cent ABV): ★★★★★★

Staropramen
(5 per cent ABV): ★★★★

January 16

At the risk of being a hypocrite who solemnly preaches against the perils of favouring one pub and then proceeds to commit the very same sin, back to the Burton Bridge tonight. However, I've sat through enough court cases (on the Press bench rather than in the dock, I hasten to add) to be able to put forward some points in mitigation: (1) I didn't want to disappoint Eugene, who expects a good frothy one when he has braved the mayhem of the drive from Manchester; (2) tonight I had a different beer. So there.

Having treated his imagination to a thorough work-out with a spell on the *Sunday Sport*, Euge is intent on seeking new horizons (excuse me if I avoid the phrase "making a clean breast of things") and come March is bound for Hong Kong to do some freelancing. He estimates this will deprive us of each other's wonderful company for the better part of a year, so it is now crucial that we two ardent beer-hunters embark on an expedition to Belgium: the delay otherwise would be too cruel.

We formulated an early set of plans over a couple of pints of **Burton Bridge Bitter.** Eugene fancies Ghent, whereas my vote goes to Antwerp – particularly since I yesterday received a birthday card from Kulminator supremo Dirk, the basic gist of which was: "Wishing you a happy one – now come back and drink more beer."

After the Bridge we picked up some Singapore chow mein from Master Leong, proprietor of my local Chinese takeaway, spiritual guru and all-round source of wisdom. Last year, upon learning he had been troubled by stomach pains, I took him a bottle of Küppers Kölsch, having read that the sublimely delicate family of beers from Köln (Cologne) has a strange knack of settling the digestive system: it did the trick, although ever since he has been reminding me to secure him an entire crate.

A laudably cosmopolitan night: Bridge Bitter (robust, hoppy, malty and fruity), Singapore chow mein (bloody hot) and then, in a bid to get us into the mood for our proposed break, a 750ml corked bottle of **Lefèbvre Happy Beerday.** I spotted this at the excellent Bottle Store, Leicester, back in November and had been saving it for a special occasion. Having ruled my birthday not sufficiently special – and determined not to fall prey to the lamentable marketing ploy behind that ridiculous name – I decided that tonight, despite not being extraordinary in any way, was probably as agreeable a time as any; and I was right, because the beer's not very special either.

Lefèbvre, of Quenast, near Brussels, produces some very good ales, including the Floreffe range of abbey beers and Student, a ludicrously quaffable witbier; but it also has a nasty habit of selling beers under a variety of names, and now I'm wondering whether Happy Beerday might have crossed my path in some other guise. It matters not: it is pretty plain by Lefèbvre standards, and I have already forgotten about it. I can offer praise only for the restraint exhibited in not calling it "*Hoppy* Beerday", which would have been truly insufferable.

England 1, Belgium 0. Not a result we shall see too often in the course of the year, methinks.

**Burton Bridge Bridge Bitter
(4.2 per cent ABV):** ★★★★★
**Lefèbvre Happy Beerday
(6.5 per cent ABV):** ★★★

January 18

Pool night. *The Hustler* is my favourite film and my favourite book, and each weekend, on table 15 at the Spot-On Snooker Club, my cue-carrying partner Gurminder and I stage our own humble recreation of Fast Eddie Felson versus Minnesota Fats. As befits an old-fashioned type whose ancient beliefs include that bottled beer benefits from being poured into a glass, I play a totally outmoded game: straight pool, the beautiful and intelligent name-a-pocket-and-a-ball variant practised by Eddie and Fats back in the '60s but nowadays uncommon even in America. If eight-ball is to pool what Budweiser is to beer then straight pool is the Orval of the green baize: a supreme challenge ignored by the masses looking for something far less taxing.

Eddie had his JTS Brown bourbon and Fats his "Dutch beer" (as the book mysteriously calls it) and his Tampan whiskey, but I'm not tempted to loosen my cuing arm with anything from the shelves of the Spot-On – whose role, let's face it, is to supply its members not with artisan ales but with reliable tables. Gurminder, whose interest in quality beers falls somewhere between next-to-nowt and the non-existent, consumes a massively unappealing liquid which I can only term Cold & Tasteless; this is often subsequently blamed for his defeat, and rightly so – anyone who sups that rubbish deserves to lose.

Still, when I arrived home tonight the pantry was bare and the fridge held only a beer which itself might be thought of by many as C&T: the ubiquitous **Beck's Bier**.

It is easy to make damning assumptions about Beck's, more so since it became one of those drinks invariably clasped in the hands of bottle-swigging club-goers. But it doesn't deserve to be lumped in with the pitiful likes of Budweiser and the wretched proliferation of "alcopops". Marketing forces have merely dictated that a decent beer has become popular among people who know nothing about the subject; Hoegaarden is going the same way (although the day I see someone swigging from a bottle of Hoegaarden is the day I emigrate).

Beck's, from Bremen, is a devil to classify. At a push it could be called a Pils, but it is arguably too light and clean-tasting to qualify on the strictest grounds. The brewery doesn't seem to care, anyway: Beck's Bier is the minimalist tag it has bestowed upon its product, and when that product sells as handsomely as Beck's there is no point in risking narrowing its customer base with superfluous categorization.

Believe it or not, Beck's played a curious but substantial part in persuading me to explore the realms of beer. In the late '80s and very early '90s I would often join my cohorts for a post-work pint at the Alexandra Hotel, a brilliantly earnest boozer not too far from our Derby office. NG, Guillo and our then-MD would drink Bateman's XB, while yours truly – an aimless soul back then – would do battle with the evils of the Beck's pump, even though the landlord, Mark, made no secret of the fact that he sold draught Beck's only because he was required to do so and thus made no effort whatsoever to keep it in a palatable condition.

His dire warnings ultimately persuaded me to concentrate on his dazzling array of real ales and then even dabble in a few bottled imports; and the rest, as they say, is history. Beck's – and Mark – I salute you.

Beck's Bier
(5 per cent ABV):   ★★★

January 27

Marketing men – don't you just love 'em? After an atrocious week consisting of 100 per cent work and zero per cent beer – sorry to harp on about it, but I did say January was going to be lousy – my wish finally to relax with a warming ale has been sabotaged by an outright absurdity which some pudding-head, quite incredibly, must have classed as a tremendous idea.

I have suffered a double-whammy of woe, in fact, the first blow coming when I settled down with an **Eisbrau Czech Traditional Beer** in readiness for an FA Cup match. I had a bottle of the same a couple of years ago and wasn't enormously moved by the experience; I bought it this time simply because nothing else in the disappointing range at our local branch of Morrisons struck me as beyond the hopelessly run-of-the-mill.

Great Label Notes of our Time, N° 1: "Eisbrau is a full-bodied lager beer that is brewed to an original Czech recipe. It is a smooth and aromatic beer with a distinctive hop character." Well, now the drinker knows exactly what to think – ta very much. But elsewhere on the bottle is an even more stunning bit of text: "Brewed and bottled by Pilsner Urquell."

Pardon my conspiracy theories, but I find myself drawing all sorts of terrible conclusions from this snippet of information. Is PU being slowly wound down to accommodate the production of an inferior stablemate? Is Michael Jackson's gloomy prediction of low-scale output of a

"Pilsner Urquell Classic" a step nearer? Is Eisbrau designed to make a declining PU look good? This is all most unnerving.

As if that should not be enough grimness for anyone, this most rotten of weeks had one more disaster up its sleeve – which brings me back to those aforementioned marketing men. Remember the **Sainsbury's Trappist Ale** NG bought me for my birthday? Great Label Notes of our Time, N° 2: "Sainsbury's Trappist Ale contains live yeast and will improve with age. If left to stand these natural yeasts will form a deposit. This is not harmful and if poured into the glass will improve the flavour." Translation: "We thought this beer would look the part on the shelf if we sold it in a stupid stone-effect bottle. That means, of course, that you won't be able to see the sediment during pouring and will dump it into your drink whether you want to or not. But that's just bad luck, basically."

Now, I know some people like to pour the sediment when they have a Trappist beer. I don't agree with them – and anyone who pours the sediment of an Orval, as far as I'm concerned, is committing sacrilege – but that's their prerogative. I tell you this, however: if a member of staff in a Belgian café casually flung the yeast into a customer's ale there would be trouble. And no prizes for guessing that, in spite of my gallant endeavours, I was left with the cloudiest glass of Trappist beer I've ever seen. Crazy.

At least this Sainsbury's import, unlike its shy Weissbier cousin, divulges its source: Koningshoeven, of Schaapskooi, Holland. This is no surprise: if Chimay is the most famous of the six Trappist monastery breweries then Koningshoeven – the only one outside Belgium – is without doubt the most commercial, selling its wares under myriad names and in various mildly-adjusted forms. It's a shame I didn't have a La Trappe Tripel on hand, because I'd wager there wouldn't be a heap of difference between it and the Sainsbury's version – which, despite undergoing a sediment divebombing, displayed all the honeyed characteristics of a Koningshoeven tripel.

As for that daft bottle, it has now found its true vocation: I have stuck a candle in it.

Eisbrau Czech Traditional Beer (4.9 per cent ABV): ★★★
Sainsbury's Trappist Ale (8 per cent ABV): ★★★★

January 31

First I predicted it, then I suspected it, then I reiterated it, and now I know it: January – a lousy, lousy month. And there could have been no more horribly apt climax than the events of this evening.

After work I set off for Leicester, hell-bent on surviving the rigours of the rush-hour on the M1 so I could carry out the year's inaugural Bottle Store raid. And what I did I find when I arrived? Nowhere to park; absolutely nowhere at all. I toured the block for 15 molar-mashing minutes before a fit of pique and a splitting headache – yes, sod all beer, yet still I get a headache – spurred me to cut my losses, preserve my sanity and drive home.

My fridge – which would have been jam-packed with goodies, as would the pantry, had all gone according to plan – contained a single bottle of **Pilsner Urquell.** I drank it, hoping against hope that past glories would be rediscovered and this bleakest of months could finish on an optimistic note; but, as I feared, it remained off-key. Ho-hum.

Must do better. Roll on February.

Pilsner Urquell: see January 12

February 1

After a day's brooding in the office, much of it spent trying to work out when I might have the time to zip back to Leicester in the hope of better luck parking-wise, I fell victim to sheer desperation on the journey home and called at the Wine Rack to avail myself of what I expected to be a somewhat forlorn selection. As it turned out, I was moderately pleased to discover a range including Eder's, a fine Altbier from Germany; the ever-dependable Budweiser Budvar; St Magnus Heller Bock, from Bavaria; Pete's Wicked Bohemian Pilsner, from the US; and the now-omnipresent **De Kluis Hoegaarden Wit** – better known simply as Hoegaarden.

The rollercoaster story of Hoegaarden is almost legendary – if the saga had unfurled in America someone would surely have made a monumentally serious TV movie about it – but there is no harm in whipping through it again.

Once upon a time there were scores of Belgian breweries producing quenching, cloudy "white beers", but by the 1950s – thanks in no small part to the inevitable onslaught of Pils – witbier had vanished from the scene; in 1966, however, milkman Pierre Celis reopened a small brewery in Hoegaarden, Brabant, and relaunched the style which his moaning mates said they were missing.

Pierre called his beer Oud Hoegaards, and it proved such an incredible success that it spawned imitators across the land: witbier was reborn on a grand scale. But potential disaster struck in 1985 with a fire at the brewery, and our hero was forced to seek backing from the gargantuan Interbrew group; and to this day the giant hand of Interbrew controls the De Kluis brewery, because Pierre eventually upped sticks and moved to Texas, where he created the Hoegaarden-style Celis White and, one trusts, lived happily ever after.

29

Back in the early '90s, when I first tried it, I had already read that Hoegaarden was not quite the beer it had once been; indeed, I had read that none of the De Kluis products could quite match its former self. This is difficult to prove if you've never tasted the previous incarnation, so I set about tracking down some evidence to support the claim.

At Kulminator I once ordered a 1979 bottle of Oud Hoegaards. It was bloody awful. I should never have assumed that a witbier could keep for more than one-and-a-half decades without its character suffering a radical, lip-puckering change. As if to punish me for my foolishness, immediately afterwards my Bro' and I were required to run through the streets of Antwerp to catch the last train back to Bruges – and this in the wake of not only a host of frothy ones but a meal of tornados hofmeester, a steak smeared in lashings of coronary-inducing butter. Silly.

On the other hand, when Dirk recommend I try De Kluis Diesters, the forerunner to the current Verboden Vrucht (Forbidden Fruit), I detected a terrific herbal tang which its contemporary sadly lacks. And then there is De Kluis Benedict, very possibly one of the three most exquisite beers it has ever been my honour to encounter: production was discontinued in the early '90s, a decision nothing short of heartbreaking, and now it is a case of "while stocks last" at specialist establishments.

On the strength of these past glories, then, I'm able to accept that the Hoegaarden of the early '90s was a lesser beast than the Hoegaarden of the early '80s. Moreover, I would go so far as to suggest that the Hoegaarden of the mid-'90s is a lesser beast again – particularly if the drinker heeds the moronic labelling on the UK market's 330ml bottles (the smaller, non-export-market bottles have always struck me as superior), which, I noticed tonight, scandalously advocates serving Hoegaarden at a teeth-chattering 4°C. Despite all of this, I can't pretend that Hoegaarden is not without vestiges of excellence; but its relegation from the top 10 has been sealed.

Significantly, the worst Hoegaarden I've ever come across was draught-dispensed at – you guessed it – Hoegaarden. My Bro' and I made a pilgrimage to the source and, after much piddling around and cursing of inadequate signposting, found De Kluis (the Cloister) and its adjoining Kouterhof restaurant in a quiet cobbled street; we first seized the opportunity to partake of Hougaerdse Das – a new addition to the line-up and so shockingly cold as to be nearly tasteless – and then came the Hoegaarden itself and the perceived privilege of sampling a respected beers on its home turf. Suffice it to say that had the barman emptied a bucket of ice into the tumbler it would have made precious little difference.

To add insult to injury, as we left the village we passed the most ugly, monolithic factory I have ever seen. The name on its side: Hoegaarden. That's progress for you.

De Kluis Hoegaarden Wit
(5 per cent ABV): ★★★★★

February 2

Tonight's European match-up: Germany versus the Czech Republic. From Großostheim, representing top-fermented brews, **Eder's Alt;** and from Budweis, representing the lager camp, **Budweiser Budvar**. A strange contest, granted, but there you go: such are my whims.

Budvar definitely has fame on its side, but the reasons for this are gut-wrenching. All credit to American brewer Adolphus Busch for being inspired by what he saw and sampled in the town of Budweis when he toured Europe in the late 19th century; but shame on his company for everything it has done since. Mention the name Budweiser to 100 people and 95 of them will think of the self-proclaimed "King of Beers", an irredeemably vile substance which is to beer what McDonald's is to haute cuisine; the remainder, meanwhile, will think of the exceptional Budvar,

31

whose brewers went into business 20 years too late to safeguard exclusive rights to the name which the shrewd Mr Busch had already had protected.

The phrase "class in a glass" is crass and over-used, yet Budweiser Budvar unquestionably merits such unavoidably limp epithets. Everything about is is beautiful: its pale golden colour; its fruity, hoppy nose; the bitter-sweet balance of its finish. It is up there with the greats and deserves to be a thousand times more popular than its fourth-rate namesake.

Even in the long shadow of such awesome competition, though, Eder's is by no means completely eclipsed: although not among the most renowned members of the Altbier fraternity, it is a good example of the malty, copper-coloured "old beer" style which dominates Düsseldorf and the surrounding area. I wish I had been more of a fan when I last visited the city, as I would have gleefully popped into the likes of Zum Uerige, the brewery-tavern responsible for the classic Altbier; alas, at the time I was, by my reckoning, six years old.

I must return to Budweiser for a moment, for I have an upsetting confession to make. Back in the bad old days, when I knew not what I was doing, Guillo and I would allow ourselves to be ensnared in that lunatic celebration of all thangs American, the Superbowl; and to help us soak up hours of helmet-hammering tedium we would assemble hefty quantities of burgers, hot-dogs, Kettle Chips and (oh dear) Anheuser-Busch Budweiser – and I would drink it, too. I can only beg forgiveness for my past sins.

Eder's Alt (5 per cent ABV):	★★★★
Budweiser Budvar (5 per cent ABV):	★★★★★★

February 3

The tale of my own formative beer-years reads like a Marston's inventory, as does many a Burtonian's. **Marston's Pedigree** was always regarded as *the* ale when I was a lad. Even at school – during the very last years, I might add, lest I should be accused of underage boozing – guys who didn't drink Pedi were contemptuously dismissed as "poofs". For reasons everyone somehow understood but no-one could adequately explain, even to choose Draught Bass or Ind Coope DBA did not earn the colossal kudos afforded by an undying affinity for Marston's revered flagship. Gloating *Burton Mail* reports of some hapless stranger coming to town and ending up before the beak after downing a few Pedis and making a drunken idiot of himself would leave us in hysterics, particularly if the poor soul's solicitor heaped indignity upon him by proffering a defence along the lines of: "Your worships, he simply wasn't used to the beer."

I can't quite remember why, but after a year or so of Pedigree I graduated to Owd Rodger, its barley wine stablemate. My local, the Bridge Inn (birthplace of my Dad, no less), served both from the barrel; it still does, too, and even now I've never found a better pint of either. I figured that Owd Rodger, at 7.6 per cent ABV, was something to be consumed by the half; but I still endured some vicious mornings-after – one of which, I vaguely recall, followed a grievous late session the night before I received a batch of exam results (okay, so I *was* an underage drinker).

Then came the year of Low C, the period during which I metamorphosed from a sluggish 13-and-a-half stones into an altogether more streamlined 10 stones. My devotion to the cause did the trick, and the end unequivocally justified the means; but, looking back, I can state without hesitation that I wouldn't want to spend another 12 months majoring in frosty bottles of Marston's low-calorie ale.

Now the wheel has turned full-circle: I'm back with Pedigree. Marston's number-one son has travelled far and wide since my school days, though, and standards range from the phenomenal to the frightful. Thankfully, in Burton and its environs the phenomenal can still be found. A high-quality pint of Pedi will have a hint of sulphur in the nose – a Burton trademark – a trace of apple in the palate and a finish of vast complexity. Tonight's, tasted at the lovely Royal Oak in Abbots Bromley, around a dozen miles from the brewery itself, did not disappoint.

I could be accused of bias, but there can be no disputing it: Pedigree is a classic. It's the beer which makes me proud to be a Burtonian. It's the only thing my far-flung Bro' likes about Britain. It's top-10 material. No arguments.

**Marston's Pedigree
(4.5 per cent ABV):** ★★★★★★★

February 5

In spite of yesterday's fulsome praise, Marston's is not beyond reproach. It is hard to fault its beers, but the manner in which it is wrecking some of its properties is almost indefensible.

Tonight Guillo and I decided the venue for our weekly face-filling exercise would be the picturesque Horseshoe Inn in Tatenhill, a village barely three miles from the outskirts of Burton. When last we saw it the Horseshoe was a congenial pub with space discreetly set aside for dining. Now 80 per cent of it has the appearance of one of those sickeningly homogeneous Harvester restaurants – all paper napkins, dried flowers and horse-brasses. The staff wear uniforms. The locals huddle in what's left of the bar. The **Marston's Pedigree** is too cold. Even if the food is probably flawless, the pub itself has been robbed of its soul and ruined. We necked a pint apiece and left.

Hurrah, then, for the Royal Oak, which, with noshing time running short, instantly sprang to mind. There is perhaps just as much room for those who fancy a meal, but the gormless treatment which has rendered the Horseshoe so disconcertingly clinical is blissfully absent. My faith, to a degree, has been restored.

Anyway, Marston's has felt the full force of my wrath: to punish the wrong-doers for corrupting the Horseshoe I shunned the Royal Oak's admittedly splendid Pedi and opted for a **Greene King Abbot Ale.** That should dent Marston's profits to the tune of roughly 0.0000003p. The temporary switch in allegiance from Staffordshire to Suffolk was more than worthwhile, for Abbot is a satisfying drop: fruity, hoppy and intensely bitter.

Of course, an inevitable and tantalizing question arises: if it tastes this good so far from home then how does it taste in Bury St Edmunds? If Marston's insists on destroying its pubs then I could soon be willing to flit to East Anglia to find out.

Marston's Pedigree: see February 3

Greene King Abbot Ale
(5 per cent ABV): ★★★★

February 8

The loathsome likes of Budweiser, Coors and the astonishingly execrable Miller Lite do a sizeable percentage of American beers a gross disservice. While the giants persist in trotting out the usual trash, it is no exaggeration to claim that the micros of the US presently produce more beers of interest than any other breweries on Earth. Many outstanding manifestations of Stateside invention are easily found in Britain, among them the principal products from Anchor, of San Francisco; the Altbiers from St Stan's, of Modesto, California; Samuel Adams Boston Ale and Boston Lager; and the award-winning Wicked line-up from former Californian home-brewer Pete Slosberg.

Pete began with a Wicked Ale, added a Wicked Lager and has now conceived so many Wicked things that he is surely condemned to an eternity basting in the fires of perdition. While the flippant titles he confers upon them have a devilish allusion, though, his creations have been a godsend to me, since their availability in the otherwise unappealing pubs near my workplace is often a saviour when it comes to snatching a swift one to break up the boredom of a Sunday duty.

The sight of **Pete's Wicked Bohemian Pilsner** on sale at a Wine Rack branch illustrates just how far Pete has come. A man who once had to hide his stocks from the sheriff's department in Palo Alto when the brewery he used there went into receivership now has his wares mass-marketed in the UK – an encouraging turnabout for the other US brewers prepared to have a stab at something other than "wet air".

My gut reaction when I first sampled Pete's Wicked Bohemian Pilsner was: "Blimey – this gives Pilsner Urquell a run for its money!" Surely it can't be that impressive? Maybe not; but every time I have a bottle I am more won over by its refreshing hoppiness and floweriness.

Let's not get too carried away with its chances of taking Britain by storm, however, because the last time I nipped into one of those unappealing pubs mentioned above the barman took perverse pleasure in informing me when I ordered a bottle: "I haven't sold one of these for ages – not since you last came in, come to think of it." And I hadn't been there for two months. Sales of Budweiser seemed to be going just swimmingly, of course.

Pete's Wicked Bohemian Pilsner (4.9 per cent ABV): ★★★★★

February 10

Folk are always telling me: "I don't read the papers – there's nothing in 'em." Not so! In *The Times* last week there was a set of tokens with which Eugene and I will be able to secure accommodation in some jolly nice Belgian hotels for but a few Francs: this just goes to show that, although we might write a load of tosh, we journalists are not daft.

Fuelled by a powerful combination of pork scratchings and **Burton Bridge Old Expensive**, we tonight managed to settle on an itinerary for our proposed weekend jaunt: travel by Eurostar to Brussels and hopefully enjoy a bit of cuisine à la bière at one of my favourite restaurants, the Spinnekopke; catch a train to Ghent and spend a night there; and round things off with a night in Antwerp. All being well, late this month or early March should see us back on Belgian soil – the first time we've hit the ale trail together since Euge, cynical hack that he is, blagged us a freebie from the Belgian Tourist Board umpteen years ago.

The Old Expensive – or OX, as it is sometimes known – was delightfully vinous and warming, as befits the strongest regular ale on the Burton Bridge's books; but, without wishing to imply an iota of disrespect, I care not. Already my mind is elsewhere. De Kluis Benedict, here I come.

**Burton Bridge Old Expensive
(6.5 per cent ABV):** ★★★★

February 15

Sometimes you act against your better judgment and, most likely because of some bizarre compulsion to prove yourself wrong, press ahead with things you're confident are doomed to disenchant. Today – with one notable exception – has been awash with such misguided acts.

First I persuaded myself to take a drive into the Peak District, even though I was well aware that doing so would have only two results: (1) make me yearn for my MG, which normally doesn't emerge from hibernation until April; (2) further increase my hatred for the Fiat Punto foisted upon me by my employers. Now, I accept that beggars can't be choosers, but the Fiat is such a shambolic piece of junk and so distant from what anyone with even a droplet of oil in his veins might deem a car that it saps my will every time I turn the key and hear the diesel engine clatter and splutter into life. But off into the Peaks I nonetheless went; and within five minutes I was left totally crushed after being passed by an MG identical to my own. Most distressing.

Then, having returned from the weekly pool marathon, I resolved to snuggle down and watch a video. And what did I select in preference to various cinematic triumphs, even though I presumed it would be garbage? *Tango and Cash*, starring Sylvester Stallone and Kurt Russell. After a quarter of an hour's worth of bullet-strewn carnage it became obvious that my presumption had been well-founded and this was a film to be avoided at all costs; but, maybe because I was fascinated by how brain-bogglingly abominable it could get, I stuck with it to the very end – which, in case you're interested, had Sly and Kurt suddenly deciding to shoot or blow up anyone and anything unlucky enough to stand before them (no surprise finale there, then).

Two disasters foreseen, two disasters realized and senselessly prolonged – and then came a third: **St-Omer Magister**, a "premium French lager". I anticipated the worst when Gurminder presented me with a bottle, since for him the magical words "premium lager" are usually sufficient testament to a beer's brilliance; but it's the thought that counts, and common decency – not to mention the cause (or curse) of necessary research – moved me to give it a go. If nothing else, it was undoubtedly appropriate that I feasted upon its lager-by-numbers insipidness while being tortured by the thought-provoking escapades of Stallone and Russell: not because Magister is about as refined as a can of Tango and a thorough waste of cash – though that much is certainly true – but because, like the movie, it is plainly rubbish. A Fiat Punto of a beer.

All of the day's wrongs can be forgotten, however, thanks to my inspirationally concluding proceedings with **Becker's Pils**. Like Magister, Becker's bears a "premium" badge; but here the exalted addendum is validated. Even when compared with Rhineland Pilsners, all of which are wonderfully dry, Becker's – from St Ingbert, Saarland – is extraordinary: it is not only dry but supremely bitter – and it packs one of the mightiest noses of any Pils, German or otherwise.

I have loved this anonymously-packaged beer ever since I noticed it lurking in Morrisons just days after first reading about it; and my suspicions that kismet might be steering me towards a classic were strengthened shortly thereafter when I went to the Dram off-licence in Sheffield and found a Becker's glass on sale for just 75p. Everyone to whom I have recommended it has been converted, amazed that such a tremendous drink should be stashed among the Stella Artois and Molson in their local supermarket. To be frank, there really is no excuse for anyone to cram their fridge with the likes of Magister when a 10-bottle box of one of the best Pilsners on the planet can be picked up for a fiver. It should be bought by the truck-load.

St-Omer Magister (5 per cent ABV):	★★
Becker's Pils (4.9 per cent ABV):	★★★★★★

February 16

It is a matter of no mean regret that I have not made it to Bavaria at some point during the past five years or so. Not just Bavaria either: save for an hour snatched at PJ Früh in Köln –

en route to a funeral near Bonn, believe it or not – my first-hand experience of Germany's brewing capitals has been zilch. The trouble is that Belgium always seems to win the final vote when my Bro' and I come to pick a beer-hunting holiday: the lure of Antwerp is just too much, especially for him.

My Mum is German – scant wonder that a man with a Burtonian father and a German mother should become interested in frothy ones – so trips to see relatives were commonplace back in the '70s and early-to-mid-'80s. Despite my tender age, these excursions were not without hop-related incident. I had my inaugural heavy session and consequent hangover in the company of my Uncle Willi when I was about 16 – a routine tale of "No, Mum, I'm all right" assurances followed by much staggering into walls and ultimately being carried upstairs, genuinely green around the gills, by my Bro'. My declaration in the bar of the Hotel am Posthof, Nienburg, in 1991 – "No, let's carry on – I've got my second wind now" – has also become legendary, as has the sorry performance at breakfast the following morning.

Visits after 1991 have been few and far between, however, and have reaped little reward. I was working in Berlin on the night of reunification and the days leading up to it, but I was so ferociously busy that I didn't lay my paws on a glass until the evening before heading home; moreover, I didn't know then about Berliner Weisse, whose towering acidity is so challenging that the style struggles to find favour outside its home city (if and when I return I shall drink it as if it were going out of fashion – which, by all accounts, it is).

And then there was the aforementioned whistle-stop at Früh, once a brewpub but now – production having moved elsewhere – merely the bar-cum-restaurant of the most renowned of Kölsch breweries. My Bro' had rightly surmised that, since we had spent the previous evening supping nine-year-old Westmalle Tripel at Kulminator ("beer heaven", as he astutely termed it), whatever we came across that day would be a downer; and there was also our aunt's funeral waiting at the end of the journey, of course, so we weren't in too jolly a mood. Well, we were definitely less than overawed: a combination of a rambling, labyrinthian lay-out and a motley crew of volatile, sozzled customers made Früh appear almost hostile. I reckon we caught the place on a bad day; we shall have to try to catch it on a better one before too long.

Bavaria remains the German destination of choice, though. Munich seems the obvious base for operations; but there is also much to be said for heading in any direction you fancy and wending through village after village, every one of which is liable to brew its own beer. Above all, I would love to see the Weltenburg monastery, which stands on the banks of the Danube and produces a multitude of very fine lagers and a virtuous Weissbier or two. Ah, you can always dream.

In the absence of a draught Asam Dunkel Bock in Weltenburg's chestnut-shaded courtyard, then, I shall have to make do with an **Allgäuer St Magnus Heller Bock** – a mouthful in every respect – while watching *The Morecambe & Wise Show*. Not quite the same, is it? But, though the backdrop is a tad lacking in grandeur, I can't complain about the beer.

Bocks – strong lagers of between approximately 6 and 8 per cent ABV – tend towards maltiness; but St Magnus, which is brewed in Kempten to a recipe purportedly dating back to 1712, is also blessed with a distinctly hoppy finish. It is on the pale side for a Bock – many are amber or even dark – but no less charismatic for that. The overall effect is badly let down only by the typically naff notes which adorn the bottle: "Full of character!" (witness the exclamation mark for the hard of understanding) is perhaps a trifle knockabout for a label bearing a coat of arms and a halo-wearing saint.

Sound stuff, anyhow – but, like many a Bock, dangerously drinkable. Two more bottles and I could almost have believed I was actually in Germany; three more bottles and, for all I would have known, I could have been on Mars.

41

With that in mind, I reverted to **Becker's Pils** during a before-bed viewing of *The Legend of Hell House* – although I am forced to admit, with the benefit of hindsight, that the superlative nerve-settling qualities of St Magnus might well have come in useful.

Allgäuer St Magnus Heller Bock (7 per cent ABV): ★★★★

Becker's Pils: see February 15

February 17

My prediction of a February dominated by ale is proving way off the mark. There have been numerous opportunities to take advantage of the pantry's climatic accuracy, sit basking in the glow of a roaring fire and nurse something warming and top-fermented; but opportunities to actually *buy* something warming and top-fermented, it pains me to report, have been pathetically scarce.

For around eight years now I have obtained the bulk of my beer from three shops: Small Beer, Lincoln; the Dram, Sheffield; and the Bottle Store, Leicester. Each has its own peculiar strengths, but they *nonetheless* share a disgraceful fault which cannot be ignored: they're too far from Burton. Dicing with death on the M1 or crawling along the infuriating A46 (where do all those caravans come from, for God's sake?) is a shattering ordeal at the best of times, and the lure of a haul of goodies at journey's end must invariably be weighed against the abject misery of the journey itself; I have also occasionally been dealt the vicious blow of arriving to find that precious shelf-space once graced by the likes of Rochefort and Westmalle has inexplicably been claimed by the likes of Hooper's Hooch and Diamond White, which is enough to severely dent anyone's enthusiasm for high-mileage beer-hunting.

Combine the distance problem with a hectic period work-wise and you have a recipe for... well, certainly not a recipe for ale. Hence my recent drinking at home has relied heavily on whatever I can cadge from supermarkets and off-licences of a less specialized ilk – which means lager, basically. There's nowt wrong with that, as I stressed at the start of the year; but the striking of a better balance before I am robbed of the pantry's assistance would be a welcome development.

Ho-hum – there's always the pub. Time was again short tonight, so the Burton Bridge got the shout once more when Guillo and I wracked our brains: excuse our paucity of imagination. Continuing my progress through the Bridge's portfolio, I opted for arguably my favourite: the sweetish, malty, chocolatey, ruby-red **Burton Bridge Burton Porter**. More often than not a brewery which dabbles in a variety of styles emerges from the exercise as a jack of all trades, but Burton Porter further illustrates that the Bridge is very much an all-round master; never do I underestimate my outrageous fortune in having it so near.

By the way, I know of just one porter which I prefer to the Bridge's: the immaculate interpretation from Anchor, of San Francisco. Locating any in this country was irksome enough several years ago, but the tragedy is that now – even if I could be bothered to do battle with the caravans – I fear I would not find it stocked by any of my prohibitively remote suppliers.

**Burton Bridge Burton Porter
(4.5 per cent ABV):   ★★★★★**

February 23

One of the most indelible lines in *Auf Wiedersehen, Pet* came from Barry Taylor, the show's archetypal boring Brummie. Exasperated by the ill-concealed disinterest in his laudable bid to enrich their lives with more varied activities, he mournfully conceded that his workmates would forever be obsessed with just three topics: "Sex, relegation and 'the best pint I ever 'ad'."

I clearly recall my first "best pint I ever 'ad". I had gone to Oxford to check on my clever-clogs friend Tim, who was studying there, and we kicked off a day-long pub-crawl with a round of Samuel Smith's Old Brewery Bitter at the Three Goats Heads. The historic importance of the event initially escaped me, I must admit; but later, when I recounted our excesses in a missive to my Bro', the significance suddenly dawned on me. The "best pint" title has changed hands countless times in the ensuing years, of course; yet Samuel Smith's, the oldest brewery in Yorkshire, has always held a place in my affections since that momentous day.

Like the Burton Bridge, Samuel Smith's, of Tadcaster, doesn't make a single duff beer. OBB remains one of my British favourites, and the other product available on draught, Museum Ale, runs it reasonably close. Among the bottled range, the Imperial and Oatmeal Stouts are superb (not to mention much admired by my nonagenarian Gran, bless her), while Taddy Porter is heaven-sent for anyone still intrepid enough to risk eating beef.

And then there is tonight's choice, **Samuel Smith's Old Brewery Pale Ale**. Burton-on-Trent popularized pale ales in the mid-1800s, with Tadcaster volunteering a northern riposte later in the century; Marston's Pedigree and other Burton beers might still be regarded as such, although – the terms having overlapped – they are billed as bitters. I can only be grateful for not having discovered Sammy's during my school days, because I would surely have been beaten up if I had meekly suggested that a Yorkshire beer was almost as good as – if not equal to – the all-conquering Pedi.

Old Brewery Pale Ale is not at all far-removed from Museum Ale, but I prefer it to its cask-conditioned partner. Like many pale ales, it is not the colour you might expect:

more blushing than pale. It is pleasantly malty, less winy than Museum and – like all Samuel Smith's beers – well-rounded. It may never have the emotional tug of that OBB in Oxford with Tim – indeed, every OBB I've had at the Three Goats Head since has been less and less praiseworthy – but its calibre is irrefutable.

Quite where **Schwanen Schöfferhofer Hefeweizen** fits into this picture is a moot point – save for the fact that it is the other beer I had today. I was hoping for a taste of something foreign at lunchtime, as tradition dictates that the drudgery of a Sunday duty is interrupted only by the problem of ferreting out a tolerable tipple within half a mile of the office; but I was reduced to orange juice – resplendent with decorative peel and enough ice to sink the Titanic – in the face of a Pete's Wicked Bohemian Pilsner drought (was there a mad rush for it, with thousands of youths abruptly turning their backs on Budweiser, or did the pub merely give up trying to flog it?). The Wine Rack provided both the Sammy's and this incongruous German chaser.

There would have been a link if I had procured a Weissbier from the Ayinger range, since Samuel Smith's has a bizarre tie with that brewery; but Bavarian-brewed Ayinger beers – as opposed to their under-licence imitations – very seldom reach British soil. Anyway, Schöfferhofer is perfectly capable of standing on its own: it is an above-average Weizen, offering a short-lived but dense head, a very fruity palate, a sour finish and – most intriguingly – a label daubed with a drawing of the aristocratic Peter Schöffer van Gernstheim (I know not who he is, but he looks like a slimline Brian Blessed playing Falstaff).

Much as Sam Smith's will perpetually be associated with "the best pint I ever 'ad", however, Schöfferhofer will long hold another title: "the best glass I ever broke". This catastrophe occurred not tonight but nigh on two years ago, during a careless spot of washing-up. The trauma was such that it seems like yesterday. What a waste. What a clumsy prat.

**Samuel Smith's Old Brewery Pale Ale
(5 per cent ABV):** ★★★★★

**Schwanen Schöfferhofer Hefeweizen
(5 per cent ABV):** ★★★★

February 24

What does a news editor do if he lends his company car to a reporter and the reporter, for reasons too extraneously complicated to examine, ends up abandoning it 100 miles from the office? And not just 100 miles from the office, you understand, but in one of the most remote villages in the Lincolnshire Fens.

And not just in one of the most remote villages in the Lincolnshire Fens, like, but outside the home of a convicted murderer. Parked right up against his hedge, in fact. With a mobile phone on the passenger seat. And this convicted murderer has had a bit of a rotten day, all things considered, because the front page of a national newspaper has accused him of a second killing.

Well? What does the news editor do? Accord the reporter a vicious verbal roasting? Demand that he go and fetch said car? Applaud him profusely for marooning the Punto in a place where it might get nicked? No. The news editor counts himself fortunate to have a friend who offers to drive him to the Fens that night; he consults his *Good Pub Guide* and pinpoints a decent hostelry en route; and he and his friend have a slap-up meal and some beers and charge the bill to the company. Every cloud has a silver lining.

The A52 heading north from Derby is among the grimmest of roads, the so-called scenery which flanks it becoming increasingly featureless with every mile, and by the time you reach

Grantham, birthplace of Mrs Thatcher and once officially branded the most boring town in the land, you experience an all-consuming desire to turn around and go home; but Gary and I had to trundle all the way to just short of Boston – and the weather, for good measure, was horrendous. Thankfully, Gary is among the most jovial individuals you could wish to meet – despite being nicknamed Glummo – so we succeeded in maintaining a light-hearted air, defying our ridiculous situation, our bleak surroundings, the torrential rain, the gale-force winds, the lack of radio reception and our being in another Punto.

I had earlier established that the pub I had chosen – the Peacock in Redmile, a picture-postcard village in the Vale of Belvoir, around five miles off the A52 and thus well-hidden from the hapless motorists who rumble past in painful ignorance – served food until 10pm (how very un-British to offer customers meals at a civilized hour). Glummo and I reached my Punto – still intact, alas – at 9pm, were within a dozen miles of Redmile at 9.45pm, found ourselves choking on the exhaust fumes of a crawling lorry for 10 frazzling minutes (seldom does one venture into Lincolnshire without this happening), screamed into Redmile, whizzed past the Peacock without seeing it, left the village, executed our respective U-turns, careered back down the main street, saw the pub, parked, ran inside, briefly managed to get lost in the building itself (which is also an hotel) and finally dashed into the bar at 9.58pm.

"Are we too late for food?"

"No, sir."

What a pub: strangely majestic (French chef, impeccable cuisine, cordial staff) and yet without a hint of pretension (British ale, stripped wooden furniture, jolly locals). Perhaps the catharsis of putting behind us the day's stresses and strains figured heavily, but we really felt we could have stayed there forever. My meal – bacon and scallop salad with a red pesto dressing, followed by venison sausages with mashed potato and onion gravy – was nothing less than delicious.

47

And then there was the **Timothy Taylor Landlord**. My encounters with Landlord are normally confined to the Victoria, a backstreet boozer which skulks at the rear of Lincoln Castle (home to the city's Crown Court, where I have spent many a mirthless hour) and boasts bacon butties which have no peers. How uplifting to find its unparalleled balance of malt and hops is as sensational with a £30 feast as it is with a two-quid artery-clogger at the Vic. It is a stunning drink, so marvelously distinctive that anyone who has sampled it should soon be able to identify it in a blind tasting. With apologies to Marston's, I believe it is the best beer in Britain – and it has certainly won enough awards to support this opinion – and that Timothy Taylor, of Keighley, Yorkshire, is probably the best brewery; and I can't be more forthright than that.

Typical, though, that Glummo and I should stumble across an absolutely stellar bitter when both of us are at the wheel. We dared permit ourselves one each and then, moaning at life's injustices, switched to after-dinner coffee and contemplated the myriad joys of the remaining slog along the A52. Every cloud has a silver lining, but it can still rain.

**Timothy Taylor Landlord
(4.3 per cent ABV): ★★★★★★★**

February 27

Tomorrow I shall revel in the splendour of Brussels and Ghent; tonight... Stoke-on-Trent. Although he has worked wonders in organizing our foreign break, Eugene was somehow defeated by the vagaries of the British railway network: apparently unable to plot a sensible path from Manchester to Burton, he had to be picked up from Stoke station. If ever I needed encouragement to flee blighty for Belgium – and I don't, ta – this provided it, because I have always regarded Stoke as the place which gives my home county a bad name. Mention Staffordshire to people and they think not of Cannock Chase, the Manifold Valley, the moorlands or even Britain's brewing capital: they think of the Potteries, and the Potteries, to be ruthlessly candid, ain't pretty.

Curious, then, that Euge should choose such a gloomy locale to unexpectedly announce such a beautiful event: James Patrick Eugene Henderson, long-time Lothario and beer-loving breaker of hearts, is going to be a daddy. He's seriously chuffed; I am more than somewhat gobsmacked.

I wasn't going to have a frothy one until we were pounding the Grand' Place, but this definitely called for a toast. Stoke having rightly been ruled out as a venue for such a profound piece of glass-raising, we relied on the Robinson fridge – which offered only Becker's, Beck's, **Staropramen** and, to Eugene's rapture, Pilsner Urquell. Something of deeper meaning to us – an Abbaye des Rocs, say – would have been more expedient, but I suppose we'll have ample scope for that in the next few days.

The adventure begins tomorrow; and it begins at 4.30am, disturbingly enough. An early night for me, then, while Eugene – his stamina seemingly undiminished by his recent achievement – watches my *Bilko* tapes and cogitates the tribulations of fatherhood.

Staropramen: see January 12

February 28

My ideal start to an extended weekend of beer-hunting would not be a 4.30am wake-up and a Punto ride to Watford Junction, but such are the necessary evils of travelling from Burton to Belgium. At least the car wheezed into life without the need for a frenzy of key-turning and accelerator-pumping: many are the mornings when it withstands my determined efforts and I am sorely tempted to reward it with a Fawlty-esque damned good thrashing.

Call me a bumpkin, but I detest London. To stand (no danger of sitting down, naturally) on the train from Watford to Waterloo and hear folk whisper in grave tones about stoppages on the Bakerloo Line makes me despair of humanity, because that's no bloody way to live. The Underground sums up everything which is wrong with not only the capital but Britain as a whole: it is ancient, crumbling, overcrowded, ramshackle, often inefficient, scores of years out of date and generally wretched – yet we try to pass it off as acceptable by labelling it "charming", "authentic" or even, quite incredibly, "romantic". Such guff might fool American tourists, but it shouldn't fool us. Still, it all helps me yearn even more for Belgium.

Having completed our commando training in commuting – a piece of cake for Euge, who, as a veteran of Hong Kong's Mass Transit System, has been battered into sardine-tin carriages by club-wielding guards – we arrived at the Eurostar terminal. Imagine a messy collision between the worst aspects of a British Rail station and Heathrow Airport and you get some picture of the scene: moving walkways, endless expanses of white, one man checking hundreds of passengers' tickets. We were travelling "standard" class – aye, I remember t'days when we were allowed to call it "second" class – and took our designated seats in the near-deserted Coach 18, ready for the off at 8.55am.

We pulled away bang on schedule and shortly thereafter were greeted by a trolley-dragging Poirot-lookalike offering drinks. Eugene began as he meant to go on by ordering, to my dismay, a can of Stella Artois (he has a twisted affinity for it, he says, because he once stood alone for an hour at Leuven station); Poirot, with a smile and a commendable command of the deadpan, commented simply: "Enjoy your breakfast, sir." Having won our hearts, he went on to provide further entertainment by displaying a narrow grasp of both technology and the English language, furiously stabbing at his calculator before telling a lady who requested a cup of tea: "That will be 190 Francs, sir."

50

Without him our sunny dispositions would have been severely challenged, because there's not an enormous amount you can do on a train – particularly an ultra-fast train which travels at approximately 50mph on British tracks (has anyone heard of the word "investment"?). Having scanned the in-house magazine (whose "What's on in Belgium" section advocated visiting Binche and being pelted with fruit at the town's carnival – cheers) and stared vacantly at our reflections while chugging through the Channel Tunnel, Euge and I were reduced to drawing up a list of never-before-tried beers we were keen to trace: I racked up 14, Euge nine. Otherwise points of interest were limited to the hilarity of Ashford station's being repackaged as Ashford International (no-one got on, no-one got off – what a surprise); the announcement shortly after we emerged from the Tunnel that the train had hit its maximum speed of 300km/h (or, for we backward British buggers, 186mph); and Eugene's sorry slide from Stella to Kronenbourg to Carlsberg.

The train glided to a halt in Brussels in plenty of time for us to wander to the Spinnekopke for a bite of lunch. It has taken me years to formulate a practical passage to this cosy restaurant, which is located in the slightly far-flung and not very attractive Place du Jardin aux Fleurs: on previous sallies, once with Euge and once with my Bro', I have become hopelessly lost in decaying residential streets and ended up being accosted by children, beggars and assorted loonies, but practice has made perfect. The Spinnekopke is famed for its cuisine à la bière, a subject on which its owner, Jean Rodriguez, has written a book; Euge is an erstwhile chef and once even penned a series of articles on beer cuisine for a magazine (although the naughty so-and-so had shamelessly plagiarized all the recipes), so eating there is almost educational for him.

The first beer I ever drank in Belgium was **Orval**. It was already my all-time favourite prior to that, and it still is now. Produced by one of the country's five monastic breweries – the Abbaye Notre Dame d'Orval in the tiny hamlet of Villers-devant-

51

Orval, Luxembourg province – it has the most fantastic amber/orange colour, an indescribably captivating bitterness and an unmistakable hint of candy. It is also a great aperitif, and I've developed a habit of having one as I peruse the Spinnekopke's menu. Euge and I know we're back where we love to be when we clunk Orval glasses while choosing our starters.

I settled on coquilles St Jacques cooked in one of the three ales from another of the Trappist breweries, Rochefort; and fillet of pork cooked in **Het Anker Gouden Carolus**, the strong brown ale made in Mechelen, between Brussels and Antwerp. I stuck with Orval for the coquilles but had a Gouden Carolus – very deep red in colour, with a sweet-and-sour character and a certain bitterness – with the pork. It was all truly blissful; and the best thing for a Briton in Belgium, of course, is that every restaurant, regardless of price or pretension, serves magnificent chips as a matter of course. What a welcome.

Afterwards the day took a temporary dive. First, armed with the indispensable *Good Beer Guide to Belgium and Holland*, we went looking for Beer Street, a bar allegedly harbouring the largest selection of draught frothy ones in the history of the hop – only to discover that, as far as we could tell, its address had been taken over by a couscous house. Since it is our wish to one day own a Belgian bar of our own, Euge and I are invariably distressed when we come across such a failed enterprise; I recall our grief when we turned up at the Pavane, Antwerp, to find it has vanished from existence (as had our taxi, meaning we had to walk miles back to the city-centre – which may have accounted for a modicum of our melancholy).

We then moved on to the Falstaff, a renowned rococo/Art Déco restaurant with 22-hours-a-day opening times and an adequate beer-list. When I made my inaugural visit back in 1994 I instantly fell for the place, but since then it has exhibited an uncanny capacity to disappoint: it's just little things which annoy, like serving a drink in the wrong glass or bringing two thick Englishmen who ask for "chips" a bag of ready-salted crisps. On this occasion the letdown was two-fold: (1) advertizing Hoegaarden Speciale and then admitting to not stocking any; (2) dispensing instead the coldest, nastiest **De Kluis Hoegaarden Wit** I've ever tasted — substantially worse than the rubbish foisted upon me at the brewery and almost sufficiently iniquitous to warrant a further downgrading. My patience with the Falstaff is wearing extremely thin, and it could soon join the Mort Subite — savaged in 1996 when my Bro' and I caught the staff stirring a glass of dead gueuze, their dire intention being to render it presentable after it had languished behind the bar for God knows how long — in the "Once-Great Brussels Bars I Don't Visit Any More" file.

Our faith was restored, however, on the other side of the Bourse, where we popped into Cirio. This café, with decor similar to the Falstaff's, has more than a touch of the British seaside about it, because it is constantly packed with old dears. It should stage the World Silly Hat Championships. I have huge difficulty in visualizing a pub in the centre of a bustling British city in which scores of OAPs cheerily sit around and sip strong beverages while bow-tied waiters attend to their every caprice. I adored it: it was just so *Belgian*. Nice beer, too: **Friart St Feuillien Blond**, a stupendously hoppy ale from a once-dead brewery between Charleroi and Mons. And we got our first free bowl of nuts, which is always a mark of superiority. When I'm 60 I must remember to go back in the hope of getting lucky.

We were fleetingly tempted to knock the top off one on the Grand' Place before walking back to the station, but we decided against it. Rents there are so vast that a bar which isn't tied to a massive brewing group has about as much hope of survival as anyone (apart from Scottie) who wears a red shirt on Captain Kirk's *Enterprise*; the beers are therefore criminally overpriced and usually restricted to the likes of Hoegaarden (boo, hiss), Jupiler (a bland lager which somehow contrives to be the country's biggest seller) and the uninspiring Leffe range of abbey ales (nice glasses, shame about what's in 'em). Aside from the cost and quality concerns, the Grand' Place is also one of those spots – like Manhattan or Blackpool – which are best viewed at night, when they can be seen in all their illuminated glory.

Onwards by train, then, to Ghent, provincial capital of East Flanders. Eugene had been before, but this was my first exposure to a town described by the *Good Beer Guide to Belgium and Holland* as "without the instant charm of Bruges or the spectacular bars of Antwerp". Hmmm. If it were possible to gauge somewhere by its railway station – BR would have been proud of its dourness (as opposed to the stations of Bruges and Antwerp, both of which have buffets equipped to shame 90 per cent of British pubs) – then Ghent was not poised to impress; but my dread was unfounded.

Our hotel, the Holiday Inn Crowne Plaza, was no mean cab-fare away; but a guy who is used to a Fiat Punto can't really complain when he's being ferried around in a black Mercedes. We watched a few episodes of *The Simpsons* on cable, made up for lost sleep and generally steeled ourselves for the night ahead – which began, needless to say, with another expensive waft in a Merc, this time back into town.

Ghent by night makes for a reasonably winsome spectacle – more Amsterdam than Bruges, I think, but none the worse for that – and hard against the glittering River Leie, on the edge of the old town, is the Waterhuis aan der Bierkant, whose name apparently derives from a typically crazy (not) slice of Belgian humour involving the transposing of words. The Waterhuis is something of a brown bar (as was unfortunately illustrated, to my disdain, by the layers of dust gathered on the glasses kept on higher shelves) and has a solid array of beers. I kicked off the night's pleasures with a **De Kluis Hoegaarden Speciale** – except it wasn't too much of a pleasure, to be honest, since Speciale (misnomer alert) is merely a lame winter interpretation of Hoegaarden; why does the brewery waste its efforts on such witlessness when it could reintroduce Benedict to the line-up?

Next up was one of the abbey beers from Union, of Jumet, the chief ale-brewer of the leviathan-like Alken-Maes group. Abbey beers should not be confused with the Trappist style: whereas the latter term describes only the products of the Belgian monasteries of Chimay, Orval, Rochefort, Westmalle and Westvleteren and the Dutch monastery of Koningshoeven, the former is applied to any old tosh made by a commercial brewery in imitation of a Trappist ale – and, believe me, there are some poor imitations about. Many abbey beers are worthy wanna-bes – St Bernardus, Benedict (RIP), Het Kapittel – but many more are shockers. **Union Cuvée de l'Ermitage** – which, like the aforementioned Leffe, is presented in one of the most opulent glasses ever created – is among the better examples: very dark, very assertive, a trifle cloying.

We left the Waterhuis when the sounds of Bronski Beat began blaring from unseen speakers – such music is not notably conducive to the appreciation of holy ales – and ambled a hundred yards or so down the riverbank to the Witte Leeuw (White Lion), a spacious pub which somehow emerges unhurt from a crash of ancient and modern (a trick notoriously beyond the average British inn). Had we been in England we would have been told to neck a quick 'un and go home; but in this altogether more civilized land, though the clocks read 11.30pm, we were able not only to drink to our hearts' content but to indulge in some late-night nibbles – mushrooms on toast for me, shrimp croquettes (the house speciality) for Eugene. The **Bavik Witbier**, from the village of Bavikhove in West Flanders, was plain but afforded suitable refreshment for the assignment which lay ahead: tracking down the acclaimed Hopduvel café.

No sooner have I worked out a route to the Spinnekopke than I have another map-reading disaster on my hands. Knowing the Hopduvel was down an anonymous terraced street we were unlikely to flounder into by sheer chance, we hired yet another taxi: the driver courteously delivered us to the Hopduvel warehouse, several streets away from

our planned destination, but we didn't realize as much until
the silly sod had shot off into the darkness. With much
referring to the *Guide* and even more strolling in the wrong
direction, we trudged along deserted roads until we at last
espied Rokerelstraat, an East Flanders version of Coronation
Street. It was worth the trek.

The Hopduvel is a TARDIS. The *Guide* brands it as such;
so, too, quite by coincidence, did Eugene. From the outside it
appears barely more than a door in a terraced row, but inside it
is multi-levelled and multi-roomed. I suggested, though, that
we ignore its various nooks and crannies and sit at the bar,
arguing that doing so would give us the best opportunity to
meet the owner, Antoine Denooze, a leading light in the
Belgian beer revival; and the gambit paid off, because he
served us.

The first beer you order when you go into a top-flight
café sets the tone for what follows. When, without
consulting the 500-strong list, I ordered 1991 Benedict for
my Bro' and myself upon entering the Kulminator a chap
at the bar immediately turned to us and said: "You must
know about beer." If you can prove you know your stuff
then conversation will follow and friendships will be
forged. If you ask for a Skol then you can expect short
shrift. We opted to wow Antoine by requesting two
bottles of **La Binchoise**, a very dry Wallonian pale ale
from the fruit-chucking town highlighted in the Eurostar
magazine: within minutes we were chatting away.

Antoine, it transpired, is Michael 'Beer-Hunter'
Jackson's best mate: "I introduced him to Belgian beer," he
said, thus laying a claim to being *the* catalyst for the revival
in his nation's brewing fortunes. A number of years ago he
also invented a celebrated kruidenbier (spiced beer),
Stropken, and, knowing this, I ordered a couple; but what I
didn't know was that his recipe had long since been tampered
with and left a shadow of its former self as **Slaghmuylder
Stropken Grand Cru**: "It used to be better," he remarked with
obvious disgust, bringing relief to a pair of trembling Englishmen
who had been terrified to admit they didn't think much of it.

By now our host was recommending beers for us to try from his selection of 120-plus: **Bosteels Tripel Karmeliet** was among the finest secular tripels I've ever had – golden, spicy and warming – but came in a glass which showed that the breweries' keenness to outdo one another in the receptacle stakes is getting out of control. I cannot begin to do its hideous chintziness justice: you'll have to go to Belgium and see it for yourself.

With the clocks now nudging 3am, the Hopduvel's custom consisted of the intrepid Englanders and the sagacious Eric, Antoine's big buddy, who struck me as being to the Hopduvel what Norm was to Cheers. He sat at a corner of the bar and drank Johnnie Walker Black Label with Coke and ice, waxing lyrical about his and Antoine's days as salesmen. "Money does not mean happiness," he assured me. "Being able to come here for a drink and then going home to my wife... that is happiness." I told him I would remember his words of wisdom when I had bought a bar and was utterly skint (although he perhaps ought to check it's all right with his wife first); I also promised I would one day return and bring him a bottle of Lagavulin single malt – on condition that he keep it well away from Coke and ice, of course.

Antoine rounded off the proceedings with a present for us: a 1986 bottle of **Het Anker Gouden Carolus**. It was never going to be anything less than excellent. It was more sherried than its modern-day counterpart at the Spinnekopke, as one would presuppose, but it was also smoother and yet somehow more challenging. "Not everywhere gives you free beer like this, eh?" said Antoine; indeed not.

All good things must come to an end, alas; and, the vintage Gouden Carolus having been savoured at length, we had to say au revoir. Eric graciously offered to chauffeur us back to the Holiday Inn, but – though our knowledge of Belgian drink-driving laws is far from comprehensive – we thought this unwise and politely declined; I shall, I trust, see him and Antoine next year – if not sooner.

To put it mildly, not a bad day. I love this country.

Orval
(6.2 per cent ABV): ★★★★★★★

Het Anker Gouden Carolus
(7.6 per cent ABV):   ★★★★★

De Kluis Hoegaarden Wit: see February 1

Friart St Feuillien Blond
(7.5 ABV):   ★★★★★

De Kluis Hoegaarden Speciale
(5 per cent ABV):   ★★★★

Union Cuvée de l'Ermitage
(7.2 per cent ABV):   ★★★★

Bavik Witbier
(5 per cent ABV):   ★★★

La Binchoise
(6.8 per cent ABV):   ★★★★

Slaghmuylder Stropken Grand Cru
(6 per cent ABV):   ★★★

Bosteels Tripel Karmeliet
(8 per cent ABV):   ★★★★★

Het Anker Gouden Carolus: see above

March 1

Yesterday I got up at 4.30am and felt dog-rough; today I got up at 11.30am and felt... well, dog-rough, basically. What a difference a day makes. Why is it, pray, that the air-conditioning systems in hotel rooms have only two settings –

"freezing" and "total dehydration"? Given my groggy state, I thought my bravery in enduring a restorative cold shower was worthy of a chestful of medals: it had the desired effect, but much self-pitying moaning was to be heard. Still, in spite of an initial paucity of zest, what better way to start the month than with Antwerp beckoning?

First, though, Eugene and I killed a couple of hours by sightseeing in Ghent. There were two highlights: (1) the Trollekelder (Troll Cellar) bar, whose window is filled with a profoundly unsettling bunch of homicidal-looking gnomes – possibly the most unappealing display ever devised by a disturbed mind (although the bar, closed when we took our turn at being alarmed, is said to be very good); (2) the wonderfully-named Loony Land – not, as you might expect, a museum dedicated to the UK but a shop selling cartoon-related merchandise. The low-point of our aimless tour was a midday visit to the Galgenhuisje, one of the tiniest hostelries imaginable and purportedly a brown bar of some repute: the only other punters vying for space were a sneering pair who must have been knocking back Westmalle Tripel since breakfast, and their less-than-charming conduct persuaded us to perform a swift about-face. The tourist trail having been given the gentlest of poundings, we adjourned to the Vrijdagmarkt, a square in the northern part of the old town, for an alfresco seafood lunch before commencing a lengthy but nonetheless enjoyable march to St Pieters station.

The buffet/bar at St Pieters deserves a brief mention, for it is quite the most abominable establishment I have ever come across in Belgium. Compared to its counterparts in Bruges and Antwerp, it is a bona fide atrocity – almost BR-like in its awfulness, in fact. The decor is nightmarish, with plastic tables, plastic chairs and plastic plants in abundance and a ludicrous network of interconnected lamps weaving its way around the furniture. Nuts are absent, but nutters are prolific. All that can be said in its favour, to be frank, is that it serves beer – although the ambience was such that I had a Coke. Most distressing.

And so to Antwerp, where the cognoscenti are inexorably drawn to some of the most brilliant bars to be found anywhere. Many a town or city is blessed with a classic, and some even have two, but Antwerp has at least three absolute belters: the Elfde Gebod (Eleventh Commandment), the Groote Witte Arend (Great White Eagle) and the finest it has ever been my privilege to experience, Kulminator (named after the super-strong Doppelbock from Bavaria's EKU brewery, whose wares owner Dirk pedalled for a living many moons ago). Legend has it that there was once a fourth Mecca for the hop-encrusted, the Pavane, on the outskirts of the city; but, as cited earlier, this monastic-style venture had already expired when Euge and I gallantly sought it out three years ago.

Another Mercedes whisked us to another Crowne Plaza, this one again located by planners entranced by the ethereal beauty of ring-roads. More episodes of *The Simpsons* were viewed; by now I was a die-hard fan and considered them hysterical. Eugene, his appetite insatiable and his greed boundless, ordered a club sandwich and frites to tide him over until dinner; it cost a wallet-thinning 250 Francs, yet still the miserable git who brought it to our room was miffed not to receive a tip. A prolonged bout of channel-hopping discovered *Grandstand* and the British football results, but even a Preston triumph and Euge's consequent temporary revitalization could not prevent our falling asleep. We eventually headed back into the city at 9pm, having ensured record profits for Belgian cabbies everywhere and sworn not to take another taxi unless irredeemably legless.

Café Pelgrom (Pilgrim), a candle-lit cellar bar attached to a restaurant which (not unlike Britain) is famous for its beef, was our first stop. We got lost looking for it, of course, even though I once went there with my Bro'; but no matter. Provided you are not driven insane by flickering flames and can manage to breathe in an atmosphere which makes the output of a

Holiday Inn air-con seem like a sea-breeze, Pelgrom is a laudable eatery – particularly if you're enamoured with steak.

Sometimes, as on this occasion, a chirpy old chap dressed as a Pilgrim entertains waiting diners with a magic show. He soon won our undying admiration when, upon learning we didn't understand a word he was saying, he assured us: "Do not worry – I do a Tommy Cooper trick for you!" I tried some **Haacht Haecht Witbier** – ultra-wheaty and highly quaffable, from Boortmeerbeek, near Leuven, Brabant – but didn't do an efficient job of burying my head in the mug and, as I had feared, was duly chosen to assist the Pilgrim in a two-rope trick; I came perilously close to buggering it up due to predictable communication problems, but it was much fun.

My initiation into the black arts accomplished, I tucked into a well-earned fillet of Angus in bearnaise sauce, accompanying it with Antwerp's most renowned ale: **De Koninck** – The King. Brits who visit the city derive much merriment from the fact that they can nip into any bar and demand a "bolleke", the 33cl glass used for the ubiquitous local brew. I've had the odd bottle of De Koninck at home, but these have been desperately lame compared to the draught version sampled on the beer's own territory: for one thing, they lacked the tremendously rocky head which tops a measure from the tap. Perhaps the word most applicable to De Koninck is "balance": it is so balanced that it can come across as being rather simple. It is tantamount to sacrilege to say so, but I've always deemed it bordering on the boring; yet it is almost universally hailed as a classic. Regardless of which echelon of excellence it should inhabit, I cannot deny that it goes damned well with beef; and to leave Antwerp without having supped one would be like leaving Burton without having downed a Pedi – it's just not done.

Our next call was a toss-up between the Great White Eagle and the Eleventh Commandment. Neither revels in an especially noteworthy beer-list, but then neither really needs one. The Great

White Eagle has an exquisite courtyard in which drinkers have been known to be serenaded by a string quartet; and adjoining one side of this yard is, of all things, a chapel – convenient for overindulgers wishing to repent, I suppose. The Eleventh Commandment – with every spare inch of its floor, windowsills and shelved walls bedecked with religious icons and paintings – may be the most visually arresting bar on the planet. A tough shout; but the Great White Eagle ultimately conquered, for no other reason than it was the nearer of the two.

To our disquiet, the courtyard was practically empty; worse still, its former centrepiece, an outlandish chunk of modernist sculpture which the *Good Beer Guide to Belgium and Holland* dubbed *Cement-Mixer Hit by Meteorite*, appeared to have gone. But our concerns that this precious café's popularity was on the wane were allayed by the bolstering sight of a packed interior: the bar was, if anything, significantly busier than we had ever seen it. One thing which had remained exactly the same was the **Palm Steendonk**: a witbier of uncommon strength from a brewery near Brussels more associated with its pale ale, it is among the more interesting challengers to Hoegaarden's lopsided crown and is the beer we invariably end up choosing at the Great White Eagle. We imbibed at an extremely leisurely pace – no disgrace in Belgium, where folk are not scorned for failing to neck half a gallon at last orders – and, convinced that all was well, set off for Kulminator.

I often think that much of Kulminator's allure would be lost if the premises were situated at the heart of the city. As it is, you have to leave behind the bustle of the centre and pick your way to Vleminckveld, a singularly unspectacular street, to find this most elegant of cafés. A regular once told me that no-one in Antwerp really knew of it; indeed, the majority of its customers are usually aficionados from far afield who have heard or read about it. With supremely knowledgeable owners in Dirk and Leen, more than 500 different brands in stock – a mighty achievement even by Belgian standards – and a discreet sophistication arising out out of a reverence for beer, Kulminator is probably all the more attractive for being slightly off the beaten track: such a gem might be horribly tarnished it if were sandwiched between a burger-bar and a nightclub. Despite its comparative remoteness, the place was full when we walked in at 11.30pm, with Dirk and Leen busily flitting between the bar and cellar.

I instantly noticed that Dirk, who last year sported a Trappist-style skinhead with his infamous beard, had rocked the fashion world by growing a quasi-Afro: he rather resembled a white Gil Scott-Heron, although I quickly accepted that the chances of his bursting into a rendition of *The Revolution Will Not Be Televised* were less than slim. Actually, the chances of Dirk's bursting into anything are not enormous: it was three years before I heard him do better than a begrudging mumble. It is easy to misjudge him, because he doesn't speak much English (why should he, after all?) and is frequently so engrossed in frothy ones that he has the air of a man who would render Victor Meldrew loving and gregarious by comparison; but if you do succeed in getting him talking — ask for a decent ale and you'll be well-set — it is a revelation of Biblical proportions.

I had sent Dirk and Leen a vintage Guinness postcard to say I would be popping in, and as soon as I reached the bar Leen greeted me by proudly declaring: "We got your card last week!" I was astonished to be recognized, but then these are special people. Dirk struggled for a few seconds until I pulled from my pocket the Guinness postcard he had sent me in January, whereupon he obviously recalled those nine-year-old Westmalle Tripels and excitedly showed me how he had kept my thank-you letter in his visitors' book (in which, incidentally, my Bro' and I proudly occupy page two; my Bro' will be very chuffed to hear he is still the only New Zealand resident to grace this hallowed tome).

Euge and I shared a table with four Americans: as far as we could tell, one of them was a Kulminator devotee who thought he was doing the others an honourable deed by bringing them to a fantastic bar. They paid him back thus: his friend gazed glumly into a two-thirds-full ballon, making clear that he had no intention of draining it of its contents, while the two women sipped Coke and issued foul-mouthed opinions about everything from the lack of coffee to their night out in general. I never thought I'd feel sorry for an American, but this poor soul merited sympathy aplenty in the face of such phenomenally graceless behaviour. If anyone I took to Kulminator conducted themselves so despicably I would chuck them into the street and direct them to a four-pack of Stella Artois.

Our suffering Statesider had been unsuccessfully recommending Piraat to his gloomy companions, but we knew we could improve on that. A **De Kluis Benedict** and an **Abbaye des Rocs** – both dated 1991 and presented in bottles delicately sprinkled with dust, a testament to tranquil repose in the cellar – brought back all my fondest recollections of previous visits: 1994, when Eugene and I, seeking something extraordinary to reward ourselves for overcoming a disastrous spell of map-reading, tasted them for the first time and quickly concluded they were two of the most sublime beers ever created; 1995, when my Bro' and I could only spoil ourselves for an hour or so before making a frantic (and stomach-churning) dash for the station to catch the last train back to Bruges; and 1996, when we were granted an audience with Dirk and Leen. Piraat might be okay, American pal o' mine, but bottles of Benedict and Abbaye des Rocs contain more than just beer: they're full of memories.

Why did De Kluis axe Benedict? Whatever the reason, I shall never be able to accept it. Dirk had growled dismissively when I told him I was planning to go to Hoegaarden: I understood why when I saw how cynical and commercial it was. Breweries have to make money, and Benedict – dark, smooth and contemplative, somewhere between one of the stronger beers from De Kluis and the Westmalle monastery's dubbel – might not have been bringing home the bacon. It is annoying – even frightening – that such a noble ale can be condemned to the dustbin of history; but such injustices are perpetrated the world over, and the bigwigs will doubtless gesture towards their profits and claim they made a shrewd decision if middle-of-the-road nonsense like ice-cool Hoegaarden Speciale sells thousands more units.

Whereas Benedict is essentially dead, Abbaye des Rocs – a strong brown ale of mammoth complexity, with wave after wave of aftertastes and a lingering butterscotch character – is on the up-and-up. Born in the garage of a former civil servant – an inauspicious start – it can now be found in Britain (albeit seldom in corked bottles, which impart a much richer flavour). There was a time when my Bro', Eugene and I concurred that it was unquestionably the pre-eminent frothy one; my Bro' stands by this opinion but has a nascent affection for Benedict, Euge has since nominated Duvel (Belgium's archetypal "strong golden" ale), and I say both Benedict and Orval must enter the reckoning. Naming any beer as the undisputed champ really is an impossible feat – although the pursuit of the ultimate drop is what beer-hunting is all about, of course – but Abbaye des Rocs, as far as I'm concerned, will forever be there or thereabouts.

Bizarrely, following the thrill of back-to-back Belgian top-tenners, I ended the night by taking advantage of Dirk's cosmopolitan approach and choosing something German: **Löwenbräu Triumphator**, the Doppelbock from Munich's most widely-known brewery. Some of the best cafés in Belgium won't even sell lager, let alone foreign products, a stance which can be parochially beneficial but might also be criticized as narrow-minded: after all, can anyone claim that Pilsner Urquell or Paulaner Salvator are undeserving of a place alongside Chimay Grand Réserve or Liefmans Kriek? Kulminator will stock anything which Dirk and Leen class as worthy, irrespective of method of fermentation or country or origin, and so should it be. Triumphator – dark brown and malty, thick yet dangerously drinkable – is a beer of quality, and quality ought to be the prime prerequisite when compiling any menu.

With much waving and handshaking, we left at 2am. By then only a hardcore of stalwarts loitered at the bar, and among them was the man who helped make my number-one session at Kulminator so unforgettable – the man who, having overheard my request for two bottles of Benedict, turned to me and delivered that most satisfying line: "You must know about beer."

My friend, that's why I come to Antwerp.

Haacht Haecht Witbier (5 per cent ABV):	★★★★
De Koninck (5 per cent ABV):	★★★★
Palm Steendonk (6.5 per cent ABV):	★★★★
De Kluis Benedict (7.3 per cent ABV):	★★★★★★★
Abbaye des Rocs (9 per cent ABV):	★★★★★★★
Löwenbräu Triumphator (7.7 per cent ABV):	★★★★

March 2

Daft Ideas of our Time, N° 1: "Hey, why don't we walk to the railway station?" It is one thing to stride back to your hotel with the spring-in-the-step insouciance occasioned by a night of strong beers; it is quite another to drag your weary frame and your baggage several miles the next morning. But, masochists that we are, we did it. This was, as it happened, one of the less interminable legs of a thoroughly wretched journey home.

We caught the train back to Brussels and, with around an hour to spare, headed to the Falstaff for a farewell carbonade flamande. Unfortunately for us, it appeared that the rest of Brussels had made similar plans. Snugly squeezed in at a table which had been kindly set aside for dwarves, we waited in vain for a menu before storming out after five minutes of being ignored. Having disappointed yet again, the Falstaff has now exhausted my patience: I hereby pledge my allegiance to Cirio, even if such a switch in loyalty requires me to invest in a silly hat and a Zimmer frame.

With time running short, we hastily availed ourselves of the nearest frittur and then hurried to the Eurostar terminal. All of this meant, of course, that my final beer of the trip was the Triumphator; Eugene grabbed a can of Jupiler with his frites, but I felt that a tin of fizzy trash was hardly a fitting denouement. It occurred to me that it was wrong to sign off with a German beer; worse still to spend half a day in Belgium without tasting even a single frothy one. My failure to end the weekend in an expedient manner nagged at me as I climbed aboard the train; but, save for suddenly crying "No!" and embarking on a dramatic sprint to the Spinnekopke, there was nowt I could do about it.

We travelled first-class from Brussels to Waterloo. This entitled us to a complimentary glass of champagne ("No, thanks – I've got to drive when we get back to London"), free wine ("No, thanks – I've got to drive when we get back to London") and what was comically billed as a three-course meal. As ever, the train rifled through France and became virtually motionless in Kent. The ordeal was so fist-clenchingly tedious that, apart from sleeping, we could only gaze in silent fascination at the first-class lamp which adorned our first-class table and wonder whether it would ever be turned on by some unseen controller – which, of course, it wasn't.

Daft Ideas of our Time, N° 2: "Hey, we can take the Tube all the way from Waterloo to Watford. Let's do it!" Ninety minutes of pure torture. Waterloo to Leicester Square on the Northern Line. Leicester Square to Piccadilly on the Piccadilly Line. Piccadilly to Baker Street on the Bakerloo Line. Baker Street to Watford Met on the Metropolitan Line. Much sitting at stations boasting no signs of human life. A carriage which seemed to have numerous tons of bricks dangling beneath it. A sense of total hopelessness. Emerging from Watford Met to discover it is in the middle of a residential area and nowhere near Watford Junction. And so on.

There wasn't even any respite to be found at the car-park: the Punto, heartbreakingly, was still there. To hear it clatter and cough was to know that I was back on British soil. I safely deposited Euge at Stoke station – a minor detour of 120 miles – arrived home at 11.30pm, went to the fridge and whipped out a **Becker's Pils**, adamant that the day should not go by without a respectable beer passing my lips. I definitely needed a drink after 11 hours of exploring almost every useless form of transport known to man.

Now my post-hols purgatory begins: ritual dictates that I must survive at least a week without touching a frothy one of any description. Precisely why I punish myself thus I honestly don't know, but I assume it is just one of those stupid things people do in a bid to feel happy about themselves. Provided no-one comes up to me in the street and brandishes an Abbaye des Rocs in my mush, I'm confident I can tough it out; besides, as my experience at PJ Früh proved, any beer-hunting carried out in the immediate aftermath of a Belgian jaunt is unavoidably shunted into the sidings of anti-climax.

I shall be brave.

Becker's Pils: see February 15

March 13

My self-imposed lay-off has been moderately taxing but far from unbearable. There have been a few distractions which cried out for a frothy accompaniment – engrossing films, agreeable meals, European Cup quarter-finals – but I have done my penance and paid my dues without too much grief.

The weirdest thing happened last week: I was offered beery celebrity in the pages of the *Daily Star*. The day after my Eurostar/Tube/Punto marathon I proudly told anyone who cared to listen that I had spent the weekend imbibing abroad, and one of the *Star* blokes was stunned to learn that Trappist monks made beer, that such beer was even available in this country and that a beer of 7 per cent ABV was viewed as of average strength in Belgium; he was, moreover, truly in awe to hear that someone should dedicate a few days to investigating these matters.

"We should do a story on you, Robbo," he said, enthusing as only we hacks can. "You know, the man who travels hundreds of miles and forks out hundreds of pounds just to have a pint."

A pint? Indeed. "I don't think it's that rare, to be honest, mate," I told him.

"I think it's amazing."

"I suppose if I told you I live in Burton-on-Trent, brewing capital of Britain, and still see fit to make such trips then you'd think it was even better."

"Really?"

"And I suppose if I told you I have hundreds of beer glasses from around the world so I can drink every beer from the right glass…"

He was becoming positively apoplectic, but I had to decline his offer – even though he promised to include a plug for my book, which was jolly generous of him. I couldn't help picturing a cheesy photograph of a sad sod surrounded by glassware and holding up a foaming Orval for the camera, possibly beneath a headline along the lines of "Beer-hunter Neil is a glass act". I have no qualms about earning a living writing such drivel, but I'd rather not have it written about me.

Anyway, back into the swing tonight with something of an oddity: **Zámek,** which hails from the Samson brewery in Budweis, home of Budvar, but is branded "Czech Pilsner Lager". Surely it is not a Pilsner but a Budweiser? I can understand its not being billed as a Budweiser, since confusion would inevitably ensue – as would a writ from Anheuser-Busch, no doubt – but to slap it with the appellation which should be reserved for products emanating from the town which rivals Budweis as the centre of Czech brewing seems misguided and defeatist. When the Czechs themselves ride rough-shod over the term "Pilsner" then respect for brewing traditions really is plumbing the depths.

To my disbelief and concomitant delight, I found Zámek – which I came across in Morrisons – so, so bitter that something like Becker's was reduced to puniness by comparison. It is by no means objectionable, but it might just be too much for many palates. Certainly those who are accustomed to run-of-the-mill Pils are in for a shock if the marketing/misnomer employed on the label nets some extra sales; but then that might just do some good.

All in all, not a bad way to return to the fray. It's nice to be back.

**Zámek
(4.5 per cent ABV):   ★★★★**

March 14

I need to haul myself to Leicester and boost the coffers of the Bottle Store, not just because I'm short of supplies but because I have been set a diverting task: I must obtain some British beers which will impress the French. My mucker John, of *The Sun*, is off to see friends in France – one can only hope he has a sounder relationship with the natives than his paper does

– and is anxious to astound them with a selection of this land's foremost bottled ales. At the moment I have in mind Pedigree, Landlord and Sammy Smith's Oatmeal Stout; beyond those three I'm rather stumped – and I'm not even sure I'll be able to lay my paws on the Landlord, which would be a bit of a tragedy.

My endeavours should reap some reward, for John – whom I have been schooling in frothy ones – proposes to drive into the Ardennes to visit Chimay, the source of Belgium's most famous Trappist beers. I already have a surplus of Chimay glasses, but if he can pick up something quaint then my crusade on his behalf will be more than worthwhile. I'm bloody jealous of him, to be frank, but there you go.

Meanwhile, I must make do with scraps from the supermarket. This time a fortnight ago I was at the Hopduvel; tonight I sat at home with a **Staropramen**. Well, at least some trace of my Belgian escapades persists: BBC2 is showing *The Simpsons*.

Staropramen: see January 12

March 16

There was more than a hint of spring in the air today. It was an ideal day for jumping into the MG, ridding it of its roof and cruising to a country pub for a pint in the garden. Only one problem: the MG is still in hibernation, so thoughts of trundling to a bucolic hostelry went out of the window.

Instead I took in a Lotus exhibition, ogling lots of beautiful motors which I could not afford. I then traipsed around the circuit's motorsport museum, where I stood before a row of gleaming McLarens and paid tacit homage to my hero, the late Ayrton Senna, after whom my MG is named. The afternoon was indubitably entertaining; and yet as I drove back to Burton in the accursed Punto I couldn't escape a fed-up feeling, wistfully yearning for what I can't have and what I have no more.

71

I called in at the Wine Rack and bought an appropriately woeful bag of beers: Pete's Wicked Ale, Carlsberg Elephant, **Holsten Pils, Amstel Bier** and **Tiger Lager Beer**. The Wicked Ale, easily the star of the show, was put away for a more inspiring juncture, while my fleeting care for the Elephant had faded by the time I flopped down in front of *Coronation Street;* but I polished off the other three while watching the *Street* and an episode of *Columbo* (*Columbo* is like a classic beer: I can enjoy it over and over again and derive no lesser fulfilment each time). They made for a grim night's drinking.

Something has been lost in the translation where the label notes for Holsten Pils are concerned: it is touted as "the original Pils", which is plainly claptrap. Given its incredible proliferation in pubs and clubs, it is very possibly the only so-called Pils many myopic swiggers ever try; but I believe the "original" title belongs to some effort from Czechoslovakia, like. There may be substance in the fact that in its home city of Hamburg the beer is correctly known as Diät Pils, signifying it is a low-carbohydrate offering for diabetics (in Britain, of course, people took "Diät" to mean "diet" and were outraged when they got fat after downing a gallon every evening); but this may be crediting the spin-doctors with a tad too much slyness. I suspect it is merely a try-on, because – even allowing for the geographical abuse of the term – Holsten Pils isn't strictly a Pils at all.

Despite the scandalous nature of its labelling, it is a fair beer: dry and hoppy and, because all the sugar is turned to alcohol (as innumerable commercials have informed us through the years), packing a light-heavyweight punch. However, with its fatuous packaging and its insufferable in-your-face advertizing, it is so patently aimed at the "yoof" market – and therefore those who couldn't give a toss about what they gulp, as long as it looks the part when clasped in their hand – that it somehow irritates me. Ho-hum.

Amstel and Tiger are similarly mundane. Countless years ago my Bro' lived in Amsterdam, and this month he moved to

Singapore: if he can remember the taste of Amstel from his Dutch days then he'll be reassured by Tiger, since both are close cousins of the omnipresent Heineken. Amstel is the cleaner-tasting, Tiger the hoppier; both are pleasant enough but the epitome of ordinariness. Boring, to put it bluntly. I must confess that why I bought them is now a mystery to me.

Yet I cannot complain, ironically enough, because today has reinforced the urgency of storming the Bottle Store ASAP. It has also accentuated the importance of having heaps of money to lavish on a Lotus Seven. I shall attend to the former tomorrow; the latter, I'll wager, will have to wait.

Holsten Pils **(5.5 per cent ABV):**	★★★
Amstel Bier **(5 per cent ABV):**	★★★
Tiger Lager Beer **(5 per cent ABV):**	★★★

March 19

There is nothing wrong with drinking alone, but drinking in company is usually twice the treat. I mention this because today I bade farewell to Eugene, who flies to Hong Kong on the 21st and is unlikely to grace blighty again until Christmas at the earliest. Since my Bro' remains ever-distant, I am rapidly running out of supping partners who stipulate anything more than a pint of bitter or a bottle of Beck's. It is comforting, then, to be cultivating interest among other acquaintances: such philanthropic and educational work brings me satisfaction and, from a selfish view, fosters potential for future glass-clunking.

Before setting a course for Manchester, where Euge and I would knock the top off a couple for the last time in who knows how long, I played the part of the Beer Fairy this morning. The much-awaited trip to the Bottle Store two days ago yielded more than I had dared expect – including, just weeks after I had bemoaned its lack of availability over the past few years, Anchor Porter – and, as well as assembling a tidy array for myself, I was able to grab the selection John had requested for his French hosts and some stout for my Gran; today I passed these goodies on to their eager recipients.

John and I, sneaky journalists that we are, arranged a sinister 9.30am assignation in a lay-by just off the M42, halfway between Burton and John's Warwickshire home. I handed over a box of Samuel Smith's Oatmeal Stout, Imperial Stout, Taddy Porter and Old Brewery Pale Ale; Burton Bridge Burton Porter; Marston's Pedigree; Timothy Taylor Landlord; Sarah Hughes Dark Ruby Mild, brewed at the Beacon Hotel in Sedgley, near Dudley; Shepherd Neame Masterbrew, made in Faversham, Kent, by the brewery which claims to be the oldest in England; and George Gale's Prize Old Ale, from Portsmouth. John also wanted to take some pint glasses with which to wow his Chanel-and-Lacoste-wearing chums, so I gave him my last two "Make Mine a Marston's" straight-siders (another was dispatched to New Zealand in '96, so at least I'm doing the business when it comes to spreading the Marston's gospel). He swore he would not leave Chimay without securing me a tub of escavèche, the fish dish favoured by the locals as an accompaniment to Chimay White, so I keenly anticipate his return in a fortnight or so: he shall suffer my wrath if he fails in his quest.

Having delivered more Sammy Smith's to my Gran – who was clearly in need of a Tadcaster tonic, as she was feeling off-colour and was confined to bed – I called at the Marston's shop to replace my France-bound glassware. This curious little establishment – announced by an easily-missed sandwich-board and a window display featuring such diverse delights as Marston's sweatshirts, Marston's darts and Marston's cribbage-boards – is hidden away next to the brewery's ornate central entrance, which boasts wrought-iron gates and a brass nameplate but is not often used. Inside there is barely enough room to swing a bottle of Pedi, yet the shop is an Aladdin's cave for admirers. As my new glasses were being wrapped I glimpsed a pile of stupendously hideous Pedigree T-shirts, so I bought one for my Bro' and one for Euge: the might of Marston's shall descend upon the East shortly. The cost of my haul? A grand total of £7.40, which in Singapore or Hong Kong would probably land you a bottle of second-rate lager: perhaps Britain isn't so bad after all.

The thrash to Manchester has become no less dreadful since I last subjected myself to it. The M6 is evil enough, but the Younger's Kestrel Lager brewery on the outskirts of the city is a vision from the very bowels of Hell. Nowadays there is also the disconcertment of witnessing the Hulme Arch, a titanic boomerang which – with no motive apparent – has been rammed into the ground near a busy junction: Eugene assures me it serves no purpose whatsoever, yet a quarter of a mile before it loomed large I passed a billboard declaring: "Reasons to be cheerful... The Hulme Arch!" Am I missing something here?

Eugene and I were to meet at the highly idiosyncratic Circus Tavern, Portland Street, incongruously perched on the fringe of Chinatown. A tiny terraced pub, it has a lilliputian bar adorned with just two pumps – both of which, amusingly, dispense Tetley Bitter, from the Leeds brewery rated as the world's most prolific producer of cask-conditioned beer. Space is at a premium – only 20 to 30 customers can be accommodated – but I managed to snuggle into a corner with *The Daily Telegraph* and have a quiet read. I had travelled many miles but still arrived bang on 1pm, as scheduled; Eugene, true to form, came bounding in 25 minutes later, by which point the sports pages had been extensively thumbed.

I have never known the **Tetley Bitter** at the Circus to be anything other than first-class: creamy – almost milky, in fact – and delicately golden, with an enduring head and a dry but quenching aftertaste. I would happily have downed two or three in such sincere surroundings, but having to drive afterwards limited me to a pint: cruel, yes, but there can be no alternative in such circumstances. Euge and I traded appreciative sighs before I presented him with his Pedigree T-shirt and an Abbaye des Rocs glass, both designed to help him stay strong during what could be months of being denied a tolerable drop; he in turn gave me a pair of single-malt miniatures which he picked up during a recent weekend in Edinburgh.

After an hour's shopping I whisked him to his flat in Didsbury; and then it was time to say goodbye. "I've got no-one to drink with now," I told him mournfully; but my sorry plight was not sufficient to dissuade the callous bastard from jetting off and leaving me in beer-hunting limbo. Bugger. I shall miss him coming round to nick all my best ales. Bon voyage, mate.

Perhaps I could manipulate Guillo into widening his scope beyond Staropramen and the Burton Bridge. Tonight I shoved a Becker's Pils in his direction as we settled down with a takeaway from Leong and yet another European Cup quarter-final; and he liked it a lot, which was encouraging. The path from there to Orval is a tricky one to tread, but – as Eugene's prospective neighbours are wont to declare – a journey of a thousand miles begins beneath one's feet.

With Guillo relishing his Becker's, I spoiled myself rotten and opted for an **Anchor Liberty Ale**. The presence of Anchor makes San Francisco the only city in America which really appeals to me; the brewery is famous for its Steam Beer, but the rest of its range also exudes excellence. Liberty Ale was created in the mid-'70s after Anchor's owner, Fritz Maytag, had toured a handful of Britain's most celebrated breweries – among them, spookily enough, Marston's – to learn the secrets of ale-brewing. An all-malt beer, it has a hugely fruity bouquet and a terrifically dry, hoppy finish. All of Anchor's wares are exemplary, but Liberty Ale is right up there with the greats. What a day: I have lost a boozing buddy but gained a top-tenner.

Incidentally, I did permit Guillo a sip of Liberty. He raved about it, too, so he could yet come to cherish the elite. But by then he had already drained two Becker's; and, faced with the drive home, he couldn't risk a glass of anything else. How unfortunate: all the more for me.

Tetley Bitter (3.7 per cent ABV):	★★★★★
Anchor Liberty Ale (5.9 per cent ABV):	★★★★★★★

March 20

A pool-playing beer-lover such as myself knows that two seminal items originate from Brooklyn, New York: (1) the Balabushka cue; (2) Brooklyn Lager. The late George Balabushka was to pool cues what Stradivari was to violins: examples of his work are much sought-after and now fetch thousands of dollars in the States, and the odds of my ever owning one are roughly equal to the odds of my becoming World Pocket Billiards Champion. The award-winning **Brooklyn Lager** represents a revival of the all-malt beers of late-19th-century America, when NYC was dotted with more than 100 breweries; and I would have thought the odds of my finding it in Britain were roughly equal to the odds of my running a rack at straight pool – that's 15 balls in 15 shots – which are, I'm afraid, as damned near nil as it is possible to get.

Hurrah, then, for the odds-defying Bottle Store, which proffered rows of the stuff and has thus given me my first taste of it. Brooklyn Lager was the brainchild of home-brewing journalist Steve Hindy and banker Tom Potter, who set out to replicate the local lagers of pre-Prohibition (after Prohibition, of course, the growth of national leviathans like Anheuser-Busch, coupled with the effects of the Depression, further decimated the ranks of interesting beers in the States). It was contract-brewed by Utica-based FX Matt until the new Brooklyn Brewery took over.

Brooklyn Lager is ale-like in many ways: rich, full-bodied, very malty and with a long, long finish. If even a dozen pre-Prohibition lagers were as commendable then I can't say I'm surprised that people reacted to the taps' being turned off by equipping themselves with "heaters", screeching around the streets and machine-gunning each other: I would have been a trifle miffed myself to be robbed of such glorious frothy ones. I hesitate to harp on about it, but how Americans can consume zillions of litres of Budweiser when beers like this abound I do not know; for much the same reason that Britons consume zillions of gallons of Carling Black Label, I guess – because they can't be bothered to unearth owt better.

Seek and ye shall find. A Balabushka of a beer.

Brooklyn Lager (5.1 per cent ABV):

March 22

Oh, momentous day! Oh, happy, happy world! The journalist in me says it's too good to be true, but true it is: tonight, for the first time in my life, I ran a rack. Fifteen balls in one visit. I'd done it before on a cruddy 6ft-by-3ft table, but to do it on a 12ft-by-6ft is altogether a different proposition. By such petty accomplishments is my humble existence immeasurably enriched. If a juggernaut had crashed through the walls of the Spot-On and squashed me into the carpet seconds after I made that 15th ball – the six, gently rolled into a corner bag – I would have died a contented man.

Why did it happen? Not, I admit, because of my encounter with Brooklyn Lager and any attendant microscopic traces of George Balabushka. Most likely is my scanning of *Willie Mosconi on Pocket Billiards*, a book written in 1948 by the

19-time World Champ: it taught me I was frequently guilty of striking the cue-ball with inadequate authority, so I brought extra conviction to my game – with instant results. Just to put things into perspective, however, although my highest run now stands at 15, Willie Mosconi once potted 526 balls on the trot. Hmmm.

Actually, Brooklyn Lager would have been an ideal after-match beer; but, exasperatingly, I had none left. Instead my exploits were toasted with **Anchor Porter**, which, though devoid of any pool connection, was pertinent enough: I had to wait years to rediscover it, just as I had to wait years to run a rack – and, much like my coming of age on the green baize, it was worth that wait.

More than those of any other nation, quality American beers habitually possess label notes which are salutary rather than senseless. US micro-breweries customarily wrap theirs around the neck of the bottle, and they are concise, informative, accurate and intelligent – the very antithesis of the asinine and condescending garbage to be found elsewhere. It would be foolish to expect a brewery to portray its inventions as anything but magnificent – how welcome it would be if Miller Lite came garnished with a "Don't touch this – it's utter crap" warning – but surely it is not inconceivable to transcend a stream of meaningless prose which amounts to "Drink this – it's bloody ace!"? Anchor Porter's notes are on the flowery side – let's face it, the final sentence is almost absurd – but nevertheless say it all: "The deep-black colour, the thick, creamy head and the intensely rich flavour of Anchor Porter, made in San Francisco since 1974, have earned this delicious and unique brew a worldwide reputation. It is aesthetically pleasing and wholly superior in every respect [blimey!]."

How can you top the frothy one which topped running a rack? By moving on to **Anchor Steam Beer**, universally applauded as one of the giants of the scene. Steam beer dates back to the Californian Gold Rush, when ale-brewers in San Francisco sated the influx of lager-hungry East Coasters by employing a lager yeast at ale temperatures. Fritz Maytag was so appalled when he ordered a Steam Beer back in the mid-'60s and was cordially informed that Anchor was about to fold that he bought the brewery, struggling for a decade before it at last became profitable; like Pierre Celis, of Hoegaarden fame, he is a beer-hunter's hero.

Anchor Steam Beer – which is thought to have earned its name from the heavy carbonation of the Gold Rush brews – is fermented in uncommonly shallow vessels and emerges with an enthralling combination of ale fruitiness and lager freshness. It is a very special beer – although I must say that now I consider its stablemate, Liberty Ale, to have a slight edge.

What I knock back when I run *two* racks will have to somewhat awesome; but at least, bearing in mind my current rate of improvement, I'll have about 20 years to come up with something. I wonder what Willie Mosconi downed after that sequence of 526?

Anchor Porter **(5.7 per cent ABV):**	★★★★★★
Anchor Steam Beer **(4.8 per cent ABV):**	★★★★★★

March 23

I'm not having much luck when it comes to matching a frothy one to a mood. Last night I attained a landmark in my pool career just a day after drinking the beer I would have deemed the perfect reward (okay, that Balabushka link is less than tenuous, but give me some credit for my twisted imagination). Tonight I watched a documentary about *Star Wars* director/producer George Lucas and was caught out once more.

Even speaking as someone who at the age of eight had a poster of the *Millennium Falcon* on his bedroom wall, I can take or leave George Lucas and his *Star Wars* fixation. I like cheering for Darth Vader and listening to the perturbing wail of the TIE fighters, but I don't care too much for anything else – particularly the role the movies played in inciting Hollywood to put bums on seats with special effects rather than such minor concerns as brilliant scripts or perceptive acting. Of greater note than his contribution to cinema, I say, is where Lucas was born: Modesto, California, home of the St Stan's brewery, which makes formidable interpretations of the Düsseldorf Altbier style.

So there I sat, beholding endless shots of Modesto, with nary a St Stan's in sight on either my gogglebox or – more upsettingly – my table. Annoying; very annoying, come to think of it, because I picked up a Dark Alt at the Bottle Store and then put it back down again. I hit upon a solid compromise, though: **Anchor Liberty Ale** (for Lucas now spends much of his time in San Francisco) in my St Stan's glass (for, to my perpetual shame, I have no Anchor glass). I am nothing if not resourceful; besides, having to fall back on Liberty Ale isn't exactly a hardship, whatever the mood.

Anchor Liberty Ale: see March 19

March 27

I have no time for people who needlessly grind themselves into the dirt through alleged overworking. There is a thin line between commendable commitment and farcical fanaticism, between diligence and death-wish, and no-one ever wheezed with their dying breath: "Crikey, if only I'd spent more time in the office." Furthermore, most of those who claim to put in 20 hours a day are normally just thrashing about and achieving bugger all: I knew a man who prided himself on being the first to arrive in the morning and the last to leave at night, and yet he succeeded only in bringing his company to its knees. Sheer madness. Having said all that, I would love to be at my desk now: Easter, in my opinion, is no time to be lumbered with a load of days off.

The trouble is that everyone else is on a break, so all attempts to do anything or go anywhere are likely to be thwarted by gridlock. This would not be so disagreeable if Ayrton were available, since I'm quite prepared to languish in a traffic-jam if everyone can gawp at my Roadster; but, with the Mogster a week or so from resurrection (excuse the sacrilege), the notion of stewing in the Punto is not one which fills me with elation. Hence my decision to skulk indoors and chip away at a mountain of unwatched videos accumulated over untold eons – beginning with four episodes of *A Touch of Frost*, David Jason's dour detective drama.

If you reckon that's a dismal way to spend the day – and it was, for eight hours' absorption of *Frost* does not constitute a barrel of laughs – then spare a thought for the Norwegians. They have to cope not only with a veritable superfluity of frost but with a government which has done its best to tax frothy ones to the point of extinction. Locating beers of more than 4.5 per cent ABV in Norway would be a mission worthy of Jim Phelps and his team, for the bureaucrats have dealt them such a severe hammering that they are now either sold only in shops abiding by reems of ridiculous regulations or exported. Norwegian politicians, it appears, cannot rid themselves of the idea that a Scandinavian who slurps anything stronger than a standard lager will promptly jump into a longboat and embark upon a spree of raping, burning and pillaging.

Confronted with this abject lunacy, Norway's oldest brewery now even exports to Britain. Its hesitancy in doing so and the petite scale of its operation may have much to with its name: Aass – a monicker which upon initial examination ranks alongside Belgium's Slag Lager and that other Scandinavian titan, Krapp loo-roll. You may think "Get your lips round an Aass" has the makings of a slogan to woo Carling Black Label disciples by the thousand, but titter ye not:

it's pronounced "Orse", as the label for **Aass Classic** is not slow in stressing (how about "Put your money on an Aass", then?).

Aass Classic is the brewery's rebadged Pilsner. Like all the beers from Aass, it conforms not only to Norway's preposterous rules but to those of the infinitely more sensible Reinheitsgebot, Germany's 1516 Purity Law. The label's assertion that it is "rated as one of the great classic beers of the world" is news to me, but it is evidently a more-than-competent Pilsner. So as to spare its home nation years of unrelenting carnage, it weighs in at precisely 4.5 per cent ABV. Phew. Careful, now, guys.

Aass Bock, meanwhile, has been brewed with not an iota's consideration for the good folk of Norway. At a thoroughly reckless 6.5 per cent ABV, it has the power to spark revolution, bring down governments and possibly provoke thermonuclear warfare. Crates of it are hurried from the country under armed guard and in lead-lined containers. Foreigners who irresponsibly expose themselves to its dark and unusually creamy richness jeopardize their very being.

Even with my frothy ones to soothe me, by the time the credits rolled on the fourth instalment of *Frost* – which ended with the eponymous hero weeping over the open coffin of his Detective Sergeant – I was mildly distraught. A superlative programme, yes; but very depressing. At least I was able to console myself with the knowledge that worse things happen in Norway.

Politicians, eh? Silly Aasses.

Aass Classic **(4.5 per cent ABV):**	★★★★
Aass Bock **(6.5 per cent ABV):**	★★★★

March 28

It has just occurred to me that I am a pudding-head: the month is about to pass by without my having drunk a single bottle of Märzen, the beer nowadays associated with the Munich Oktoberfest but nonetheless named after the German for "March". Märzen is so-called because in pre-refrigeration days March was the last month in which it could be brewed before being lagered. Whether it is better enjoyed in October or March is neither here nor there – the weather is much the same during both, so there can be no real expression of preference based on that regard – but if a beer is named after March then I am bound to class that month as expedient a period as any in which to pour one. Only one problem: no Märzen.

What was I thinking of at the Bottle Store? I actually eyed a Spaten Märzen and said to myself: "Nah, don't fancy that." Maybe I was preoccupied with John's requirements for his French excursion: if that escavèche is not already nestled in his suitcase, perhaps with a gold-ringed Chimay Cinq Cents glass by way of a bonus, I shall chin him. I also neglected to buy any Easter beer – even though I espied some Boskeun (Easter Bunny), from the Dolle Brouwers (Mad Brewers), of Esen, Belgium. I know that at the start of the year I advocated not being a slave to the beer calendar, but this is just a pathetic performance.

Might as well be 100 per cent off-the-wall in the light of such gormlessness: I soaked up John Frankenheimer's *The Manchurian Candidate* with an **Oechsner Weißbier.** Weißbier has nothing to do with March or Easter (or even Manchuria); but it doesn't automatically follow that it will be unpleasant if sampled on anything other than a summer afternoon in Bavaria (oh, if only...). Oechsner Weißbier is pale for the style but throws a towering head and is typically turbid, fruity and then sour; the family-run brewery, based in Ochsenfurt, also makes a challenging Schwarzbier.

A check on the pantry revealed the assortment which should

take me through the remainder of Easter: Pete's Wicked Ale, Carlsberg Elephant, St Georgen Bräu Schwarzenbock and – cheers – Mönchshof Weihnachts Bier. Scholars of German will recognize that the latter is a Christmas beer. Bloody marvellous.

Oechsner Weißbier (5.2 per cent ABV): ★★★★

March 29

Like Laurel and Hardy, Steptoe and Son or fish and chips, beer and sport make a splendid couple. This is not to suggest that running a marathon with a crate of Rochefort 10° swilling around your belly is a smart idea; nor is it to suggest that decanting a glass of Foster's over the head of the spectator seated in front of you – a fate which once befell me on Sydney Cricket Ground's notorious Yabba's Hill – is riotously funny. I mean to say that the practice of poring over the twists and turns of a sporting event, either there and then or courtesy of the cathode ray, is almost invariably enhanced by the addition of some frothy ones (the obvious exception being, as in many cases where drink is concerned, when you lack the intelligence to distinguish between sociability and loutishness).

Certain sporting occasions will forever make me think of certain beers, and vice versa. I can't recall who won the 1991 Australian Masters, but I still tremble at the memory of the lukewarm Victoria Bitter my Bro' and I courageously stomached while pursuing Greg Norman around Sydney's Lakes course (golf pundits have accused Norman of being a choker, but we did our own share of choking that day). I savoured two bottles of Köstritzer Schwarzbier, brought back from Germany by my ever-selfless Mum, while the last round of the 1995 US Open unfurled on screen. My Bro' and I staged our own Weissbierfest after dragging the portable TV on to the patio to watch The Open in 1996 (the weather was so hot and bright that the beers were ruined and the picture was invisible, but c'est la vie); and so on.

The observant may have inferred that my Bro' and I have a soft spot for golf. He has a handicap of three and plays as often as he can, although membership of clubs in Singapore is so prohibitively expensive that his scores could be poised to rocket. My handicap is that I can't stand playing the bloody game, which is without question the most frustrating ever devised: having quit at the grand old age of 14 – coming out of exile only for a round in Sydney on Boxing Day in 1991 (on the 18th I missed a hole-in-one by inches and then four-putted, which did little to quell my desire to get back to retirement) – I remain an avid follower of the fairways and a student of course architecture.

Just to prove it is not the exclusive domain of golf tournaments, though, the beer-and-sport list also has a nostalgic berth for none other than the Boat Race; and the frothy one which shares that berth is Hoegaarden. I must state categorically that never in a million years would I watch the Boat Race by choice: I could grouch for hours about how futile it is – a "race" which limits its field of entry to two can hardly be judged meaningful – but suffice it to say that anyone who doesn't study at Oxford or Cambridge or isn't impressed by such dubious British "traditions" should pay it no heed. My hatred for this most vain of regattas notwithstanding, several years ago I was forced to sustain a full helping of it at a Belgian household Eugene and I were visiting.

Our channel-switching hosts, the Jeurissen family, were so dumbfounded to come across such rot on BBC1 (they were used to rot of another kind: *Neighbours*) that they saw it through to its outcome, peppering their commentary with reflective phrases like "stupid English". They also seized the opportunity to mock all things British; unable to blame them, we joined in. Afterwards, amid gasps of worship from we guests, Mr Jeurissen opened his drinks cabinet to reveal a stack of

Hoegaarden tumblers; and these, as if to further ram home Belgium's superiority, were duly filled. It was Mr Jeurissen who obtained me my first Hoegaarden glass, so I will always be in his debt – even if he did subject me to the Boat Race in its horrific entirety.

Well, there it was again this afternoon: the dazzling spectacle of two boats scything through filthy waters while a BBC chap screamed with excitement as the crews' respective oars – gosh, be still my beating ticker – almost *touched*. Wowser. With neither Mr Jeurissen nor Hoegaarden to bring frivolity to the proceedings, I sought refuge in ITV and a sport many would denounce as even drearier: Formula One.

Although I steadfastly defend it against charges of monotony, F1 holds a terrible place on my role of beer-and-sport reminiscences. On May 1 1994 Eugene and I went for a Sunday-lunchtime drink at the Three Stags Heads, Wardlow Mires, Derbyshire, a remote farmhouse inn popular with walkers, and en route heard that there had been an horrendous crash during the early laps of the San Marino Grand Prix; by the time we left the pub, stepping back into the beautiful sunshine, the radio was reporting that the driver involved had been declared brain-dead. The driver was my hero, Ayrton Senna; the beer was Kelham Island Pale Rider.

No such fitting frothy one for today's qualifying session at Ayrton's home GP: instead a bottle of **Carlsberg Elephant** was reluctantly plucked from the fridge. Christened in honour of the imposing statues which form the gates of Carlsberg's Copenhagen brewery, Elephant is very much a Danish bock; it has never designated itself thus, but its strength and maltiness fulfil the criteria. I was once fond of it but am now simply sanguine; yet it is definitely more deserving of attention than the witless Carlsberg Special Brew, the beer whose get-you-wrecked-quick infamy spawned a glut of syrupy loopy-juices and made oblivion accessible to down-and-outs everywhere.

Talking of loopy-juice, Marston's Owd Rodger – a loopy-juice of no mean calibre, I hasten to emphasize – features in one last beer-and-sport blast from the past. On the night of Frank Bruno's inaugural scuffle with Mike Tyson I had four pints of OR and was then dim enough to devour a duck curry: by the time the bell sounded for round one, of course, I had been violently ill and had collapsed into bed. Desperate days.

Carlsberg Elephant
(7.2 per cent ABV):   ★★★

March 30

Strangely overcome by a startling resolve, I heaved back Ayrton's cover this afternoon to gauge how grievously winter had ravaged him. He bore not a speck of grime, let alone a patch of rust, yet I still washed and polished him. Predictably, his battery was as flat as a sash-marked lambic; but I will deal with that anon.

Exhausted by my three hours' determined graft, I sat down with some frothy ones and Stanley Kramer's *On the Beach*, the film described by *Halliwell's* as "about the most downbeat production ever to come from Hollywood". One of those end-of-the-world movies of the late '50s and early '60s – when the industry was obsessed with the Cold War and trotted out doom-laden fare like *Dr Strangelove*, *Failsafe* and *The Bedford Incident* – *On the Beach* is almost two-and-a-half hours in length and tells the bleak tale of a northern hemisphere obliterated by atomic bombs and a southern hemisphere waiting for the radiation clouds to arrive. The beers were about as uplifting.

Most people have a fixed concept of Christmas beers –
dark, warming, sufficiently potent to leave you slumped face-
down in the mince pies – so **Mönchshof Weihnachts
Bier**, from the great brewing town of Kulmbach, Bavaria,
comes as something of a jolt: it is bottom-fermented, pale
and, by German standards, not extravagantly strong. Maybe
it is better as an Easter beer. Maybe, since Kulmbach (and
Mönchshof in particular) is renowned for dark and malty
lagers, the brewery was striving to offer something different for
the festive season: Mönchshof, after all, is best-known for its
Kloster Schwarz Bier, christened "the black Pils". Maybe *On
the Beach* was just getting to me.

St Georgian Bräu, of Buttenheim, Franconia, is acclaimed
for its Kellerbier, a very hoppy, very dry, unfiltered lager of
low carbonation; I hadn't heard of **St Georgen Bräu
Schwarzenbock** but had been looking forward to trying it
since acquiring some at the Bottle Store. Alas,
Schwarzenbock is leagues beneath Kellerbier: it is ruby-
red, malty and powerful but somehow banal – arguably
the biggest disappointment of the year so far, given my
haughty expectations. To be fair, the radiation-
threatened Fred Astaire was gassing himself by over-
revving his Ferrari when I emptied my glass; but I
cannot hold him solely culpable.

I could identify with Fred's death-by-classic-car
whim, but *On the Beach* contains an even better scene
for the discerning drinker. Early in the film, with the
radiation clouds still five months away, a pair of snobs in
a snooty gentlemen's club lament the wine committee's
"lack of foresight" in failing to presage that Armageddon
would leave them with less than half a year in which to
polish off 400 bottles of vintage port; later, the clouds
having descended, the club is shown again, this time
deserted save for the stoical wine-waiter – who, still dressed

in his uniform and brandishing a silver tray, treats himself to a nip of said port and, with an approving nod, quietly prepares to await the inevitable. What a wonderful way to go.

Mönchshof Weihnachts Bier (5.6 per cent ABV): ★★★★

St Georgen Bräu Schwarzenbock (7.3 per cent ABV): ★★★

March 31

Easter Day at work. Yes, it's humdrum; yes, it's lonely; but it whacks vegetating in a queue of caravans somewhere in the Peak District. The major snag is finding an eatery near the office: it's either McDonald's or a pub-chain boozer – and they're pretty much the same thing.

Decent pubs are being increasingly overwhelmed by a craving for the homogeneous. The peculiar, the authentic and the unique are being steamrollered by the lookalike, the soundalike and the tastealike. Why is it impossible to drive five miles without passing a McDonald's? Because people want to be able to mosey into any joint in the world and eat the same sort of burger at the same sort of table next to the same sort of plant. Soon it could be impossible to drive five miles without passing a pub where you can drink the same sort of beer at the same sort of table next to the same sort of ersatz bookcase.

Not all pub chains are rubbish – I know of at least two which are outstanding, in fact, although both (significantly?) are relatively small concerns – but most of the larger ones, with their uniformed staff and their photofit interiors and their universal menus, are both clinical and cynical. They create jobs and attract punters aplenty; but a pox on them if they eventually rob us of proper pubs.

Detesting McDonald's more than just about anything on the planet, I dauntlessly elected the pub-chain boozer and sauntered into the Babington Arms, a conveniently-situated branch of the JD Wetherspoon empire. Suitably unmoved, I had a **Beck's Bier** and exited with no shortage of alacrity.

Beck's Bier: see January 18

April 4

A number of beery matters are coming to a head (pun intended – sorry). Most, sadly, are not turning out as I had wished; but at least I can report that one has brought a modicum of success, albeit not via the envisaged route.

Pessimism and resignation prevailed when I heard that John had been back from his hols for the best part of a week: since he hadn't been in touch, I could only presume he had miserably failed to obtain me a memento from Chimay. I told myself that perhaps those scathing of the Fourth Estate were right: you should never trust a journalist – especially one from *The Sun*. I decided that I would refrain from according him the promised chinning, having carefully considered (1) his valued custom and (2) his size (6'4" or thereabouts); but no escavèche, I thought, and no gold-rimmed glass. Damn.

My worst suspicions were seemingly confirmed when we finally spoke. "How did you get on at Chimay, then, John?" I asked.

"Well, we didn't actually get there in the end."

Yes, here we go. "How so?"

"The car broke down."

Uh-huh. Trying to let me down gently. Rightio. So I was right, then: no escavèche, no gold-rimmed glass. Marvellous.

The car's electrics went up in smoke, said John, robbing him of indicators and windscreen wipers. Two-and-a-half days of potential travelling had been lost by the time a French garage cannibalized one of its own models to rectify the fault.

He stopped for a Chimay Red in Bruges on his way home, but that was as close as he got to Trappist territory.

He was full of apologies – each of them unnecessary, for I, as a Punto owner, know more than most how one's dreams can be ruined by the shortcomings of one's motor – but ruefully conceded that he had, as I feared, returned sans escavèche. And then he promptly brightened up what had become a dark day: "But my French friend did give me a glass…"

"Yeah?" I said, suddenly rejuvenated.

"A Chimay glass…"

"Yeah?"

"Gold-rimmed…"

"Gold writing?"

"I'll just check… Yes."

Fate had lent a hand: John's host had presented him with the very glass I wanted. And in due course John will present it to me – in exchange, as is only fair, for one of my standard Chimay glasses, as I can't expect him to expand his appreciation of Trappist ales without the benefit of his own kelk. Pity about the escavèche, but you can't have everything; besides, maybe one day I should cut out the middle-man and simply trundle to the Ardennes to fetch some myself.

Incidentally, the selection of British frothy ones which John took across was a real hit with the recipient, René. John knew this to be so, because his chum, having studiously examined them, neglected to open a single bottle and hurriedly stored them away for a solo session. Obviously keen to cement Anglo-French relations, René sent me a couple of corked bottles of 3 Monts, a bière de garde from the St Sylvestre brewery, for which I am extremely grateful. Salut, René; and salut, John – I never doubted you for an instant.

The news is otherwise grim; and the grimmest of all is that my Bro', who was set to visit before this month was out, is now unlikely to be with us until late summer. He is so busy settling into his new position that he can't even pop across for some scheduled extra training from Rolls-Royce. A mutual mucker who also works for R-R was in Singapore recently, and he told me that he and my Bro' were very much the worse for wear after a night of Tiger; but I find this of scant comfort, because my Bro' deserves to get utterly wrecked on artisanal Belgian ales rather than on bland Asian lagers. As if being unable to knock the top off a few with him were not distressing enough, I have been saving a gargantuan pile of *Bilkos* for us to tackle – it is our favourite programme, as it was our Dad's – and am not sure how much longer even my deep reserves of willpower can stop me from watching them alone while nursing some consoling beers.

Another no-show is my Kölsch-loving Uncle Henny. He was to come to England next month, but now my Mum is journeying to Germany instead. Thus any hopes of congenial evenings spent downing copious amounts of Früh and Küppers have been thrown out of the window. I shall find solace only if my Mum crams her suitcases with Richmodis – Henny's preferred brand and, since he introduced me to it at his house last year, now also my own – before she steps aboard the flight for Birmingham.

I thought a bottle of **Pete's Wicked Ale**, the founding product of the Wicked range, might raise my spirits. I thought it would be impossible to remain glum after reminding myself of its copper-red colour and its rich, malty palate. But when I realized it was the last beer in the pantry – indeed, the last beer in the house – all the gold-rimmed Chimay glasses on Earth wouldn't have brought a smile to my face. This month can only get better.

**Pete's Wicked Ale
(5.1 per cent ABV):**

April 5

With the cupboard bare and no opportunity to shoot to Leicester or Sheffield in the near future, I was again left to scratch around at the Wine Rack today. Excluding those already sampled this year, I was met with a forlorn assortment of frothy ones: Michelob, Coors, Whitbread-brewed Heineken, Corona, Stella Artois Dry ("Dry" equals "tasteless"), San Miguel, various cans etcetera. After much depressing deliberation I went Dutch and opted for Grolsch Pilsener (known in Britain as Grolsch Premium Lager, a name which inadvertently avoids offending Pilsen but lumps an above-average beer in with the Carling Premiers of this world) and **Oranjeboom Pilsener**.

Oranjeboom, of Breda, is nowadays controlled by Interbrew, overlord of De Kluis. Interbrew's intervention might have heralded a reduction in character among the Hoegaarden beers, but the same is unlikely with Oranjeboom's: they are almost devoid of character already. Oranjeboom Pilsener is dreadfully dull, with even its label smacking of a particularly dour period of the '70s; and yet, for reasons I am unable to fathom, I cannot pretend to dislike it and might even go so far as to declare that I prefer it to both Heineken and Amstel, the similarly duff Dutch Pils against which it should be measured.

Eugene claims to remember a time when Oranjeboom was sufficiently beloved in Britain to merit its own advertizing jingle. This must have been back when Allied Breweries had sought to gain a foothold in Europe by buying Oranjeboom; it would also solve the riddle of why a relative of mine who worked for Allied casually mentioned a few years ago that 50-odd Oranjeboom glasses were gathering dust in his pantry. Unfortunately – or perhaps fortunately – I struggle to recall the ditty Euge so kindly reproduced, and I don't think a call to Hong Kong is really necessary. I can only muse that anyone who was able to come up with a rhyme for "Oranjeboom" must have been one hell of a lyricist.

Oranjeboom Pilsener (5 per cent ABV):

April 6

Shame on the man who doesn't admit his mistakes. Having been so wary of the Babington Arms earlier this week that I risked only a **Beck's Bier** before fleeing, I was viciously rebuked by my dear mate Phil, worshipper of Pilsner Urquell and La Trappe Tripel, who berated me for not trying any of the cask-conditioned ales: the **Courage Directors**, he said, was first-rate.

I confess that I had been narrow-minded apropos the Babington Arms' handpumped fare. I had based my approach on the evidence of some atrociously cold bitters at another JD Wetherspoon pub in Derby and had no intention of tossing more money down the overflow. Keeping British ales in acceptable nick is not easy, and I am — arguably to my detriment — sceptical of any boozer which doesn't immediately strike me as up to the job. But I was willing to heed Phil's advice and wandered over for a lunchtime drink — only to discover that an erroneously prescient cohort had a bottle of Beck's waiting for me.

I drained the Beck's and then chanced a half of Directors (so-called because it was originally brewed for the top-nobs at Courage's Bristol brewery). It was rather on the chilled side — almost as cold as the Beck's, to tell the truth — but eventually, to my surprise, the beer's well-balanced, rich, fruity characteristics were perfectly apparent. Quite a revelation, I must say. A lesson has been learned: sizeable pub-chains are capable of serving ales in satisfactory condition.

Honourable type that I am, I stand prepared to admit my mistake. To myself, that is. I haven't admitted it to Phil, of course. And the pub itself is still rubbish. So there we go.

Beck's Bier: see January 15

Courage Directors
(4.8 per cent ABV): ★★★★

April 10

As the French say: "Tout vient à qui sait attendre." It has been an agonizing wait – two years, five months and 10 days (not that I'm counting, like) – but the curse of the Fiat Punto has at last been lifted from me. No longer must I be cloaked in automotive gloom. No longer must I start the day by disturbing the neighbours with the rattle of dodgy tappets and the screech of an errant fan-belt. No longer must I drench my shoes in diesel. After 46,703 miles, the ordeal is at an end. I am now the keeper of a shiny, comparatively luxurious, blissfully quiet, petrol-engined Ford Escort. Although not wishing in any way to advocate drink-driving, I felt the happy event cried out for a celebratory frothy one.

With the setting sun bringing dramatic relief to the hills which separate my village from the next, it was one of those evenings which beg an excursion to a country pub. Guillo and I, blessed with half an hour to kill before the kick-off of a Cup-Winners' Cup semi-final, agreed that a visit to the Bridge Inn was well overdue: this meant the Escort's inaugural run was a scintillating round-trip of approximately one-and-a-half miles, but the meagre scope for pleasure at the wheel was more than assuaged by the vast scope for pleasure at the bar.

As I mentioned earlier, my Dad was born at the Bridge; I don't know whether it was a sense of history or a regard for the best **Marston's Pedigree** in the cosmos which shaped his partiality, but he preferred to do his supping there, too – and I

can't say I blame him. Unless Marston's inflicts a particularly
repulsive refit upon it – and this, I trust, is unlikely – it will
forever occupy a spot in my heart. It stands next to the
Trent & Mersey Canal – into which my Dad, in a state of
what might be politely termed "confusion", once casually
stepped after being invited on to a barge for an after-hours
top-up – and to sit in the garden, Pedi in hand, and watch
the boats chug past is one of life's simplest treats.

My true halcyon days at the Bridge came during my sixth-
form years. My pals and I must have been something of an old-
fashioned bunch, because while others of our tender age were
cutting a debauched swathe through the Friday-night club
scene we were paying homage to Marston's in a cheery local.
After four or five Pedigrees – or, God forbid, a few glasses of
Owd Rodger – we were usually ready to accompany the
resident pianist, the venerable Mack, with slurred renditions
of Sinatra classics and the likes of *We'll Meet Again*. Ah, the
Bridge Inn Choral Society: dear, dear. We would often
jump into a car at lunchtime and race to the Bridge for a
pint and a sandwich, removing our school ties
beforehand so as not to appear too youthful; I remember
occasionally attending a German class in the afternoon
while still sporting my "I visited the Bridge Inn" T-
shirt, which made me feel extremely cool at the time
but now, looking back, makes me feel a trifle silly. I
doubt whether today's sixth-formers follow our lead –
slurping bitter in a tranquil pub is probably not
considered very "phat" – but I must admit that if I
behaved in such a way myself nowadays I would be flat
on my back: where the hell did we put all those frothy
ones?

I may have become more sedate with the passage of
time, but the beer is as fantastic as ever. Some people are
scornful of ale served from the barrel, but I've yet to come
across anyone who has been disappointed by the Bridge's
gravity-dispensed Pedigree. Aside from the magnificence of
the beer itself, there is something profoundly charming about
watching the barman disappear with a tray of empty glasses and

return minutes later with a plethora of pints: the interval is exquisite. A northerner of my acquaintance once colourfully dismissed straight-from-the-cask beers as "pisswater", obviously aghast at the absence of an abiding head; conversely, legend has it that my Dad once stunned a German waiter by complaining that his foaming lager contained too much fluff and not enough liquid – a point he sought to prove by shoving his finger into the glass until he reached something wet. Each to his own, but I won't have a negative word said about my local's nectar.

Guillo and I had an unrushed pint apiece, emerged from the pub and remarked how dazzling my Escort looked, picked up a takeaway from Leong (who launched a vicious attack on my paymasters, refusing to accept that they hadn't accorded me a BMW; I admire your sentiments, Leong) and sat down to the game. Since John had called at the office earlier in the week to drop off the Chimay glass – and what a beauty it is – and the bottles of **St Sylvestre 3 Monts**, we were able to swill something ostensibly out of the ordinary. If mainland Europe dominated on the pitch, though, England took the honours off it: Pedigree 1, 3 Monts 0.

Like Germany's Märzen, bière de garde was originally brewed around March and then laid down in anticipation of those summer months not conducive to brewing. The name means "beer to keep"; Phil, who is singularly unmoved by the style, insists it should mean "beer to keep and forget about" (cheers, Phil). I must confess that I find it one of the less exciting sorts of frothy one, although that is not to imply it should automatically be deemed uninteresting or poor: Kölsch is not the most thrilling kind of beer in existence, yet I consider Richmodis and Früh absolute classics. 3 Monts – named after a trio of hills near the brewery and presented, like many bières de garde, in a champagne bottle – is pale, dry, malty, fruity and pleasingly warming; it is also alarmingly drinkable, and I was genuinely amazed when I studied the small print and read "Alc vol 8.5%". I am quietly impressed.

The crucial task for the coming days is to obtain some beers for the US Masters, which climaxes on Sunday; and in so doing I shall spare a thought for my poor Bro', who had the opportunity to jet to Augusta with a wealthy New Zealander friend but then had his fantasies shot down in flames when he was sent to Singapore. To compound his despondency, he has just discovered that the tournament is not even *screened* in Singapore. No celebratory drinks for him this week, methinks.

Marston's Pedigree: see February 3	
St Sylvestre 3 Monts **(8.5 per cent ABV):**	★★★★

April 13

As ever, the US Masters made for a bewitching scene; yet, having been denied the time to whip to the Bottle Store, I didn't possess a beer to do justice to the drama. Still, at least I actually saw it: my Bro' will have to wait until I send him the tape.

I could – and maybe should – have headed for Leicester at some juncture during the past three days; but, because I put Ayrton on the road this week, my spare time has been geared towards blasting along leafy lanes rather than thundering up and down the M1. Apart from the remaining bottle of 3 Monts and a surplus of Becker's, my supplies offered only **Grolsch Pilsener**. Grolsch, I concluded, was not fit to accompany the golf but would suffice for the altogether less enthralling spectacle of the weekend's Grand Prix, a typically processional affair conducted around a glorified go-kart track.

Many moons ago, when he worked in Amsterdam, my Bro' would come home with crates of Grolsch piled high in his car. I loved it, and when the crates' contents had been exhausted I would buy it in cans (oh, the innocence of youth) from the supermarket. Even now, a decade later, a couple of those crates lurk in the garden – discreetly concealed betwixt fences and conifers, of course – patiently waiting for the day when I get round to securing a refund on the bottles. When I went to Amsterdam myself, expecting to wallow in a veritable sea of Grolsch, I was gutted to discover that 95 per cent of the bars were contracted to Heineken or Amstel: reality can be cruel sometimes.

In these enlightened times – yeah, right – Grolsch can be found on draught throughout the UK; it is also brewed and bottled under licence by Bass. Both versions are wretched, and one can only be thankful that the original – complete with swing-top bottle, the aborted phasing-out of which turned into a marketing coup for the brewery in the '50s – is still imported from Gelderland. Grolsch enjoys a lengthy conditioning and is then left unpasteurized, allowing its fresh, floral, hoppy character to survive undiminished.

The brewery – the Netherlands' largest independent – also produces an excellent Mei Bok, the appropriate glass for which my Bro' proudly displayed at his Amsterdam flat. Several years ago, when I asked if I might add said glass to my collection, he was forced to reveal that he had broken it. Maybe, after all, he deserves to miss the Masters.

**Grolsch Pilsener
(5 per cent ABV):**

April 17

I seem to have earned a certain infamy. When I strolled into the Bottle Store this evening a member of staff instantly dashed from behind the counter and, bracing himself for my clearing of the shelves, handed me a capacious cardboard box.

"You're psychic," I told him.

"No," he said, "I'm used to it."

The spoils were plenteous indeed. There were some new wares from Oechsner, including an irresistible Schwarzbier mug, and two of the world's finest frothy ones: St Georgen Bräu Kellerbier and Rauchenfelser Steinbier, both from Bavaria. Stocks of La Trappe which had exceeded their ridiculous "best by" dates were on sale at cut prices: ironic, since a Dutch or Belgian café-owner with any nous would charge extra for a vintage drop. I also bought some De Kluis Hoegaarden Grand Cru and Verboden Vrucht, although I was mildly upset to see that the packaging of these beers has again become increasingly functional and inversely attractive. The load was completed by Westmalle and La Gauloise, from Belgium; Asahi Super Dry, from Japan (about which I am already having the gravest doubts); and **Schneider Aventinus**, from Kelheim, near Munich.

I polished off the latter tonight, and it was nothing less than sensational. The standard (if "standard" is a fair word) Schneiderweisse is *the* Weissbier and a stalwart of my top 10; Aventinus, the brewery's Weizen Doppelbock, cannot be far behind. It is named after the historian who first described Bavaria, Johannes Aventinus; I have never liked historians – well, I didn't like my history teacher – but I shall make an exception in his case. Aventinus is tawny, dark brown, rich and fruity, sweet and sour, challenging, rewarding, ultimately smooth and generally superb. I recently read that it can be an unrivalled bedtime drink on a warm evening, and that's an assertion from which I cannot dissent: after but one bottle I was a model of late-night contentment.

Tracking down Weissbier in Britain is a cinch now, but the Doppelbock interpretations are elusive beasts. Apart from Aventinus, the most common is probably Pikantus, which is made by Erdinger, the biggest producer of Weissbier in Germany (and therefore anywhere). The Bottle Store hasn't stocked any Erdinger for a while, but the Dram or Small Beer might just hold a surprise or two. Perhaps the time has come to indulge in an optimistic thrash to Sheffield or Lincoln; in the meantime, though, I shall steadily wade through my latest acquisitions and hope that each brings as much joy as tonight's choice (even if I know all too well that the Asahi Super Dry could be the worst beer of the year so far).

Schneider Aventinus
(8 per cent ABV):

April 18

Black mood, black beer: having loitered in the office to assist in the mending of a wayward computer, I ambled into the car-park tonight and was met with the horrifying sight of my eight-day-old Escort minus wheeltrims. So that's what you get for trying to be helpful. My car now looks like a CID patrol vehicle; and so it shall stay, too, because I'm not providing some bloody-minded toe-rag with further amusement by forking out for a new set of tear-off frisbees. Blimey, such scandalous happenings are enough to drive a man to drink.

I drowned my sorrows in **Oechsner Schwarzbier**, a frothy one as dark and foreboding as my disposition. Schwarzbier has been the subject of a revival similar to that of its opposite in nomenclature, Weissbier, with the reunification of Germany allowing a style once confined to the East to find favour elsewhere. The epitome is Köstritzer Schwarzbier, from Bad Köstritz, which I haven't tasted since 1995; but others are appearing with encouraging regularity, and they are invariably worthy of investigation. A Schwarzbier is normally tinged with hints of red, but it will nonetheless be notably blacker than other dark lagers; it will taste chocolatey, roasted, sometimes toffee-ish, and will be quite dry. I believe Oechsner's is the most satisfying Schwarzbier I have encountered thus far, although I would relish the chance to pit it against Köstritzer in a direct comparison.

Without wishing to perpetuate the cycle of crime by condoning violence, I bet the git who stole my wheeltrims wouldn't recognize a quality Schwarzbier if I broke a bottle of it over his head. Which, make no mistake, I am sorely tempted to do. I shall now go away and seethe for an hour or so.

Oechsner Schwarzbier (5 per cent ABV): ★★★★★

April 19

I often despair at how creations which lean towards the quirky and not the customary fail to garner the appreciation they deserve. Take, for example, the TR7: it became an icon for all things crappy and '70s, merely because it was an ugly chunk of British Leyland trash. I was frequently met with howls of derision when I recently mooted owning a TR7, with only a few cognoscenti (or lunatics, if you prefer) applauding my intentions; I chickened out in the end, troubled by the likelihood of having my tartan interior remorselessly mocked. **Rauchenfelser Steinbier**, a frothy one unique in nature, is a TR7 of a beer: it is curiously old-fashioned, somewhat silly when viewed with a modern outlook and very much an acquired taste – but it should be welcomed rather than rebuffed.

"Steinbier" means "stone beer", and the name is derived from the ancient process used to make Rauchenfelser. The wort is poured over rocks heated to 1,200°C, caramelizing the malt; the rocks are then removed during primary fermentation and later placed in the maturation tanks to aid in secondary fermentation. The overall effect is to give the beer a smoky flavour which most people to which I have kindly exposed it, alas, have found revolting. One of my friends – I can't recall the culprit exactly, but it was either Eugene or photographer Stuart – likened drinking Rauchenfelser to "tonguing a urinal" (a disturbing outburst which raises questions I am happy to ignore), and even my Bro', by his very silence, betrayed that he was finding it tough work; but the loss, I'm afraid, is theirs.

Rauchenfelser is top-fermented, brown, smoky (although not overwhelmingly so) and very dry. I have heard it attacked as "fishy", but the only thing I find fishy is people's reluctance to entertain a classic frothy one whose peculiar charms might not be immediately apparent. I once read that some folk require at least five litres of smoked beer before they develop a liking for it; I would have developed an undying affection for virtually anything after five litres, but I guess it's still a notion worth retaining for when the doubters are next in town.

Long live the TR7.

Rauchenfelser Steinbier (4.9 per cent ABV): ★★★★★★

April 20

My heap of unwatched videos is attaining Empire State Building dimensions, so tonight I resolved to knock it down a tier by tackling the second series of the long-forgotten *Murder One*. I have cherished recollections of the previous run's final two instalments, because I lapped them up with my Bro' while we drank practically every Trappist beer known to man; but everything about tonight's session was a desperately limp imitation of its predecessor, with German lagers instead of Belgian and Dutch ales, no Bro' and – most crucially – no Ted Hoffman.

When my Bro' made his '96 pilgrimage to Burton he was already conversant with how the Byzantine complexities of *Murder One's* initial series disentangled themselves, since the shows had been screened on Sky TV in New Zealand long before BBC2 aired them for we dishless British types. He steadfastly defied my pathetic pleas for him to put me out of my misery, but – devious and traitorous hack that I am – I succeeded in conning the identity of the murderer out of him by phoning up and pretending to have uncovered the details elsewhere. "I never guessed it was... oh, I've forgotten his name now," I told him, and he very graciously provided me with the missing monicker: there's one born every minute.

With neither of us due a shock, then, we added spice to the proceedings by ploughing through all the Trappist frothy ones on which I had been able to lay my hands. After Chimay Red and White (in champagne bottles), La Trappe Quadrupel, Westmalle Dubbel, Orval and Rochefort 10° – the latter of which I wisely avoided – Mickey Mouse could have been unmasked as the killer for all we cared. Hoffman & Associates having signed off, we did ourselves no favours by staging a *Bilko*fest until well into the early hours. I was so appallingly knackered the next morning that I could barely keep my eyes open – which turned out to be a tad embarrassing, as one of my former editors popped into the office and found me asleep on the picture-desk; my Bro', meanwhile, commented at the end of the day that he "could have been sick at any minute". Hurrah.

We always credited Ted Hoffman with being the "hook" where *Murder One* was concerned. Bald as a coot and jug-eared, he spoke in gravelly whispers and was intriguingly shifty, almost anti-heroic. What future could such an iconoclast possibly have, you might ask, in the land of Miller Lite? Answer: no future at all. Americans complained that they couldn't "relate" to him; and so Ted, the expository dialogue of the second series was quick to point out, took extended leave "to rescue his marriage". He was swiftly usurped, with painful predictability, by a man more in keeping with the Hollywood ideal; a man with a full head of hair; a man who didn't inspire me to grope for something as cultured as a Trappist beer but who still, thanks principally to the naffness of his script, forced me to take refuge in a bottle.

Rocked by Ted's clumsily-handled exit, I raided the fridge and came away with an **Oechsner Märzen** (weeks too tardy for

March and months too early for October, but no matter). My admiration for Oechsner grows apace: Weissbier, Schwarzbier, Märzen – all competent. Many a Märzen is gradually drifting away from the firm-bodied, copper-coloured lager which should typify the style – the Märzen sloshed around at the Oktoberfest is definitely less than faithful – but Oechsner's is reassuringly fruity and malty, and it saw me through the evils of the Ted-dumping with no mean aplomb.

With Ted's immaculately-coiffured replacement straining my patience, I upped the stakes and resorted to the pale, malty, warming **Oechsner Heller Bock**. Bock is an April–May beer, but adhering to the calendar was the last thing on my mind: I needed something potent to get me through the monumentally feeble stabs at courtroom drama. In years of reporting cases I have never seen a lawyer rip a witness to shreds with one question, yet it took only minutes for a single rapier-thrust inquiry to leave some hapless fool blurting out an earth-shattering revelation in the Ted-less *Murder One*. Sipping Chimay while relishing a masterly performance is one thing, but seeking solace in strong lager while suffering a tirade of tosh is altogether different: either the programme improves or I (1) stop watching or (2) become a drunkard.

Oechsner Märzen **(5.5 per cent ABV):**	★★★★
Oechsner Heller Bock **(6.8 per cent ABV):**	★★★★

April 24

I was sitting in the office this afternoon, lazily cogitating a menu for an evening of European football, when NG suddenly piped up: "Hey, you'll be able to have a Summery one soon." He was referring to **Burton Bridge Summer Ale**, and it slowly occurred to me that "soon" was not quite the word: with BST well underway, I could have a "Summery one" when I next went to the pub – and that, I decided, would be tonight. As if to celebrate such a propitious circumstance, NG and I risked boring to death anyone who happened to be in the vicinity by launching into a prolonged bout of praise for this sublime beer, our worship culminating in a stupendously lousy piece of wordplay from yours truly: "Yes, I could murder a Summery one. Indeed, there'll be a Summery execution tonight." Well, it made us happy.

I was due to meet Guillo at 6.30pm, but an unanticipated act of minor lunacy from *The Sun* delayed my departure and left me almost 45 minutes late. With a quarter of an hour until kick-off, we faced the dilemma of abandoning our trip to the Burton Bridge or missing much of the first period of the game: a case of weighing a pint against a half, you might say (oh, aren't I the punmeister today?). To my relief, Guillo agreed that the maiden Summer Ale of the year took precedent. I can't say I regretted our judgment that the beer was a more pressing concern.

Although the Bridge was playing heavily on the seasons by also offering Spring Ale, the lure of Summer was too much to resist; I might come to lament this if I return anon to discover that Spring is no more, but at least I'll be able to reassure myself that I was only obeying my instincts at the time. Summer Ale is so quaffable that real determination is required to avoid draining a glass in a solitary gulp. It is light, fruity and deliciously quenching. I have nary a qualm about putting it forward for top-10 status and would go so far as to suggest – in the heat of the moment – that I rate it as highly as Timothy Taylor Landlord, my favourite British beer for three or four years. The downside is that its very brilliance threatens to prevent my drinking anything else at the Bridge in the coming months; but sometimes we must be brave and accept hardship.

I had planned to uncork the leftover bottle of 3 Monts during the second half, but, my mood for it curiously short-lived, I jettisoned it for an after-match **De Kluis Hoegaarden Grand Cru**, an excellent dessert beer.

I first tried Hoegaarden Grand Cru in the early '90s, when I was familiar only with Hoegaarden Wit and fancied getting to grips with its stablemates. I bought some from Small Beer, bounced it around the car during the journey home from Lincoln and then eagerly poured myself a glass. Having sustained a jarring ride and been granted no latitude for recovery, it emerged from the bottle cloudy and ruined. An ignorant pudding-head, I concluded that I despised it. Thankfully, time and experience have reformed my initial opinions: now I rate Grand Cru very loftily indeed, as do my Bro' and Eugene.

The essentially meaningless term "Grand Cru" is often code for "overpriced and unspectacular" in the beer world, but De Kluis has hedged its bets by designating its Grand Cru a tripel: as a general rule, a tripel (usually strong and golden, with Westmalle's standard-setting example the archetype) has the beating of a Grand Cru (usually strong and unnecessarily costly, with no obvious archetype). Served in a De Kluis ballon, Hoegaarden Grand Cru generates a tight, bright-white head and looks beautiful. The beer is peachy, spicy, slightly hazy (though not cloudy in a post-A46-slog vein), warming and liqueur-like. De Kluis also makes a similar beer, Julius, which boasts almost precisely the same alcohol content but is drier, more sparkling and more perfumed; I think I prefer Julius, but it is becoming tougher to find in Britain.

I believe the last occasion I sampled a Grand Cru in Belgium was two years ago, when my Bro' and I were staying at the impeccable Oud Huis Amsterdam in Bruges and revelling in the company of Jerry, its fatalistic young barman. Having already caused us much amusement by dejectedly branding his country "corrupt" and proclaiming that he intended to emigrate to Cuba (a nation renowned for its lack of corruption, of course),* one night he asked us what the hell we were doing in a land he clearly felt held no attractions whatsoever: my Bro' and I, with the kind of simultaneous spontaneity only brothers can share, simply pointed to the frothy ones in front of us.

Jerry was incredulous, but when it came to signing the visitors' book I took the liberty of tipping him to become Belgium's Tourism Minister. He had given me an Oud Hoegaards glass, so I knew he would see the light eventually.

Burton Bridge Summer Ale (3.8 per cent ABV): ★★★★★★★

De Kluis Hoegaarden Grand Cru (8.7 per cent ABV): ★★★★★

April 25

An incongruous feast of film and frothy ones tonight. The films were both grisly tales of the the seedier side of life in London: *Up the Junction*, a sporadically jovial but remorselessly squalid depiction of working-class folk in Battersea in the late '60s; and *Villain*, a *Sweeney*-esque caper about gangland goings-on in the early '70s (featuring koshes à gogo, a fleet of MkII Jags, the obligatory "strip-club scene" and Richard Burton as a brutal boss with dodgy sexual predilections and an even dodgier East End accent). The beers were **Westmalle Dubbel** and **Westmalle Tripel**, which for me conjure up visions about as far removed from The Smoke as it is possible to get.

Before last year I casually acknowledged the Westmalle beers as classics but was in no position to reflect upon them in any wider sense. The monastery's products are credited as the benchmarks for dubbels and tripels everywhere: the former a dark ale of around 6 per cent ABV, the latter a golden ale of around 8 or 9 per cent ABV. They have played an important part in moulding beer history. They are universally hailed as greats. Fair enough. But now they mean much more to me, because in '96 my Bro' and I tasted them at Westmalle itself; and the memory of that afternoon is indelible.

Our attendance was required in Germany for the burial of our Aunt Brunhild, so we seized the chance to spend a day or two in Belgium and partake of some frothy ones before and after the event – a piece of opportunism of which Brunhild would surely have approved. Since we would be grieving at the funeral, we vowed to spare no expense in enjoying ourselves otherwise. We flew to Antwerp, hired the flashiest car available – an Audi A4 – and checked into the Antwerp Hilton, where our room was roughly the size of my house.

All credit to my Bro', for it was he who came up with the idea as we lay on our beds and indolently digested CNN pictures of Americans charging around and frantically bellowing orders in the wake of the bomb at the Atlanta Olympics: "Shall we go to a monastery, then?" It seemed the perfect proposal: the world was going crazy on the box in front of us, so where better to escape to than the peace of a Trappist abbey? We consulted a map and saw that Westmalle was less than 20 miles away; Koningshoeven, home of La Trappe, was just a little further adrift, across the Dutch border. With the afternoon sun shining and our Audi gleaming every bit as brightly, we equipped ourselves with the *Good Beer Guide to Belgium and Holland* and set off.

The vagaries of Antwerp's one-way system meant we joined the ring-road in the wrong direction and duly found ourselves sitting at a huge swing-bridge on the edge of the docks, a dilapidated district whose ambience of menace and decay would have left the location scouts for *Villain* in a state of ecstasy. If Regan and Carter had come screeching around the corner in an M-reg Granada I would scarcely have batted an eyelid. It was bleak to a quasi-surreal degree. Having deduced that (1) we had taken a wrong turn and (2) we should retreat ASAP, we roared off on the correct course and were almost instantaneously motoring through characteristically flat Belgian countryside, passing the village of Oostmalle before arriving at the outskirts of Westmalle.

Although it is basically a one-street village, we managed to go astray after espying a signpost which had clearly been erected for the purpose of misleading stupid Englishmen. It read "Monasterium Magnificat", and our reaction was immediate: "Aha! Must mean 'magnificent monastery'." We followed the pointers through fields and woodland with an increasing sensation of nearing our goal, but after a few minutes we drew into a car-park and were confronted by a building which, though unmistakably religious in appearance, was plainly not the Abbey of Our Lady of the Sacred Heart. Having inspected the blacked-out windows and absorbed the eerie hush pervading the area, we concluded – rightly or wrongly – that we had stumbled upon the local crematorium. There ensued a dignified but expeditious exit, my Bro' and I thankful that we had seen the error of our ways before bursting in and politely requesting two Dubbels from a party of weeping mourners.

In fact, the monastery does not exactly advertize its presence – a discreet notice at the start of a tree-lined approach is the limit of its self-promotion – but it has scant hope of escaping the attention of tourists while the Café Trappisten commands space on the opposite side of the road. The Westmalle crest is plastered on everything from the café's walls to its terrace umbrellas, from its menus to its beer-mats, and the word "overkill" inexorably springs to mind. Restrained it ain't; indeed, given the withdrawn nature of its neighbour, it is less an amusing antithesis and more a borderline obscenity.

The hush of the abbey was infinitely more appealing than the secularized crudeness of the café, so we rumbled along the driveway and pulled into Westmalle's outer courtyard. There was one other car but no indication of the slightest activity; and it was very, very quiet. Before us were two imposing wooden doors, the gateway to the abbey itself; next to them was a pull for a doorbell. The scene was wonderful in its serenity, but to stand in that courtyard was like contemplating a bottle of Westmalle Tripel: all very nice, but you know the real treat awaits *inside*.

"Well," said my Bro', "what do we do now?"

"Not a lot."

"Can't we go in?"

"They're Trappist monks, man. They can't even talk to us."

My Bro' briefly pondered this disadvantage before declaring: "I'm going to ring the bell."

"If you ring that bell," I said, daunted by the prospect of disturbing the Brothers, "I'm legging it."

While we took photos and kicked our heels, however, something happened: a man with a garland of flowers walked up to the doors and, to our disbelief, knocked on them – and a Westmalle monk, dressed for gardening rather than prayer, duly answered. My Bro' swooped, rushing up to the pair and inquiring in his best slow-and-loud English-for-foreigners voice: "Can we come in?" The monk smiled, shook his head, took the chap's blooms and closed the doors; and thus ended the historic but ephemeral meeting between Brother and Bro'. Bereft of the floral ammunition necessary for a further audience, we were left with no alternative: we retired to the Café Trappisten for a frothy one.

The beers were perversely sub-standard – served on draught and needlessly chilled (shades of Hoegaarden's tap) – but we couldn't complain. To sit on the terrace, the abbey peeking through the trees, the sun beating down, and drink Westmalle while nibbling cubes of fatty meat dipped in the most fearsome mustard imaginable was positively unforgettable. The entire episode easily fell within the "I wish this could last forever" bracket; but it was machiavellian to stretch things out when my Bro' had to drive us back to Antwerp, and so we were Hilton-bound after an ultra-leisurely Dubbel and an even more unhurried Tripel.

Westmalle Dubbel is a reddish dark-brown, sweet, malty and faintly chocolatey; sometimes, sadly, it seems to suffer through travelling. The Tripel is lager-like in its incredible paleness and is warming, somewhat herbal, yet dry and delicate; like the Dubbel, it has an enormous hoppiness. Granted, a Westmalle savoured while watching Richard Burton deliver a masterclass in cut-throat razor techniques doesn't quite yield the romance of a Westmalle savoured within a barrel-roll of the abbey; but that should not detract from the illustriousness of these superlative beers.

Westmalle Dubbel (6.5 per cent ABV):	★★★★★★
Westmalle Tripel (9 per cent ABV):	★★★★★★★

April 27

How tempting it is to dismiss today with that phrase much-abhorred by journalists: "No comment." Why, I ask myself, should I dignify with prose one of the most deplorable beers I have ever consumed? Why should my keyboard endure a hammering because of a frothy one whose lameness beggars belief? And, more saliently, why did I buy the stuff in the first place? Well, as Spinal Tap's Nigel Tufnell said: "I'm a professional – I'll rise above it."

Without prejudging too much, I knew **Asahi Super Dry** was going to be bad; but never in my wildest nightmares did I dream it would be *that* bad. Begging Ted Hoffman's forgiveness for reversing court procedures, before presenting the evidence I would like to offer my defence: I committed a cardinal sin by buying a bottle without scrutinizing the label, subconsciously banking on my purchase being the well-respected Asahi Black. At least I took my punishment like a man: I drank the bloody garbage, even though I had not an iota of incertitude about its potential to perturb.

To put it bluntly, Asahi Super Dry is tasteless. Literally. It is like coloured water or, as someone once described an equally insipid American lager, wet air. Asahi, of Tokyo, led the fad for "dry" beer, the craze proving eminently popular in (where else?) the US. The thinking behind it totally defeats me, because if people want a beer which tastes of nothing at all then I can only assume they don't even *like* beer: oxymoronic or what? Perhaps those who endorse it merely crave a method of getting drunk which makes no demands on their taste-buds; if this is so then might I suggest vodka? I am dismayed that the culture which gave us *The Book of Five Rings,* Honda engines, Kurosawa films and *Pacman* can be responsible for such fatuous drivel.

Very much at the other end of the lager spectrum is **St Georgen Bräu Kellerbier**, whose dryness should not be confused with that of Asahi's ghastly effort. Brewed uniquely in the region of central Franconia, Kellerbier is an unfiltered, low-carbonation, very dry and hoppy lager; St Georgen Bräu's example, rusty red and fabulously hoppy, is arguably the classic of the style. Would-be naysayers are vexed by a lager devoid of fizz and crystal-clarity – "It's got bits floating in it!" – but all are won over in time.

The tragedy, of course, is that Asahi Super Dry, with its full-page adverts on the back of the broadsheets' Sunday supplements, is seen as trendy; St Georgen Bräu Kellerbier, meanwhile, is rarely even seen. Consequently, if you placed bottles of each in the average pub or nightclub, maybe even going so far as to sell them at an identical price, the majority of customers would choose one of the worst beers on the planet and ignore one of the best. Something's wrong somewhere, isn't it?

Asahi Super Dry
(5 per cent ABV): ★

St Georgen Bräu Kellerbier
(4.9 per cent ABV): ★★★★★★

April 30

Tomorrow is the anniversary of Ayrton Senna's death. I would like to mark it by spending the day in my MG, zooming to the Three Stags Heads, Wardlow Mires, or the Peacock, Redmile, or even the Falkland Arms, Great Tew; instead I'll be at work, and that I resent intensely.

My attitude has not profited from today's exertions, during which I toured the East Midlands in pursuit of an objective so absurd that I will not discuss it. It is frustrating enough to dawdle behind the lorries and tractors which clog the roads around Melton Mowbray and Grantham, but the dallying becomes intolerable when your timetable doesn't allow a restful stop-off at a rural inn. I passed within three miles of the Peacock and also glimpsed a picture-postcard thatched hostelry in Waltham-on-the-Wolds, but my schedule curbed my longing for a cathartic pint. I came home with an awful headache and a nascent yearning for the becalming frothy one I had been so callously denied.

Two kindred beers from Belgium did the trick: **Du Bocq La Gauloise Brune** and **De Kluis Verboden Vrucht**. Both are dark, strong and mellow – just right for soothing an advanced case of acute aggravation. Once I would have put money on Verboden Vrucht trouncing La Gauloise Brune; but now I believe the latter is smoother, sweeter and more herbal, closer to the beer Verboden Vrucht was years ago. Although Du Bocq's offering seems to have improved and that of De Kluis has almost imperceptibly deteriorated, I wouldn't like to select one or the other as the better: both are excellent.

Incidentally, Verboden Vrucht has possibly the most luscious label ever: it shows the Rubens painting of Adam and Eve in the Garden of Eden, with Adam poised to bring disaster to paradise not with an apple but with a glass of Verboden Vrucht (Forbidden Fruit, see). Yet the labelling on the rear of the bottle is as disenchanting as the labelling on the front is beguiling: it recommends serving the beer at 6°C, a temperature which is too frosty even for a lager and is an unequivocal insult to a powerful ale.

Now I'm annoyed again.

Du Bocq La Gauloise Brune (9 per cent ABV):   ★★★★★

De Kluis Verboden Vrucht (9 per cent ABV):   ★★★★★

May 3

Last month I extolled the virtues of Westmalle Dubbel and Tripel and conceded that my glowing assessments, to a significant but tolerable extent, were clouded by an expedition to the abbey where the beers are adoringly crafted. How the same radiant attitude might have applied to the ales from Koningshoeven; but no. When I think of my sally to Koningshoeven I think only of denial – of tyrannical, compassionless, savage denial – and I blame one man for this: Dutch darts ace Raymond Barneveld.

The boy Raymond – a.k.a. Barney Rubble in arrow-chucking circles – was gunning for the world title when Phil and I motored to Koningshoeven, and Holland was in the bizarre grip of darts fever. Heck, even we had sneaked a peek at the "action" after lurching back to the Antwerp Hilton, bellies bulging with De Koninck and Chateaubriand, the night before hitting the road. Never did I dare suppose, however, that the affliction for oche-idolizing had spread to the secluded sanctuary of a Trappist monastery.

Koningshoeven was not exactly a cinch to locate. I had no difficulty in navigating to Westmalle – the Dubbel at the Café Trappisten was still chilly, yet the privilege of drinking within sight of the source survived – but map-scanning savvy acceded to indiscriminate page-jabbing over the border. A garage attendant finally furnished us with a hand-drawn sketch which solved the riddle of how to reach the august spires jutting above far-off woodland; his primitive scribblings will forever be the bookmark in my copy of the *Good Beer Guide to Belgium and Holland*. After all the palaver, all the arbitrary pounding of disparate trails, we craved reward; and the omens were incredibly auspicious when we were simply waved through by the Brother at the gate.

Amid the neo-Gothic cloisters stood the brewhouse and, more importantly, Koningshoeven's own bar-cum-shop. For Phil this was the ultimate, the holy of holies – the La Trappe tap; and he was not about to squander the moment.

"Mate, I am going to drink La Trappe Tripel at La Trappe," he enthused.

Wrong.

In spite of our lavishing francs, gilders and plastic on La Trappe beers, kelks, ballons, bottle-openers and towels, the secular staff were in no mood to unleash their liquid wares. They were busy, you see. So very, very busy. Busy playing bloody darts.

"Tonight we have a match," one of them announced proudly. "We must practise!" Our mumbled, inaudible reply was roughly "F★★★ing cheers" – an earnest sentiment probably not frequently expressed within Koningshoeven's walls. You'll pardon me, then, if my evaluation of tonight's **La Trappe Enkel** is conducted without the benefit of rose-tinted spectacles.

Many breweries make a dubbel and a tripel, but the monks at Koningshoeven – who appear more commercially-minded than the majority of their Belgian brethren – also produce a Quadrupel and, since 1995, a singel (Enkel). If you recognize that the names merely represent a scale of potency – like the X, XX and XXX of old – then the christening of Enkel and Quadrupel doesn't seem so cynically tacky; besides, even Westmalle brews a singel for its Brothers (though it is known, bewilderingly, as Extra).

La Trappe Enkel is vaguely Orval-ish in colour, although I doubt it is intended as a direct competitor: after all, Orval is different to any other Trappist ale – even this one, which is not only of similar looks but of similar strength. Enkel is dry and refreshing but otherwise uninspired, and appraisals of it must therefore boast the unsympathetic "for a Trappist beer" suffix (as in "That's all right, but it's nowt special for a Trappist beer"). There's nothing awry with La Trappe Enkel; but you are measured against your peers, and standards come no higher than in the Trappist sector.

Barney, this one's for you. You bastard.

**La Trappe Enkel
(5.5 per cent ABV):   ★★★★**

May 4

Today proved my instincts correct but also left me in something of a quandary, and the quandary was this: should I downgrade a beer's rating when I come across an atrocious example of what I know to be a perfectly respectable frothy one? On balance, I think not: it is stupid to rebuke the brewer for someone else's incompetence, unjustifiable to instigate a sweeping judgment on the foundation of what a mitigating barrister would term "an isolated incident". When a beer is going downhill on a universal scale – Hoegaarden is one such – then punishment is deserved; but that was not the case today. Yes, I am harsh but fair.

Why were my instincts proved correct? Because the offending ale was dispensed at the Babington Arms. The episode was a real tragedy, to be honest, because last month's Courage Directors had persuaded me that I could have faith in what trickled from the pub's pumps. I was counting on a treat when I strolled in and saw **Hop Back Summer Lightning** advertized as a guest beer, but the half I was given turned out to be essentially undrinkable.

These things happen, of course – bottom of the barrel and so forth – but the mishap definitely shook me. It provided me with that crucial piece of ammo needed to blast the place to bits.

I reverted to a cowardly **Beck's Bier** when the next round came; and that might well be the last drink I ever have there. I shall, however, derive bountiful satisfaction from recounting the horrors to Phil: it was he who advised me to try the Babington Arms' draught ales, remember, so I curse him for my enduring this calamity.

Summer Lightning, by the way, is a former class-winner in the Champion Beer of Britain competition. Brewed in Salisbury, Wiltshire, it is a pale but strong bitter with a fruity nose, a hoppy flavour and a dry finish. Despite its strength, it is perilously quaffable − when it hasn't been reduced to vinegar by some idiot, that is. I recently spotted it in bottle-conditioned form, so I might grab a couple and reacquaint myself with its true attributes soon.

Even the downfall of the Babington Arms has been overshadowed by other events, though: Eugene is back from Hong Kong after less than two months of what was scheduled to be a year-long stay. He called me from none other than the Falkland Arms, Great Tew, to which he had diverted for a pint of Hook Norton en route from Heathrow (a detour I have taken several times myself). From what I could gather before the silly sod ran out of change, he decided to cut his losses after discovering there was no steady work in HK to make his remaining there worthwhile. I can only revel in once more having someone with whom to split an Abbaye des Rocs − although I can't say I'm very impressed with the fact that he was guzzling Hook Norton Best at one of the nicest boozers in the country while I was choking on a half of pseudo-Sarson's.

Hop Back Summer Lightning (5 per cent ABV): ★★★★★

Beck's Bier: see January 18

May 7

Countless years ago, much to our amusement but arguably to no-one else's, Guillo and I wrote a television column which was syndicated in a number of weekly newspapers. It was topped with a mugshot of Guillo looking highly imperious and rather sinister; I, perhaps thankfully, was not even accorded a by-line. We referred to our outpourings as *We Hate TV*, although the papers whom we supplied were not privy to this snippet of information. To put it bluntly, we slated everything and had nary a positive word to say about anything (with the noble exception of *Police Squad!*, the unloved and short-lived series which spawned the *Naked Gun* movies). We only ever received one letter from a reader, a lady who hailed our severity but made the error of adding that she liked *Murder, She Wrote;* the next week, despite never having seen it, we launched a scathing attack on *Murder, She Wrote* and thus guaranteed that we lost our sole fan. The column was cancelled shortly after we compiled a critique of TV in the '80s and lamented that one of the largest audiences of the decade was attracted by the climax of the '85 World Snooker Championship, "when 18-million people stayed up to watch a man with a pointy stick deposit a black knacker in a sack".

I mention all this because I wonder what kind of caning we would have administered to *Murder One* if *We Hate TV* were still around. I'm sticking with it – after delaying until now it would be insane not to – but I shake my head at how deeply preposterous it is and almost incessantly ache for a sustaining frothy one to dull the daftness of the script. Tonight, as Ted's successor continued to career from one farcical plot-twist to another, **La Trappe Dubbel** became the latest beer to help me through another instalment of courtroom nonsense.

I think La Trappe Dubbel is exquisite; irrespective of the Barneveld Effect, I might even prefer it to its Westmalle counterpart. It is tawny in colour – maybe a deep ruby – and is fruity, spicy, even mildly chocolatey. Unlike the brewery's Enkel, it is not dwarfed by the giants of the Trappist echelon; indeed, it could lay a claim to being among them. If it were a television show – *Dubbel Your Money?* – I'm sure even *We Hate TV* would applaud it.

**La Trappe Dubbel
(6.5 per cent ABV):**

May 8

The first story I ever covered as a wide-eyed and innocent journalist was the tale of a woman who was arranging a school reunion. Riveting it was not (hey, we all have to begin somewhere); but it had formidable repercussions, because the photographer who chaperoned me, 6'7"-tall Stuart, has been a mate ever since.

We have been out on some lousy jobs together through the years. Before we progressed to agency work, back when we toiled for a freesheet, the nightmare task was the vox-pop – accosting unsuspecting folk in the street and demanding their opinions on subjects of shocking insignificance. We would occasionally retire to a pub on vox-pop days, sincerely fed-up with being told to bugger off by disgruntled punters who didn't want their shopping disrupted by men brandishing cameras and notepads. The spectre of a lousy job would often drive us into a lousy pub, and the lousy pub would drive us back to the lousy job; this vicious cycle, fortunately, doesn't come around quite so unremittingly nowadays.

I visited Stuart tonight and was chuffed to find he had stocked up on some reasonable ales: Erdinger, Leffe Brune and Schöfferhofer (he has long been keen on the latter). Fast-living chaps that we are, we had planned to spend the evening playing *Brian Lara's Cricket* while nursing the fruits of Stuart's fridge; but his wretched Sega kept crashing, so we hopped into the car and headed in search of a quiet pint in the Peak District instead.

We ended up in Brassington, a white-stone village near Carsington Water, where the 17th-century Olde Gate serves a marvellously fresh pint of **Marston's Pedigree.** The Gate is a tremendous pub: relaxing, convivial, its scrubbed-tabled and stone-flagged bar dominated by an antique kitchen range dotted with shining pots and pans. I was a mite inattentive, because before I ordered the Pedi I failed to espy either the Marston's Little Lambswick or the bottle of Glenfarclas (I've been slipping on single malts so far this year); but my clumsiness mattered not, for the Pedigree was top-notch. Just the one for me, though: I was driving.

Stuart and his girlfriend are holidaying in Devon next week and were mulling over nipping to Calais for a day, but I believe I have managed to swivel them towards Bruges. If nothing else, the Belgians might teach my old mucker not to keep his Leffe Brune in the fridge.

Marston's Pedigree: see February 3

May 10

I wrote to my Bro' today: I thought I would cheer him up, for he has not only been working jolly hard but has been coping with the massive blow of having to view the US Masters – the tournament he could have witnessed in person – on video, deprived of even the fundamental joy afforded by speculating on the outcome. To have your hopes built up and then dramatically dashed by fate is cruel indeed; and I speak from a position of relative empathy, because bathos reigned where today's beers were concerned.

I cannot pretend that a disillusioning frothy one ranks alongside the heartache of seeing your ambition of treading Augusta's hallowed turf demoted to six hours of two-week-old BBC footage; yet it nonetheless rankles when a beer falls short of expectations. The first of tonight's trio was only marginally dissatisfying, but the others were bona fide anti-climaxes. Perhaps the pursuit of frothy ones would become a tedious business if every beer lived up to its billing, but the drinker has a right to presume better from some of those whose products frustrate.

Black Regent, a dark lager from Regent, an ancient brewery in the Czech Republic town of Trebon, was by far the slightest of the night's evils. It is really an extremely sound beer; some might even reckon it a classic of its particular style. It is spoiled chiefly by its fanciful designation: it is strictly more Dunkel than "Black" – although maybe its marketers are attempting to distance it as much as possible from the golden lagers with which the Republic is more readily associated. It commences in a bitter and chocolatey vein and finishes with a coffeeish maltiness; but the overall effect can be a mite fleeting.

Next came **Paulaner Oktoberfestbier**, a letdown of epic proportions. The initial evidence was promising: Paulaner – one of Munich's "big six"; Oktoberfestbier – an intriguing style; and a jovial label depicting typically corpulent cartoon Bavarians, their cheeks flushed and their mitts clasped around earthenware mugs. The reality was grim: the beer was notably pale in colour (patently aimed at English-speaking Oktoberfest-goers oblivious to the copper-tinged fascinations of Märzen), malty and yet too sweet, even cloying. How anyone could sling litres of that down his or her throat without sprinting to the chunder-sinks is beyond my humble ken. However, being an equitable soul, I shall proffer a quasi-defence on Paulaner's behalf.

A beer which advertizes itself as Märzen *and* Oktoberfestbier is more likely to be of the copper/amber ilk, whereas one which advertizes itself only as the latter – as Paulaner's does – can be paler and stronger. The terms, like many in the beer world, have become blurred and confused. This might explain Paulaner Oktoberfestbier's golden hue and higher gravity; but it does not explain its mediocrity, and nor do I for one instant bid to excuse it.

I generously sought to forgive the brewery's sins by sampling a bottle of **Paulaner Original Münchner Dunkel**, but instead those sins were compounded. I am a huge fan of Dunkel beers, yet this was irredeemably bland: malty, dry, unmoving, boring. Compared to the likes of Andechs Export Dunkel or Weltenburg Spezial Export Dunkel, both of which I am struggling to track down this year, it was timid fare. I shall have to invest in some Paulaner Salvator, the undisputed king of the Doppelbock scene, to replenish my trust in the brewery.

Chin up, Bro'. I'm suffering, too, you know.

Black Regent (4.5 per cent ABV):	★★★★
Paulaner Oktoberfestbier (6 per cent ABV):	★★★
Paulaner Original Münchner Dunkel (5 per cent ABV):	★★★

May 14

This morning my Mum flew to Germany for a three-week break which will take in many of the country's renowned centres of brewing. Not that she'll notice them: the proximity of celebrated frothy ones tends to be of zero consequence to Mum, because she couldn't give a monkey's about the subject. I am forever advising her to dine at Zum Uerige, home of Düsseldorf's principal Altbier, or try an organic Spezial at Pinkus Müller, Münster, or sip a restorative Kölsch at the Malzmühle brewpub in Köln; but even Uncle Henny's fondness for Richmodis cannot sway her. She invariably returns to Britain with a glass or six to swell my cupboard-busting clique – my hobby is well-known among her friends and relatives, and their altruism is laudable – but she cares not about what is poured into them. It is utterly deflating to think that she will have been chauffeured through Düsseldorf today without the

idea of knocking back a Diebels even entering her brain.
Lamentably, while she was shunning opportunities about
which her hapless son can only dream, the closest I came to
mainland Europe was via the pantry's provisions.

Leaving Guillo to erode my reserves of Becker's (it
struck me that I have fashioned a monster whom I might
not be able to goad into trying anything else), I again refused
to make use of that lingering 3 Monts and instead chose
Staromost, a Budvar-like Bohemian lager, and **Schwaben
Bräu Das Schwarze**, an elaborately-presented Schwarzbier. It
would be tricky to come up with two bottom-fermented beers
more contrasting than these – save for Asahi Super Dry and
something worth drinking, of course – but my pre-opening
predictions about which would delight and which would
dismay were, to my embarrassment, back-to-front. The
lesson for the evening: never judge a frothy one by its bottle.

The Bottle Store, where I bought these beers, is cleverly
arranged so as to shepherd the hesitant customer towards
what he or she desires. There are not only sections for
Belgium, Germany and the UK but further sub-sections
dedicated to (for instance) Trappist ale, Weissbier and
porter. There is even what might be loosely termed an
"old East European" section, wherein lurk some
decidedly old-East-European-looking frothy ones:
brutal dark beers from Poland, obscure pseudo-Pilsners
from the former Czechoslovakia, quirky lagers from
Hungary – each, like Staromost, packaged with all the
panache and allure of a Trabant.

A Staromost bottle has the air of something out of a
Christmas cracker. No: on second thoughts, it has the air
of the cracker itself. Its label – a sickly combination of
gold, red and green, with laughable '60s-style lettering –
somehow contrives to be both minimalist and hideous.
You can only be sceptical of the contents when you gaze at
the sheer awfulness of what surrounds them. When you
remark that the label notes amount to a scintillating nine
words – "Brewed and bottled at the brewery, Most, Czech
Republic" – you question the wisdom of your purchase and ask

yourself: "Okay, what have these people got to hide?"

In fact, the beer is as palatable as the bottle is pitiful. Although perhaps a tad darker, it appears to share some of the characteristics of Budvar: a hint of vanilla, gently hoppy, enormously refreshing. It is by no means a match for Budvar or other Czech Republic classics (such as Pilsner Urquell and Gambrinus), but then there is no disgrace in that: rare are those which are. All in all, a stimulating little discovery.

Tribute must be paid to the image-makers at Schwaben Bräu, of Stuttgart: they certainly know how to render the brewery's merchandise appealing to the eye. Das Schwarze comes in a swing-top bottle with beautifully restrained labelling, and the whole caboodle stands out on the shelf and hollers: "Come on, buy me!" So I admit that I fell for it.

Don't get me wrong: Das Schwarze is not bad. But it's not brilliant. It is as black as they come and possesses the chocolatey, roasted traits inherent in any Schwarzbier; yet rather more should be expected from a member of a genre which has fostered some genuinely exciting beers. The overwhelming aftertaste is an unsettling fishiness – not the lightly-smoked fishiness found in some Bavarian specialities but a sort of "Has someone been stirring this with a Captain Bird's Eye?" fishiness – and this somewhat wrecked my enjoyment, to say the least.

A salutary exercise, then, in the hazards of first impressions. There are dozens of other culprits in both the sphere of "gruesome bottle, gratifying beer" and the sphere of "pretty bottle, pretty dreadful beer" – and here, for your erudition, are some which spring to mind:

<u>"Nice bottle – shame about the beer"</u>

(1) Leffe Blond – "parchment" labels instil undue gravitas in the Leffe line -up's weakest link.

(2) Anheuser-Busch Michelob – strangely tasteful bottle, criminally tasteless beer.

(3) Moretti Birra Fruilana – smartly-attired and moustachioed gent prepares to slurp from a foaming mug of Italian lager; but we

need a glimpse of what he looked like *afterwards.*

(4) Rolling Rock – unique in featuring a bottle with an in-built mystery (why is "33" written on the back?); but scarce are those who give a tinker's cuss, such is the beer's plainness.

(5) Asahi Super Dry – flash on the outside, trash on the inside.

"Nice beer – shame about the bottle"

(1) Westvleteren – the Brothers at the tiniest Trappist monastery have to realize they'll never topple Anheuser-Busch until they start putting labels on their beers.

(2) Rochefort – approximately half a step ahead of Westvleteren in the self-publicity stakes, albeit begrudgingly.

(3) Hofbräu Dunkelgold – "don't buy our beer" alert.

(4) Binding Kutscher Alt – labelling which makes Staromost's seem the zenith of colour-coordination.

(5) De Dolle Brouwers Boskeun – whimsical but thoroughly disturbing drawing of an ale-supping rabbit (allegedly prized by collectors).

This may be asking too much, but I would like my Mum to land at Birmingham Airport with a Richmodis glass *and* a Richmodis bottle (preferably a full one). Neither can be faulted. The bottle shouldn't pose a problem, since Henny keeps several million in his fridge; but Kölsch glasses are notoriously flimsy and are vulnerable to shattering in transit. We shall see.

Staromost (4.7 per cent ABV):	★★★★
Schwaben Bräu Das Schwarze (4.9 per cent ABV):	★★★

127

May 16

I abhor alcopops. Bleedin' detest them. Teenagers do not drink them because they cherish them as the height of brewing achievement. Teenagers drink them because they like getting drunk but don't like the taste of beer. The entire enterprise is disgusting.

It is not only the manufacturers' blasé cynicism which is annoying, for there is another negative aspect to alcopops: they're crap. Simple as that. I recall when Mark made local headlines by banning them from the Alexandra, explaining to the *Derby Evening Telegraph* that anything whose creation necessitated so minute a level of skill had no place in his pub.

It would be easy to urge comparisons with the fruit beers of Belgium. Those who complain that children are being enticed down an iniquitous path might also be angered by the same nation's bières de table – low-alcohol frothy ones for nippers to consume when dining at home with their parents. But the difference between these beers and Britain's alcopops is that the Belgian products are usually commendable examples of the brewer's art: everything about Cantillon Kriek (including its presentation) is class, whereas everything about Hooper's Hooch is merely crass.

I had a brief debate this afternoon with someone who queried claims that teenagers were being led astray. He said many people – not just the young – clamoured for alcopops because they appreciated the taste. Even allowing for the possibility that kids were not being influenced, I said, I pined for the demise of something so vile and talentless. "Imagine the destruction of every branch of McDonald's," I ventured; and he succumbed to my devastating rationale.

Anyway, no Hooper's Hooch for me; not even Belgian fruit beer (I must do something about my miserly intake of lambic: copious quantities of Timmermans shall be secured anon). The night belonged instead to the magnificent **Kaltenberg König Ludwig Dunkel**, flagship of Prinz Luitpold's Bavarian castle brewery.

Our royals may invite scandal and mockery in equal doses, but not so Prinz Luitpold: he elicits only praise for his commitment to the cause of frothy ones. Can you envisage Prince Charles taking over Fuller's? Can you visualize the Queen converting Buckingham Palace into a 10,000-barrels-a-week brewery? Prinz Luitpold has prevailed at Kaltenberg since the mid-'70s and has courted infamy only in his long-running (but unsuccessful) battle to sell his beers at the Oktoberfest: Munich's leviathans have callously frozen him out of the event, notwithstanding that the marriage of one his 19th-century ancestors was the catalyst for the the original.

He was quick to enhance Kaltenberg's dark lager when he assumed control more than 20 years ago, and the result of his tampering remains one of the kings – literally – of the Dunkel world. König Ludwig Dunkel is a bafflingly complex beer: very dark and topped with a thick head, it exhibits a bitterness and robust maltiness before ending with a lasting, coffeeish dryness. It is regal indeed. How I yearn to drain a Krug's worth in the castle's beer-garden, perhaps while surveying Prinz Luitpold's jousting festival.

Would we all sleep sounder in our beds if the youth of today drank König Ludwig Dunkel rather than Hooper's Hooch? Well, I think *they* would sleep sounder, since *they* would be flat on their backs after two bottles; but I'm not so convinced about the rest of us. No, I think they should stick to lemonade – *real* lemonade, that is – until they're old enough to comprehend the value of a proper frothy one.

Kaltenberg König Ludwig Dunkel (5.1 per cent ABV): ★★★★★

May 18

I had lunch with my Gran today. She might be more than 90 years old, but she's as sharp as nails and can still rustle up a tender slab of beef and a delicious Yorkshire pudding. While she

129

played her part in readying our feast, though, I flunked my assignment by arriving sans stout; and, although she insisted she never touched it at lunchtimes, I know some Sammy Smith's Oatmeal wouldn't have gone amiss. I shall zip to the Bottle Store and procure an appropriate thank-you for her ASAP.

I spent the afternoon gunning around Derbyshire in Ayrton, but I never came across the type of picturesque country inn which would have consummated the experience – at least not one which wasn't shut. That's the catch with Sunday-afternoon drives: most of the pubs where you fancy stopping for a leisurely "I'll just sit here and stare at my snazzy car" half are closed (and most of the rotten ones are doing a roaring trade, naturally). This would not be a snag in Belgium, where end-of-the-week trips to the brewing monasteries are all the rage. Ho-hum.

With these two strikes to my credit, I turned to the fridge and selected a pair of beers from Henninger, of Frankfurt, to escort me on my traipse down *Coronation Street*. Illuminating though the sagacity of Fred Elliott undoubtedly is, I accept that a lager-and-soap combo is no competition for either a stout with my Gran or a summery bitter in a bucolic hostelry's sun-soaked garden; but there you go.

Bavaria has Weissbier and Rauchbier; Franconia has Kellerbier; Munich has Dunkelbier, Bockbier and Märzen; the Rhineland has Pilsner; Düsseldorf has Altbier; Köln has Kölsch; Dortmund has Export; and Frankfurt has... er... not a lot, basically. Henninger is the smaller of Frankfurt's two jumbo-sized breweries – Binding, Germany's largest, is its neighbour – and produces somewhat undemanding stuff in an area devoid of any dominant (or provocative) category of frothy one. Whether the presence of two colossuses whose combined annual output is in excess of four-million hectolitres has any bearing on Frankfurt's beery anonymity is open to debate.

The politest that can be said about **Henninger Kaiser Pilsner** is that it is adequate. It is smooth, faintly hoppy, far from offensive; but it takes shallowness to the verge of outright meaninglessness. It is brewed mainly for export, while Henninger's other Pils, Christian Henninger Pilsener, purportedly wows Frankfurt with its additional character (how thrilling).

Henninger Jubiläums Export, meanwhile, is based on Dortmund's Export style. "Export" is a confounding misnomer, because even Dortmund's brewers have lost confidence in their city's beer – though it is estimable – and instead gormlessly dispatch abroad their run-of-the-mill Pilsners. A model Dortmunder Export is dry, with a firm maltiness, and is a smidgen stronger than a Pilsner. Like Kaiser Pilsner, Jubiläums Export is passable but nothing more.

I can only reflect upon wasted chances.

**Henninger Kaiser Pilsner
(4.8 per cent ABV):** ★★★

**Henninger Jubiläums Export
(5.5 per cent ABV):** ★★★

May 22

My customary co-taster was tonight back where he belongs: at the bar, in my pantry and in my fridge. Who needs the culture-clash drama of Hong Kong when you can have the wholly uncultured majesty of Burton-on-Trent? Who wants to stroll up and down Nathan Road when you can fulfil all your Oriental requirements at Leong's? Who fancies a Heineken Export and a five-course meal at the Sheraton Hotel and Towers when you can nestle in a snug corner of the Burton Bridge with a pint of Summer Ale and listen as the pork scratchings grow hairs? Why abide in a news capital when you can imbibe in a booze capital? Eugene might not regard things so lightly in the wake of his abortive excursion to HK; but it's good to see him again.

His desertion and rapid return reminded me of my Mum's "retirement". Much as her colleagues bought her a hi-fi system as a farewell gift and then watched incredulously as she restarted work on a part-time basis the next day, Henderson succeeded in stinging me for an Abbaye des Rocs glass and a Pedigree T-shirt prior to his volte face. Perhaps I should broadcast my intention to emigrate and then proceed to accrue a welter of glasses and frothy ones from well-wishers before declaring: "Actually, I think I'll tough it out here." (I do not imply, of course, that either my Mum or Eugene behaved deceitfully. [That's the libel writs clubbed to the boundary, then.])

Amazingly, the night passed without the pouring of a single Belgian ale. Britain and Germany weighed in heavily, with France starring in a cameo role (Euge polished off the 3 Monts); but, despite my obtaining a few abbey beers (among them Bosteels Tripel Karmeliet, the noteworthy secular tripel we encountered at the Hopduvel), our favourite land didn't get a look-in. Weird. We are obviously out of practice.

The evening got underway at the Burton Bridge, where my bleakest suspicions were confirmed: no more Spring Ale. My overzealous quest for its Summer cousin had brought the disastrous ramification I had feared, and now I'll have to kick my heels for something like nine months before I can give it a whirl. This sorry performance just goes to illustrate the grave dangers of snubbing greatness: you never know how long you might have to wait before you stumble upon it again, so snatch it while you can.

I consoled myself with – what else? – **Burton Bridge Summer Ale**, which was as wonderful as ever, and then completed another leg of the year's tour of the Bridge's established brews with a swift half of the golden **Burton Bridge XL**. Aside from Summer Ale, XL is the least powerful beer in the Bridge's portfolio; but it is none the worse for that, delivering a rich maltiness, a trace of hoppiness and a fruity, dry palate. XL would probably be awarded the bronze medal, behind Summer Ale and Porter, in my ranking of the Bridge's consistently fine frothy ones. We paused for sustenance from Leong before adjourning to the golf course. It wasn't a real course, you understand (there's no risk of my setting foot on one of those, as I believe I've made clear), but one of the 40-odd I have painstakingly devised using a program on the most aged of my computers. I began my course-moulding exploits with linksland lay-outs, moved to parkland designs, dabbled with American concepts (water and fakery in abundance) and then, my ingenuity exhausted, reverted to the links once more: I find that in golf – as in beer – the traditional is best.

While we hacked our way around New Laphroaig GC – named in deference to the most distinctive of single malts – Eugene's swing coordination was tested by a Kaltenberg König Ludwig Dunkel and mine by a **Scherdel Premium**, a lively, quenching lager with a whisper of fruit in its moderately dry finish. Some years ago I had an agreeable Weissbier from Scherdel, of Hof, Bavaria, and the brewery's Premium is of much the same standard: above average, yes, but bereft of that elusive quality necessary for excellence. The König Ludwig Dunkel emerged as the more challenging of the two, since Eugene staggered to an 18-over-par 90. My triumph earned me an awesome £1.70 – not a sum to cause Tiger Woods palpitations, I confess, but sufficient to finance a future pint.

With apologies to my Bro', whom I only this week warned that my resistance to the *Bilko* bevy was on the wane, the night advanced to its denouement with a Phil Silvers frenzy. You can only hold out for so long when you have the funniest shows in TV history accumulating dust next to your VCR. We gallantly restricted ourselves to three; Eugene accompanied them with the aforesaid 3 Monts, while I opted for a **Pinkus Müller Pinkus Alt**.

As I mentioned earlier, Pinkus Müller, a brewery and tavern in the venerable university city of Münster, is one of the famous

German brewing institutions my Mum is so glad to spurn on her adventures. Its Alt is a curiosity, as it is unlike an archetypal Düsseldorf Alt in a variety of respects: a Düsseldorf Alt is copper-coloured, whereas Pinkus Alt is golden; a Düsseldorf Alt is all-malt, whereas Pinkus Alt is 40 per cent wheat malt (Pinkus uses only organic malt and hops); and a Düsseldorf Alt's fruitiness is tempered, whereas Pinkus Alt's is quite conspicuous.

A curiosity it might be, but it is a superb drop: fluffy, tart and delicately acidic. All of Pinkus Müller's beers are widely acclaimed, especially its Spezial organic lager. What would it take to induce my Mum or one of her chums to pop into the tavern itself and nab me a PM glass (I used a Diebels Altbeker tonight)? A call to Deutschland could be in order.

Then again, suddenly there are already enough glasses to wash. Welcome back, Euge.

Burton Bridge Summer Ale:
see April 24

Burton Bridge XL **(4 per cent ABV):**	★★★★★
Scherdel Premium **(4.7 per cent ABV):**	★★★★
Pinkus Müller Pinkus Alt **(5 per cent ABV):**	★★★★★

May 23

One of those uncommon days, one of those sporadic sets of circumstances, when I am happy to live in England. The ingredients: a fiery sun; my MG; sinuous, tree-lined lanes; a village pub; a succulent steak; and a pleasant half of bitter.

Having pondered how we could entertain ourselves before he journeyed back to his new abode in Warrington, Cheshire, Eugene and I had resolved to trundle to the East Coast resort of

Cleethorpes for some fish and chips (and why not?). No sooner had we set off in the Escort, though, than we passed a Triumph Spitfire in roof-down mode; and we knew there and then that we should execute a U-turn, go home, jump into Ayrton and rumble into the countryside. Cleethorpes was duly usurped by Abbots Bromley and the Royal Oak (where I parked Ayrton next to another MG, since we owners of the marque bask in such sad displays of camaraderie).

I must be slow, for only today did it occur to me that the Royal Oak sells **Greene King Abbot Ale** not because it is a lovely beer — although it truly is — but because of its monicker. Abbots Bromley, Abbot Ale — geddit? Blimey, I'm getting old.

With Eugene back oop north, my prime objective now is to study *The Good Pub Guide* and the *Good Beer Guide* to probe whether there is anything comparable to the Royal Oak in the Warrington area; my secondary objective is to study an atlas and formulate a scenic route for Ayrton. Put it all together and I might just enjoy another of those precious moments when absolutely everything is hunky-dory.

Greene King Abbot Ale:
see February 5

May 25

Ah, the sophistication of it all: an idyllic evening, balmy and blessed with birdsong, spent on the patio with a game of *Scrabble* and a couple of abbey beers. Does it get any better than this? Well, yes: if only the frothy ones had been as blistering as my wordplay (he bragged).

My opponent was Stuart, who didn't make Bruges part of his itinerary last week but did happen upon an inn in Devon which served draught Hoegaarden. A serendipitous meeting of England and Belgium? I must say that I have always been rather a stickler for draught *British* ales in a British

135

pub – if the pub is capable of keeping them in decent condition – because their like is to be found nowhere else, but I grant that Hoegaarden does capture a summery ambience better than most; besides, why overlook something you relish?

No Hoegaarden for the big man today, I'm afraid, but he was able to sate himself with Becker's while I tackled **Sterkens St Paul Blond** and **Sterkens St Paul Special**. Sterkens, of Meer, Antwerp province, is acknowledged for its dark Poorter (which, despite its hue, has nothing to do with porter) and golden Kruikenbier, varieties of which are sold under a host of aliases – among them St Paul Double and St Paul Triple. Blond and Special are at the lower end of the St Paul flock's ABV scale, yet one of them is still impressive; and, as is often the case with beer, it is not the one whose handle harks of haughtiness.

St Paul Blond is a cut above many "bottom-of-the-range" abbey beers, a lot of which suffer from Ford Fiesta Popular Syndrome. I used to have a Fiesta Popular, the most plebeian of Fords, and I was adamant that the people responsible for its equipment had gone about things the wrong way: instead of first determining the make-up of the Popular and then incrementally nudging towards the bells-and-whistles Ghia – i.e. improving on their basic – they seemed to have started with the Ghia and then made each successive underling a trifle more inferior than the last, ensuring that the Popular was left with a steering wheel and not much else. Take Leffe beers: the pack-leading Vielle Cuvée and Radieuse are full of flavour, but the entry-level Blond is desperately poor – as if the brewers were scared to imbue it with any stature. St Paul Blond's foremost asset is its lack of ersatz sweetness, the bane of Leffe Blond and its Popular-like genus; there is also a pleasing whiff of lemony fruit in the aftertaste.

The Special? Special it is not. It is neither brown nor ruby but something nasty twixt the two. It is soapy and drab. For something claiming to be an abbey ale – and so aspiring to imitate the grandeur of the Trappist beers – it is incontrovertibly shabby. It is an affirmation that breweries are sometimes prone to producing too many frothy ones just for the sake of it.

And the *Scrabble* score? No, I'm too kind. Suffice it to say that Stuart was constantly soothed by that phrase prevalent among dominoes players: "If you ain't got 'em, mate, you can't play 'em." He had the better beer, but I had the better tiles.

Sterkens St Paul Blond
(5.3 per cent ABV): ★★★★
Sterkens St Paul Special
(5.5 per cent ABV): ★★

May 28

As I stated previously, not many people have faith in the beers of Dortmund. Its breweries' continuing paucity of certitude in the merits of the local style, Export, means those hunting any outside Dortmund itself would do well to remember how Basil Fawlty summed up the odds when asked to assemble the ingredients for a Waldorf Salad: "There's about as much chance of finding a tin of hippopotamus in suitcase sauce." The irony of the appellation "Export" escapes no-one, but fair-to-middling Pils is more likely to be piled into a long-distance lorry departing Dortmund: the Export stays at home, dying a sluggish death.

But rejoice: I have, by an inexplicably circuitous method, snared a bottle of **DAB Export**, the version from the sprawling Dortmunder Actien Brauerei. And now cease rejoicing: for DAB Export – ah, I should have guessed – is a bit naff. It is lighter and less malty than the exemplary Exports and, damningly, barely lords it over the likes of Henninger's extrinsic interpretation. It was DAB which pioneered Dortmund's shift to Pils in 1971. Sigh.

Germany's reputation was gloriously rescued when I bounded from Dortmunder disappointment to Franconian frivolity in one effortless leap. **Heller Aecht Schlenkerla Rauchbier**, the superlative smoked beer and a compelling candidate for the Most Extraordinary Lager in the World crown, heaved me from my slough of despond with aplomb. Smoked beer is the speciality of Bamberg, a charming and historic town in Franconia. The virtues of the place and its products are best portrayed, I think, by the fact that Kulminator's Dirk and Leen were due to travel to Bamberg for a holiday the morning after my Bro' and I were introduced to nine-year-old Westmalle Tripel at their café.

"You'll be able to have some Schlenkerla Rauchbier," I told Dirk when he disclosed their destination.

"Ah, Schlenkerla!" he said, his physog a mask of surprise. "How do you know these things?"

"Because it's a good beer."

"Yes, yes. Very good beer."

Schlenkerla − the name was originally an unflattering epithet bestowed upon an ex-brewer with a monkey-like gait − may have been diminished to "good" by our mutual linguistic deficiencies, but its legitimate status would have been conferred upon it if I had known the Belgian for "top-10 contender". It is a phenomenal frothy one, its burnt flavour derived from the use of beechwood smoke to infuse the barley malt. Bottom-fermented, frighteningly black and almost unbearably intense, it is the lager equivalent of sticking your head up a chimney; and many consider it about as much fun, to be frank, so profound is its smokiness. You either loathe it or love it; or, should you wish to elevate your cognizance of the world's supreme beers, you *learn* to love it. It accounts for more than 90 per cent of Heller's yield, but even the brewery's "normal" Lagerbier has a smoky edge.

One way or another, my interest in Dortmunders has juddered to an abrupt − and grossly unjust − halt. A purely temporary aberration, I'm sure.

**DAB Export
(5 per cent ABV):** ★★★
**Heller Aecht Schlenkerla Rauchbier
(4.8 per cent ABV):** ★★★★★★★

May 29

Sometimes I feel I'm not up to owning a 30-year-old car. My
patience is stretched by the irritating trials and tribulations it
dishes out at deplorably habitual intervals. One minute I'm
bombing along with the wind in my hair and the flies in my
teeth, the next I'm being petrified by some mechanical
death-rattle; one minute I think the throaty burbling of the
exhaust signifies power and charisma, the next I think it
signifies imminent separation; one minute I want to pull
over and behold the elegance of my rag-top's lines, the
next I want to take an axe to them. Today I drove Ayrton
through the breathtaking scenery of the Peak District
and the Staffordshire Moorlands, frying my nose and
arms and getting as far as Cheshire before turning back
(no disrespect to Cheshire, which contains many
Robinson's pubs); and then, just when everything was
fabulous to a grin-triggering degree, Ayrton had to go
and spoil it all by blowing a gasket 15 miles from home,
condemning me to an inspection at Kwik-Fit and the
future misery of a repair bill.

The immediate corollary was that Guillo and I had to
cancel our proposed MG jaunt to a remote inn; I had
even been contemplating the Falkland Arms, too, until
Ayrton did the dirty on us. Instead any semblance of
novelty went out of the window – along with my smile –
and, with voluminous gasket-and-sunburn-related
grumbling from me, we resorted to boosting once again the

profits of the Bridge Inn and the Burton Bridge. So **Marston's Pedigree** and **Burton Bridge Summer Ale** filled in for what could have been anything from Hook Norton Best to Wadworth 6X: I told myself to view it not as an evening ruined but as an unforeseen excuse to strengthen my relationship with a pair of top-tenners.

I was blithe enough after a while, since both the Pedi and the Summer Ale – particularly the latter – were scrumptious; moreover, as Guillo was lumbered with the wheelman duties because of Ayrton's glitch, I didn't have to worry about my intake. I am conscious, though, that to let the current heatwave vanish without my cruising to an out-of-the-way hostelry in Ayrton would be indefensible: I shall have to ward off the superficial seductiveness of perpetual devotion to the Bridges, grit my fly-dotted teeth, dig into my wallet and have my pride-and-joy/maddening money-pit fixed.

Incidentally, what do excessive beer-drinking and a three-hour roofless drive in blazing sunshine have in common? Answer: they're a hoot at the time, but you know you'll wake up with a blinding headache the next morning.

Marston's Pedigree: see February 3

Burton Bridge Summer Ale: see April 24

May 31

It's said that nothing is sacred. Too true: I have a newspaper cutting to prove it.

I quote the *Derby Evening Telegraph,* circa May 1997: "Brewer Marston's is testing a new device designed to give its top-selling beer Pedigree a creamier texture. The Burton-based company has installed the system in 40 pubs across the country to test customers' reaction. It involves changing the swan-neck and sprinkler on the handpumps to give the beer a frothy head."

The nightmare in print was endorsed by the nightmare in spoken words on that same terrible day: a Marston's representative, interviewed on the radio, spouted garbage about having to respond to a trend towards creamier beers. Why not brew one, then? Why mess with Pedigree? Would Marston's turn Pedi black if everyone drank Guinness? Would it switch to bottom-fermentation if its patrons renounced ales? Such thinking is insultingly flawed.

Marston's asserted that the taste would not be affected − a hollow argument, because a beer is defined by more than just taste: smell, colour, appearance, texture and a hundred other things are material. If the bosses at Moortgat were to decree that Duvel should no longer decant with the most towering of heads − although the brewery would never perpetrate such an outrage − then they, too, could bleat that the taste would be unaltered; but the beer would not be Duvel. If the Brothers at Orval concluded that their ale should be bright green − and this, needless to say, is less than conceivable − then they could make the same pledge; but the beer would not be Orval. And Pedigree with a whipped dome is not Pedigree.

When I was in my mid-teens, before I had deduced that McDonald's was to be avoided at all costs, I would order a Big Mac and Coke and be asked by the automaton behind the counter: "McDonald's Cola − is that okay?" It hasn't dawned yet, but I dread the day when I walk into the Bridge Inn, order a pint of Pedi and am met with the retort: "Pedigree Super-Cream − is that okay?" My Bro' will probably never again grace England if Marston's persists in interfering with perfection simply to conciliate those who aren't even seeking it; I don't think I would boycott the nation, but Marston's pubs would be very much off-limits.

It is not impossible for a beer to change for the better: when the Riva group acquired Straffe Hendrik, a home-brewery in Bruges, the eponymous pale ale developed more reliability. Pungent and hoppy, Straffe Hendrik has become one of *the* beers of Bruges, with bollekes of it adorning table after table around the Burg and the Markt: it is almost to the town what De Koninck is to Antwerp.

Straffe Hendrik meant nothing to me when I first visited Bruges. My ignorance was such that Eugene and I repeatedly ambled past the brewery, which is situated in the old district of town, while exploring the cobbled streets for an hotel. I can't precisely recall, but I might have savoured a bottle at the Hoefijzertje (Horseshoe) café, blissfully unaware that the beer's origins lay less than 200 yards away. The brewery has the facade of little more than a house and proclaims its vocation with an unpretentious plaque, so enlightenment is wont to evade the uninformed. Even when I was familiar with the frothy one and had consulted the *Good Beer Guide to Belgium and Holland* for an address, I was astonished – if not downright dubious – when confronted by Straffe Hendrik's source.

I attempted to promote Straffe Hendrik in my own modest way during my second sojourn, which came after Eugene and I clinched a freebie from the Belgian Tourist Board by vowing to pen a "Beer-hunting in Bruges" article for a magazine. Despite my cretinous command of a camera, I masqueraded as a photographer and was charged with taking the pics for the piece. My ludicrous endeavours at recording on film the quaint splendour of the brewery eventually led to what I thought was a competent shot; but those for whom I was "working" thought otherwise and instead printed my panoramic yet totally inexpedient snap of a canal. The prose spoke of beer, but the pictures showed only water.

To this day, much to my chagrin, I have never been inside the brewery's tavern, where the optimum glass of Straffe Hendrik may await: I seem doomed to descend upon Bruges in the out-of-season months, when Straffe Hendrik's doors are as reluctant to open as Westmalle's. My Bro' and I once uncovered a fantastic draught in a discreet restaurant recommended to us by the Oud Huis Amsterdam, but I now can't recollect said eatery's location. None of this matters tonight, however, because I have found a superior Straffe

Hendrik much closer to home: **Straffe Hendrik Brune**, as plucked from the Dram, Sheffield.

A brewery which has for years produced only one beer is under pressure to come up with something outstanding when it at last doubles its range – imagine how exceptional a stablemate for Orval would have to be – and Straffe Hendrik has done so: its Brune is gorgeous, perhaps the sensation of the campaign so far. I can pay it no higher compliment than to suggest that it falls somewhere between Westmalle Dubbel and Rochefort 10°; and it does so not only in strength and shade but in character, beginning dry, becoming spicy and then ending on a warming, chocolatey note.

This is what it's all about: seizing an unknown from the shelves and discovering that you have a classic on your hands. The beer world is gnashing at your heels, Marston's; and it is the elite, not the dross, which really ought to concern you.

**Straffe Hendrik Brune
(8.5 per cent ABV):**

June 1

Why Belgium is not beloved by each and every man, woman and child is a mystery to me. It possesses not only the finest beers and the finest bars in the world but the finest chips and the finest chocolate, thereby ensuring that all generations are catered for in style. How can anyone demand anything more from a country? All right, so the scenery is less than tremendous; but who needs to go outside when there is ample pleasure in staying indoors and cramming yourself silly with frothy ones, frites and choccies?

A quiet Belgian night in for me: a pair of abbey beers and a few heavy-on-the-cocoa nibbles. I find that rich Belgian chocolate is an ideal partner to many abbey or Trappist beers, with Rochefort 10° the supreme choice when it comes to the liquid half of the duo. Just as two or three glasses of Rochefort 10° would be enough for anyone, however, so two or three Belgian chocolates are sufficient for all but the most goo-defying palates; thus, although it might sound as if I turned in a piggish performance, I actually conducted myself with the necessary restraint.

With Rochefort 10° conspicuous by its absence, I completed my study of the St Paul line-up and sampled **Sterkens St Paul Double** and **Sterkens St Paul Triple**. It is not often that the beer billed as the most humble member of a set proves to be the most impressive; yet last month's St Paul Blond has comfortably emerged with more credit than its alleged superiors, notwithstanding their greater strength and grander designations. Both the Double and Triple are agreeable, but they are hardly the most electrifying frothy ones ever created; and they definitely don't fulfil the promise propounded by their elaborate bottles, which remind me of the garish liqueurs a pal used to number among his selection of miniatures. I don't think the Brothers at Koningshoeven and Westmalle will be quaking in their boots.

The Double is smooth, soft and dark, fruity and dry. It is very drinkable, but then so it water; and the finish is about as lasting. As to the issue of whether it is genuinely a dubbel or merely one of those beers which assumes the monicker for marketing purposes, it is accurate to say that it does display many dubbel-like characteristics; but it is important to bear in mind, too, that the beer is also sold – in minutely-adjusted forms – as Poorter and St Sebastiaan Dark.

The Triple is the better of the two. It is close to Westmalle Tripel in colour and is fruity, firm and blessed with a peculiar bitterness. It lacks the panache of a top-notch tripel, though, and is forgotten too quickly. And does it qualify as a bona fide tripel? Purists might accuse it of being a dash low in ABV; and it is also sold – again in various tweaked disguises – as Bokrijks Kruikenbier, St Sebastiaan Grand Cru and St Denise.

All in all, rather a waste of nice chocolate.

Sterkens St Paul Double (6.9 per cent ABV):	★★★
Sterkens St Paul Triple (7.6 per cent ABV):	★★★

June 4

My Mum has surpassed herself, returning from Germany yesterday with a bottle of Richmodis Kölsch and the appropriate glass. When my Bro' and I took advantage of his considerable hospitality last year Uncle Henny owned nary a single Richmodis receptacle – even though Richmodis is virtually the only Kölsch he'll drink – but he has been accruing them here and there of late and now has half a dozen or so, one of which has inexorably found its way to me: he was obviously influenced by my moaning at having to sup Richmodis from a Sion glass. The problem now is to determine what occasion is momentous enough to warrant putting these bounteous gifts to use.

I was also presented with a terrific Dortmunder Union mug, kindly sent by one of Mum's friends. The lady in question, Margret, is coming to England in August and has instructed her chums to donate their unwanted tumblers, beakers and Krugs in readiness for her trip. Bless her. It is strangely rewarding to know that old dears throughout Deutschland are rummaging in their cupboards and emptying their pantries in a bid to add to my collection.

My own cupboards and pantry were subjected to a severe trial this evening, with Eugene and Stuart dropping by to test their *Scrabble* and computer golf skills and deplete my stocks of frothy ones. There was high tension on both the board and the course, with photographer Stuart hammering his pathetic wordsmith opponents at *Scrabble* and yours truly pocketing a career-best £4.25 amid controversy on the 17th green; and the beers were excellent, too.

145

With the chaps kept smiling by Pilsner Urquell, I began by granting myself the sole bottle of **König Pilsener**. Not a beer I stumble upon very often, this elegant lager (if that's not an oxymoron), from the northern Rhineland town of Duisburg, is among Germany's leading premium Pilseners. It is very dry and notably bitter (though Becker's is more so in both respects), firm-bodied, smooth and clean-tasting. The worst thing about it is its dedicated glassware, which is preposterously thin and barely capable of sustaining the shock of the pouring of the beer: I have lost two in transit and one in the washing-up, and it is perhaps only the paucity of König Pilsener in Britain which has permitted the three I currently retain to survive for as long as they have – although doubtless they will implode through the pressure of dust build-up before the year is over.

Stuart had already forged a threatening advantage by the time I drained the König Pilsener, so I sought to revitalize my fading challenge by opening a bottle of the mighty **Paulaner Salvator**. Salvator is the doyen of the Doppelbock crowd, its pre-eminence illustrated by the fact that practically every other brewery bestows an "-ator" suffix upon its own Doppelbock (e.g. Löwenbräu's Triumphator, EKU's Kulminator, Eck's Magistrator). Despite the term, a Doppelbock is not double the potency of a Bock – which is probably just as well, since many a Bock is daunting enough – and Salvator weighs in at 7.5 per cent ABV. It is very dark and quite thick, and it has the profound maltiness which is typical of Paulaner lagers; it is also extremely dry for such a powerful beer. An undisputed classic.

Here's a frightening thought: at Paulaner's Salvator Keller in Munich, where it is available on draught, Salvator is quaffed by the litre. Even allowing for the foaming German head to which my Dad infamously took offence,

146

that's a lot of Salvator. I know we young Burtonians used to laugh at outsiders' inability to imbibe Pedigree in enormous quantities, but I'm confident that if I downed two litres of Salvator I would be a danger to myself and others. Certainly half a litre didn't boost my *Scrabble* acumen, because Stuart chipped in for a 70-point win while I was still holding the Q.

And so to the golf course. Stuart, who faced driving back to Derby, could not celebrate his *Scrabble* triumph as we stepped on to the first tee; but Eugene and I, who faced driving only into sand or water, could raise a glass to his accomplishment. Eugene chose a Bosteels Tripel Karmeliet, while I opted for a more refreshing Belgian treat: **Gouden Boom Brugs Tarwebier**, a Hoegaarden-ish witbier every bit as synonymous with its home town as last week's Straffe Hendrik.

Tarwebier is arguably a style in itself, a drier and sometimes slightly sour cousin to witbier, and Brugs Tarwebier – tart, cloudy, soft, orangey, fabulously invigorating when thermometers are rising – is surely the archetype. I eschewed it for a while about three years ago, having encountered a parade of bottles containing abnormally huge chunks of sediment which alarmed all those to whom I proffered a snifter; but now I have rediscovered my liking for it, and I think I might even prefer it to Hoegaarden. I remember a pleasant afternoon at the Oud Huis Amsterdam, Bruges, when my Bro' and I watched golf's European Masters on the box while a supply of Brugs Tarwebier – released to us by barman 'Cuban' Jerry – stayed cool in a basin of cold water in the bathroom. Wonderful.

It wasn't just the Tarwebier which was sour when Eugene missed a three-footer on the 17th to hand me that

£4.25 ante. The temptation to break out the Richmodis was there, but I am not one to gloat in victory; besides, I didn't want to risk having to share it.

König Pilsener (4.6 per cent ABV):	★★★★★
Paulaner Salvator (7.5 per cent ABV):	★★★★★★
Gouden Boom Brugs Tarwebier (5 per cent ABV):	★★★★★

June 7

Britain seems to copy everything rotten about the USA; America, meanwhile, imitates everything decent about Britain. How can this be? We are overrun with fast-food restaurants, Oprah Winfrey clones, money-grabbing mega-conglomorates and youths wearing their baseball caps back-to-front; and America is duplicating our frothy ones. Fair it is not.

The lady at the Dram said she had taken a consignment of **Wynkoop Light Rail Ale** and **Wynkoop Railyard Ale** because she had never come across them before and might never come across them again. A commendable attitude: just as I was left fuming after missing out on the magic of Burton Bridge Spring Ale, she would be mad at herself if she let a couple of rarely-seen beers slip past. And it wouldn't matter if they ultimately revealed themselves to be less than brilliant: you never know if you never try.

Like the Dram's proprietor, I hadn't heard of Wynkoop; but a flick through the *Pocket Beer Book* identified it as a brewpub in Denver, Colorado, with an extensive array of British-accented products, including a Scottish Ale. Some of the beers are dispensed cold at the source, which indicates that one element of British brewing many Americans are reluctant to embrace is the employment of expedient temperatures at the point of sale (maybe they would modify their approach if they experienced some vintage British weather); I served mine at approximately 13°C.

Great Label Notes of our Time, N° 3: "Light Rail Ale has been crafted as a traditional English bitter, the style of pale ale enjoyed by such luminaries as Dickens and Churchill." I was gladdened to see Churchill got the nod ahead of John Major, who once incorporated in one of his pro-Britain speeches a ludicrous homily to the merits of "warm ale": it is no surprise that many foreigners remain sceptical of British frothy ones when the PM is spouting ill-advised nonsense like that.

Light Rail Ale is well-named. Compared with some of the English efforts which inspired it – Pedigree, for instance – it is a smidgen light in body for its strength, nearer to Burton Bridge Summer Ale than it is to Draught Bass or Samuel Smith's Old Brewery Pale Ale. Its virtues – which are by no means insubstantial – lie in its mild fruitiness, its emphatic bitterness and its all-round thirst-quenching quality.

Railyard Ale is more robust but less effective. It is deep bronze in colour and is fruity, with a hint of roastedness in the finish; but nothing about it lingers in the memory – save for the label, which, like Light Rail's, is decorated with a very chic drawing of (what else?) a train.

I shall cherish those aspects which lent themselves to fond retrospective, for who is to say whether we will see Wynkoop's wares again? Scandalous, isn't it? Two respectable beers which I'll be lucky to taste twice, yet a Big Mac lurks on every bloody corner.

**Wynkoop Light Rail Ale
(4.4 per cent ABV):** ★★★★

**Wynkoop Railyard Ale
(5.5 per cent ABV):** ★★★

June 8

"Good people drink good beer." So said Hunter S Thompson, and his words of wisdom are cited on the magnificently off-the-wall label for one of the ales from the Flying Dog brewpub. Whether it automatically follows that bad people drink bad beer – as Thompson goes on to imply – is somewhat less clear-cut, but I cannot dissent from the initial observation.

I bought the Flying Dog stuff in the same batch as yesterday's Wynkoop fare, working on the identical principle: good or bad, they might never fall into my grasp again. When I tried them I was immediately struck by a distant resemblance to the Wynkoop ales, and this was duly explained when I examined the small print and found that both are contract-brewed by the Broadway Brewing Company, Denver. The Flying Dog is in Aspen, Colorado – playground of the rich and snowblind, I understand – so it and Wynkoop are neighbours.

I was in desperate need of a beer after a sensational session of straight pool with Gurminder. While he had loosened his cuing arm with several pints of Cold & Tasteless during the epic clash, my post-game Flying Dogs acted as relief of another sort: I was fortunate to escape with my unbeaten record intact. Having led 30-3 at one stage, I found myself trailing by the 50s and but a few points up by the 70s; and then my gallant foe somehow contrived to foul three times in a row – the third was appallingly unjust – and was penalized 15 points, leaving me with an undeservedly easy 100-73 conquest. Phew. The beers didn't really equal the thrills provided by the rest of the evening, but they were worth investigating.

Flying Dog Dog Days Golden Ale is almost as pale as a Kölsch; it is vaguely tangy and moderately fruity but is also a trifle thin. I briefly flirted with the idea of awarding it a bonus mark for its title, because *Dog Day Afternoon,* starring Al Pacino, is a marvellous film which I once saw in the rather grotty surroundings of the Hotel Tourist, Antwerp; but I concluded this would be wrong. (Ah, the Hotel Tourist... Lying on my bed, listening to the remorseless thunder of diesels at Antwerp railway station through my jammed-open window, I felt like an exile from the *Blues Brothers* skit in which Elwood introduces Jake to his grubby room next to Chicago's elway. "How often do the trains go past?" inquires Jake, and Elwood merrily replies: "So often you won't even notice it.")

Flying Dog Road Dog Ale also had a tenuous Antwerp connotation for me, for I thought I detected a handful of Belgian-chocolate-like traits. Road Dog – which is touted as a Scottish ale – is dark but tinted with red; it has a lasting, thick head and a nose of butter and vanilla; and it is quite rich, with a roasted aftertaste. Intriguingly, however, I grew less enthusiastic with each sip – maybe because most of the flavours appeared to be in that creamy head (hey, perhaps Marston's were right about Pedigree – not).

Anyhow, I think Mr Thompson knew what he was talking about: the beers were in no way bad, and I feel pretty good. QED.

**Flying Dog Dog Days Golden Ale
(4.6 per cent ABV):** ★★★

**Flying Dog Road Dog Ale
(5.8 per cent ABV):** ★★★★

June 12

Back in April, in the light-headed wake of my inaugural Summer Ale of the year, I implied that the Burton Bridge's seasonal masterpiece rivalled **Timothy Taylor Landlord** for the crown of Britain's premier beer. Without wishing to insult Summer Ale in the tiniest manner, I now accept that this is not so: Landlord, I have come to realize, is out on its own.

Enlightenment came at the Peacock, Redmile, the quaint yet sophisticated pub where Gary and I found sanctuary after rescuing my Punto from the Lincolnshire Fens in February. I had resolved some days ago to drag Guillo there, convinced he would approve of the cuisine, and had warned myself to spurn the lure of the Landlord and elect another ale in the interests of research; but when I walked into the cosy bar and surveyed the pumps – Landlord, Theakston's XB, Tetley Bitter and Pedigree – I could not bring myself to honour my own tenets about avoiding adherence to any given frothy one. Landlord is just so gorgeous; and why, to be frank, should anyone be obliged to rebuff something outstanding when the alternatives can only bring relative disappointment? So call me a hypocrite – I don't care.

The Peacock has a charming restaurant, candle-lit and awash with refinement, but Guillo's proposal that we dine therein was briskly dismissed. I have fought long and hard to persuade my family and friends that beer is as well-equipped as wine when it comes to complimenting a meal, yet still I would feel a mite incongruous if I strolled into a suave restaurant – a British one, that is – with a pint glass in my paw. Frothy ones and food are de rigeur in the posh cafés of Belgium, but perceptions of plebbishness persist in Britain; I'm sure that the logical trick of rendering our glasses more attractive would alleviate the inequitable stigma.

We ate in the bar: the menu was the same as the restaurant's, and there was the bonus of the Landlord's proximity (nearer, my god, to thee). Whether Landlord was invented to consort with king prawns in lemon sabayon or sirloin steak on a bed of potato crisps and oyster mushrooms is open to debate – I suspect not, I must confess – but it was nonetheless stunning. The shame, of course, was that I could only allocate myself one pint – again.

Landlord, then, is reinstated as the UK's imperturbable numero uno, with Summer Ale a brave but remote second; Pedigree is a rather poor third and far from guaranteed a berth in the top 10 come December 31. This, needless to say, may change in the ensuing months – if not the ensuing weeks – but at this juncture I have difficulty imagining a beer which can dislodge Landlord from its pedestal. If there is a better British frothy one then I would dearly love to try it.

**Timothy Taylor Landlord:
see February 24**

June 13

Uplifting news from abroad today: my Bro' telephoned from Singapore to report locating not only the best Chinese eatery he has ever happened upon during his travels but a bar boasting more than 150 beers. For a man who has spent the past six years in Australia and New Zealand, where a phenomenal frothy one such as Adelaide's Cooper's Extra Stout is very much the exception to the rule, this is an unforeseen slice of paradise. And we thought he would be existing purely on Tiger. Both Belgium and Germany are handsomely represented, he said, and on a recent visit he had a Leffe Brune and a Leffe Radieuse (correct glass, correct temperature) and, for sentimentality's sake, an EKU Kulminator (which he deemed undrinkably sweet – cheers, Bro'). Bolstered by these tidings, I believe I shall go to Singapore next year: the notion of an Orval in Asia is too bizarre to resist.

Stirred by reminiscences of Antwerp, I accorded myself a Belgian ale: the hefty **Van Honsebroeuck Kasteel Bier**, 11 per cent ABV and punching every ounce of its weight. Van Honsebroeuck, a family-owned brewery in Ingelmunster, West Flanders, purchased a local castle in 1986, and Kasteel Bier is matured in its cellars. The uninitiated tend to find it about as accessible as the moat-protected mansion after which it is christened, for it is not a beer for beginners. Port-like, dark, malty, fruity and stupendously rich, it could never be accused of half-heartedness. Distinctive it is; subtle it ain't.

I once saw an episode of *Wish You Were Here?* in which some jammy devil was praising Bruges while unwinding on a sun-kissed terrace and clasping a Kasteel Bier. Now I know why he looked so chuffed; in fact, I'm amazed he managed to cling to his seat.

I drink a toast to the Leffe-induced contentment of my Bro'.

**Van Honsebroeuck Kasteel Bier
(11 per cent ABV):   ★★★★**

June 14

In the middle of tonight's pool game, with Gurminder about to embark upon a nifty break, I retired to my stool, took a swig from my half of lemonade and thought: "This is not right." My reflections were directed not at Gurminder's sequence of shots but at my refreshment: a veritable touch of class would be brought to our modest sporting endeavours, I mused, by the presence of a distinguished beer. I know I have hitherto asserted that the Spot-On should not concern itself with purveying fantastic frothy ones, but I can't help pondering how blissful Saturday nights would be if it did.

This is not to say, I hasten to make plain, that I am envious of Gurminder's Cold & Tasteless – that, after all, is not a distinguished beer, and I would rather persevere with my lemonade than resort to such tosh – but *I am* envious of his being able to partake of a pint during our skirmishes. There is something perversely civilized, something almost proper, about savouring a nip of beer (or whisky/bourbon) while your adversary is rattling the pockets. A capacity for alcohol in the course of a marathon stint in the smoky environs of Bennington's Billiards was one of the attributes which made Minnesota Fats the man who "shoots the eyes right off them balls"; and, while I would have no intention of either playing or boozing as much as Fats did, the trauma of witnessing Gurminder's runs would be more than eased if I could pick up an Abbaye des Rocs when I put down my cue.

My dream is to stretch this scenario to its maximum potential by competing in the Embassy World Snooker Championship and scoring a spectacular advertizing coup for those under-valued and under-exposed frothy ones in need of a wider audience. While the humourless robots who dominate snooker's professional ranks would spend their time between shots pecking at mineral water, I would dazzle the masses by ostentatiously slurping from a branded Orval/Rochefort/Straffe Hendrik/Liefmans (delete according to round being contested) glass. I might keel over once in a while on my journey to the table, and I might miscue at toe-curlingly regular intervals; but curiosities across the globe would have been pricked, which would mean more to me than £100,000 in prize money (he lied).

Alas, the chances of my squaring up to Stephen Hendry are about as plausible as the chances of my nursing a Westvleteren at the Spot-On. One way or another, then, I guess my consuming of prime frothy ones is destined to be carried out away from the green baize – which was precisely the case tonight, with my after-bout repose enhanced by **De Kluis Julius** and **La Trappe Quadrupel**.

PILGRIM ON THE PISS

Julius appears to be the least common of the Hoegaarden products, which is a shame: it is a laudable ale and perhaps my favourite De Kluis beer. As I have said before, it is similar to Hoegaarden Grand Cru but drier and more sparkling; and, whereas Grand Cru is peachy in colour, Julius is a hazy gold and topped with an even bigger and brighter head. There have been charges that – like other De Kluis beers – it is less beguiling than it was, and I must concede that its perfumed intricacies have diminished even in the years that I have known it; yet I still have an affinity for it, and its exquisite presentation cannot be criticized.

If the drinker is keen to up the ABV stakes – and I was – then there aren't many beers to which to progress after the tripel-strength Julius, but the chestnut-hued La Trappe Quadrupel is among the few which fit the bill. First brewed in 1991 as a one-off, it has become the daddy of the Koningshoeven range; yet it is superlative only in potency, a lesser sidekick to the monastery's Dubbel and Tripel. It is thick and warming, as one would presume, but predictably cloying and maybe a shade too sweet. I will acknowledge that I am a tad biased against it, for I blame it for the wretched repercussions my Bro' and I suffered after uncorking innumerable Trappist ales while watching the climax of *Murder One*'s first series; but I don't think I'm being harsh when I suggest that it is not one of the classic Trappist beers.

Are Julius, La Trappe, Abbaye des Rocs, Orval, Westvleteren et alia as prevalent in the snooker clubs of Belgium and Holland as C&T is in those of Britain, I wonder? This is something I must probe during my next excursion – although I may never be able to face our pool nights again if I discover they are.

De Kluis Julius (8.8 per cent ABV):	★★★★★
La Trappe Quadrupel (10 per cent ABV):	★★★★

June 15

And still the Richmodis stands in the pantry, patiently awaiting an event worthy of its being cracked open. There has been the odd close shave, including the decisive instalment of *Murder One*'s second series (it was junk, and I bid it good riddance), but nothing has quite demonstrated the requisite gravitas.

Plunged into despair, I sulked while gazing at an accident-marred Grand Prix, deriving limited consolation from a diverse trio of German beers which I snapped up at a Derby cash-and-carry. Said establishment, although bursting with hundreds of cans of the usual crud, had a formidable assortment of select beers: having neglected to pop in since roughly 1990, when a crate of Grolsch was the pinnacle of the store's aspirations (and probably mine, too), I was buoyed by the sight of bottles of Leffe Brune, Schöfferhofer and even La Trappe Dubbel – most of them beyond their "best by" dates (so what?) and so retailing at bewilderingly low prices.

The key find was **Kronen Premium Pilsener**. Kronen is privately-owned and the most popular brewery in its home city of Dortmund; its Export, by all accounts, is superb but – like every other Dortmunder Export – kept hidden away. The brewery is obviously eager to push into Britain (why else would its Pilsener inhabit the shelves of such a cheap-'n'-cheerful outlet?), but will it export its Export? Nope.

Kronen Pilsener has the characteristic sweet maltiness of Kronen's beers. Less dry than a Rhineland Pilsener, lighter and cleaner than an Urquell, it is flowery and refreshing, with a fluffy head and a trace of bitterness. My enjoyment of it was dimmed somewhat by the arrival of a mate who regaled me with tantalizing tales of the Guinness he had guzzled during a weekend in Dublin – the guy doesn't even *like* beer per se, yet he had been to Stout Heaven and I to a cash-and-carry – but, at 50p a bottle, I couldn't really complain.

Next up was **Löwenbräu Premium Bier**, which I had deposited in my basket only after guarding against frustration by microscopically checking the labels for the crucial words "Brewed in Munich". If I had a tenner for every time I've spotted too late "Brewed under licence in the UK" – one of the most despicable phrases in the beer world – I would have the funds to buy that fridge I've always craved for my ales. Löwenbräu beers can be something of a bugger on this front – although the most heinous offender is Whitbread, whose Heineken Export is "exported" from none other than London but is still festooned with disgracefully deceptive references to Amsterdam and Holland.

Löwenbräu Premium can often be found on draught in Britain, brewed under licence for those discerning folk who request a "Low-en-brow" rather than a "Lurv-en-broy". Unless I'm very much mistaken, it was Löwenbräu Premium which the farcical constraints of the *Daily Star*'s pub survey demanded I solicit at the Burton Bridge all those years ago. While the UK-brewed draught version is downright horrible, the Munich-brewed bottled version isn't exactly mind-blowing: it is firm and malty, as are all Löwenbräu lagers, but otherwise pedestrian.

To taste **Erdinger Weißbier** again was to meet an old friend. Although the truth eludes me now, it may well have been the first German wheat-beer of which I approved (the first German wheat-beer I actually tasted was Löwenbräu's;

but that was in days of yore, at the Amsterdam flat of my Bro', and I wasn't strictly what you'd call a connoisseur back then: "I'm not drinking that, man – it's got bits in it!"). In the early '90s, when the Weizen explosion was struggling to reach these shores, the likes of Erdinger, Schneiderweisse and Spaten's Franziskaner were fighting a lonely campaign in Britain; but I adored these cloudy, lively, foaming beers.

In 1993 or thereabouts my reverence for Erdinger blossomed when my Bro' returned from a night at the renowned Masons Arms at Strawberry Bank, Cartmel Fell, in the Lake District, brandishing an Erdinger glass. Even by the standards of Weissbier vessels, most of which are toweringly ornate (and ornately towering), it was a gem. A flute of Erdinger is every inch and ounce as enticing as a ballon of Duvel, in visual terms if nothing else.

There can be no doubt that many a Weissbier as fine as – if not better than – Erdinger has come along since, but the brewery, based in Erding, near Munich, remains a giant of the style. Because it produces nothing else, its output of Weissbier is unparalleled; and Erdinger Weißbier, with its apples-and-cloves nose and sweet-and-sour finish, will always be extolled as one of the original classics – even if I can no longer rate it as such. Even an old friend can let you down.

And what, to summon a nightmare scenario, if the Richmodis lets me down? What if all of this waiting for the screening of a seminal movie, the making of sporting history or the scooping of a National Lottery jackpot should lead only to bathos? No, I mustn't dwell on that ugly possibility.

Kronen Premium Pilsener (4.8 per cent ABV):	★★★★
Löwenbräu Premium Bier (5.2 per cent ABV):	★★★
Erdinger Weißbier (5.3 per cent ABV):	★★★★

June 19

Guillo is dieting. He says he can't squeeze into his holiday shorts and must therefore deprive himself before he and his missus zoom off to Nice next week. Surely the acquisition of some new shorts would be a less painful and more sensible option? Why should he refuse frothy ones and fried rice when a swift jaunt to Marks & Spencer would solve all his troubles? I feared the worst when he notified me of his self-imposed torture prior to trundling round; but I'm proud to divulge that the teeniest arm-twisting persuaded him to indulge in a Summer Ale, a Becker's and a Chinese takeaway (but only one of each, like – congratulations, old bean).

With the rain pelting down, I thought **Burton Bridge Burton Porter** a more eligible aperitif than Summer; my digestif, meanwhile, was **Leffe Brune**, not an outlandishly titillating beer but one which invariably stirs happy memories. My first beer in Belgium was Orval, but my first beer after departing England *for* Belgium was Leffe Brune: this was not planned, but fate made it so.

Eugene and I had whizzed down to Ramsgate to catch the jetfoil to Ostend, but a menacing breeze nixed that mode of transport and condemned us to a lengthier crossing by ferry. My previous voyages had been graced by such achievements as redecorating a packed lounge with a regurgitated portion of chips, so I wasn't particularly looking forward to bobbing on the waves again; and, whimsical though they were, I didn't envisage that the pre-launch bacon-and-sausage butties we chomped at a quayside caff would assist in maintaining my well-being. My worries were eased, however, when we plonked ourselves down in the ship's bar and cast an eye over the list of beers.

I'm not positive that I had even heard of Leffe before that moment, and I do recall that the portly Belgian steward graciously told me it was brewed by monks – which, of course, was not so: Leffe, like all abbey ales, is brewed *for* monks, the monastery licensing a commercial brewery to produce beers in its name. Sadly, Leffe glasses were not practical – if people are going to reel from side to side and bash into furniture then it is better they should do so bereft of flamboyant bollekes – but the beer was more than palatable even in a basic half-pinter. Eugene and I were joined by a leather-and-denim-clad trucker, bristling of beard and gargantuan of gut, who came from Leicestershire, knew a number of pubs with which I was familiar and, having agreed to switch from Stella Artois to Leffe ("Hey, that's all right, that!"), delved into his bag and pulled out a king-sized French stick to consummate a curious but wholly diverting impromptu feast. "Blimey," I told myself, "if you get beer like this on the boat then Belgium must be ace!"

Interbrew presides over the Leffe ales and has them trotted out by sundry segments of its empire; even De Kluis is in on the act, responsible for Leffe Tripel (the most charismatic of the Leffe beers and the only one to be sedimented). The Brune, as became apparent to me within hours of staggering off the ferry and broadening my education, is not song-and-dance material; but it is a reasonably noble brown ale, tolerably dry and spicy, albeit ending a little shy of its abbey pretensions.

Just as it intervened with Leffe four years ago, fate butted in with Becker's tonight: no sooner had Guillo announced his diet than he had polished off my last bottle of his contemporary fave, thereby removing future temptation from his path. Shall I torment my hapless comrade by investing in another haul? Shall I hamper his flab-shedding tribulations by laying Saarland nectar before him? Or is that too cruel? Hmmm. Excuse my maniacal laughter.

Burton Bridge Burton Porter: see February 17

Leffe Brune (6.2 per cent ABV): ★★★★

June 20

A thoroughly depressing evening on the roads of the East Midlands has compelled me to query the sagacity of undertaking clutch-burning treks to Leicester merely to obtain a box of frothy ones. With the nation grinding towards a state of gridlock, the satisfaction I reap from pounding the blacktop has undoubtedly been dwindling of late; and yet seldom have I endured so lamentable a foray as tonight's to the Bottle Store. From motorway to dual-carriageway to country lane, tailbacks abounded. It was suicide fodder, the kind of automotive impasse from which stories of road-rage gush like overflowing four-star. How many bottlenecks can a man be expected to tackle just to slap his mitts on bottlenecks of a more gratifying ilk?

There was a time when my thrashes up the M1 had a serene edge, for I would divide the slog into two halves – literally – by pausing for a pint (that's twice I've used that abysmal pun, and I apologize profusely). I would sit next to the fire in the snug of the Cap and Stocking in Kegworth, a village more or less equidistant from Derby and Leicester, with a Draught Bass (straight from the cask), some ready-salted crisps and a *Daily Telegraph,* utterly at peace. My refuge from the cut-and-thrust chaos of the three-lane circus became a no-no four years ago, though, when I pledged never again to darken the Cap and Stocking's doors after a pompous young buffoon behind the bar berated me for daring to say "mate" ("My name is Tarquin," quoth he). Now, despite my reservations, I might attempt to redevelop my habit of fleetingly fleeing the bumper-to-bumper drudgery of junctions 22 to 25 if motoring matters do not improve.

It was inevitable that my ordeal at the wheel should be followed by a meagre spread at the Bottle Store. It may have been that my disposition had descended into one of irrevocable grimness, but I couldn't seem to work myself into a frenzy over anything on offer. I eventually stomped off with a token cluster of gueuze, Pilsner, Altbier and Weissbier, the incessant clunking of which contributed to the myriad delights of the ride home.

Seriously fed-up, I lobbed a **Schneiderweisse** in the fridge within seconds of entering the house, twiddled my thumbs for 20 minutes and then got stuck into a soothing half-litre of the greatest Weissbier on the planet. Schneiderweisse is darker than most non-Bock or non-Dunkel wheat-beers and is heavily carbonated and firm-bodied; it begins with a discreet fruitiness, unfolds through a malty spiciness and ends tart and dry. It is, in my opinion, in a Weissbier league of its own and possibly – just possibly – adequate compensation for 90 miles of abject woe.

Well, at least the company pays for my petrol.

**Schneiderweisse
(5.4 per cent ABV):** ★★★★★★★

June 21

What a day. Almost ceaseless drizzle and a vista of dank, grey skies. I came home from the office, flicked on the telly, was greeted by a Test match, excitedly went to fetch a beer and then sauntered back into the living-room to find that the cricket had been rained off while I was raiding the pantry. Ridiculous.

My **Samuel Smith's Nut Brown Ale** forfeited a measure of its appeal with the demise of the thwack of willow on leather. Mood is vital to the appreciation of frothy ones, and it is wicked indeed when circumstances alter dramatically twixt the opening of bottle and the filling of glass. I had a stab at recapturing the desired atmosphere with a video of *The Babe,* a biopic of baseball legend Babe Ruth; but baseball, though I am not averse to it, is simply not cricket – and Sammy Smith's, though the Americans think it ultra-trendy, is better at Lord's (or should that be Headingley?) than at Yankee Stadium.

I have no hesitation whatsoever in declaring that Liefmans Goudenband, from Oudenaarde, Belgium, is *the* brown ale, but Sammy's Nut Brown is one of England's chief pretenders to the throne – though it and its cohorts cannot honestly touch the world-classic status of Liefmans. The two are vastly different – I wanted to emphasize this tonight via back-to-back tastings, but my Liefmans requires a couple more days to settle – yet the calibre of each cannot be refuted. Nut Brown is rich, gently fruity, malty and – yes – nutty; it is sometimes sold as Old Brewery Brown Ale and is yet another of Samuel Smith's illustrious bottled beers.

With Goudenband counted out and my concept of a Battle of the Brown Ales thus ruined, I threw order to the wind and dug out a **St Stan's Dark Alt**. This was the Californian interpretation of Düsseldorf's Altbier style which I yearned to have at my disposal while viewing the documentary about *Star Wars* creator George Lucas three months ago: Lucas, you'll recollect, was born and bred in Modesto, where St Stan's is based. The brewery – founded in the mid-'80s by an American ex-engineer and his German wife – makes various ales, including numerous Alts, of which I consider Dark to be the pick of the bunch.

I am not acquainted with a glut of dark Alts, although there was a scene in *Auf Wiedersehen, Pet* – which was set in Düsseldorf – in which Magowan, an Irish-Liverpudlian labourer whose proclivity for violence and loutishness dwarfed even Oz's monstrous talent for hooliganism, snatched 20-odd beakers of deep-brown Altbier from a tavern waiter after politely urging him: "Oh, ya stoopid Eric, leave the tray 'ere, will ya?" The result of Magowan's flirtation with Altbier was a convoy of ambulances; the result of mine was the recognition that St Stan's Dark – sweet, roasted, chocolatey, reddish-brown but bordering on black – is an incontrovertibly splendid beer.

The splendour of **Gambrinus** has never been in question. It emanates from Pilsen, where the Gambrinus brewery occupies the same site as Pilsner Urquell, and is consequently that most elusive of beasts, an authentic Pilsner. It has often been said that only the fame of Urquell prevents Gambrinus from being hailed as one of the exemplars of lager-brewing; yet when I used to speculate that it might even be better than its exalted neighbour – and I am still dubious about which is the superior – my contentions provoked nothing but scorn. The production of Gambrinus is less complicated than Urquell's, much as the beer itself does not revel in Urquell's multi-layered complexity; but what is lost in fruitiness, softness and depth of character is gained in firmness of body, cleanness of taste and, above all, hoppiness. And when you gulp it from a Gambrinus glass procured from the brewery itself – my thanks to Mark, landlord of the Alexandra – it is tough to find fault.

Three smashing beers, then. If only the weather could have added to the general peachiness of the proceedings, though, and if only I could have done my bibulating while

165

reclining on the patio rather than huddled next to a roaring mid-summer fire; but in Britain that's probably just too much to ask.

Samuel Smith's Nut Brown Ale (5 per cent ABV):	★★★★★
St Stan's Dark Alt (6.2 per cent ABV):	★★★★★★
Gambrinus (4.9 per cent ABV):	★★★★★★

June 26

I believe I've caught 'flu. This would be less than astonishing: our glorious climate has grown increasingly wintry as June – June! – has worn on, and the all-pervading glumness has been tainted even further by the onset of monsoon conditions. Like everything else, I am cold and wet; and this does not portend well for beer-hunting during the rest of the month. The girth-trimming Guillo is okay, however: free from 'flu and, he alleges, 9lbs lighter.

The skies were so murky tonight that I jettisoned Summer Ale for **Burton Bridge Burton Festival Ale**, an altogether more warming and contemplative drop. Summer may be a top-tenner, but even my fascination for it is dulled by the recurring thud of rain on pane. Guillo was unswayed, though, for he was in need of a faith-restorer after a dreadful pint of Summer at a pub in Leicestershire (he said he was proud to profess his intimate knowledge of the source when aspersions were cast on his judgment, withering the barman's defiance by angrily proclaiming: "Well, I drink at the Burton Bridge almost every week, and the Summer Ale there is nothing like this!").

Festival Ale is copper-coloured, strong and sweet, with a very dry finish. Despite its reputation as a "heavy" beer, I have never thought it cloying; nor have I found it too sturdy for anything but deferential sipping – although I admit that throwing it down with reckless relish is not recommended. It doesn't seem to be the most fashionable frothy one among the Burton Bridge's clientele – XL, Summer and Porter normally slug it out for customers' affections, and perhaps rightly so – but it shouldn't be forgotten.

My hunch that a period of handkerchief-blasting might lie ahead was aroused when I got home and poured myself a **Dolle Brouwers Arabier**. This deceptively strong pale ale is colossally bitter, yet I could scarcely detect the billowing bouquet beneath the immense, Duvel-like head. I was well aware, courtesy of past encounters, of Arabier's beautiful subtleties; but suddenly, tragically, my nose was not up to the job. To unbung a bottle of Dolle Brouwers beer and promptly find that you're bunged-up yourself is an unmitigated disaster, for these are exceptional frothy ones.

De Dolle Brouwers – the Mad Brewers – are three brothers who saved from oblivion a crumbling brewery in Esen, West Flanders, and evolved from award-winning home-brewers into universally-acclaimed commercial brewers. Their remarkable portfolio encompasses multitudinous types of ale – pale, golden, brown, Easter, winter – and each is absolutely first-rate. The brewery itself can be toured by aficionados, with the brothers' mother – a formidable and vocal woman, it is said – as guide. I feel I have done these estimable people a terrible disservice by sampling an Arabier when unfit for the task.

Out with the hankies – one to blow my hooter as I sneeze my bonce off, one to dab my eyes as I weep for the frothy ones my affliction is poised to deny me in the coming days. Sod it.

Burton Bridge Burton Festival Ale (5.5 per cent ABV): ★★★★

Dolle Brouwers Arabier (8 per cent ABV): ★★★★★

June 28

It's official: I'm full of 'flu. And, having hardly tasted the Weissbier I forced upon myself at the Kleenex-pulverizing conclusion to a day of Promethean misery, I can only infer that the last frothy one of the month has passed my (rather sore) lips. What a ghastly finale to the first half of the year.

This gruesome day, with its dire mixture of missed opportunities and thwarted ambitions, has mirrored much of the year so far. I started out with high hopes, delivering Guillo (who now dejectedly claims to have piled on the pounds rather than lost them – mea culpa?) and Mrs G to Luton Airport and cogitating a cross-country sortie to the Falkland Arms thereafter; but the combination of a skull-splitting headache, hideous weather and mile after mile of horrific congestion on the M1 obliterated my scope for anything remotely cordial – apart from lemon cordial, that is.

Instead of Great Tew, then, I got Newport Pagnell services; instead of a picture-postcard hostelry and a pint of Hook Norton I got an amusement arcade and a computer game which – somewhat disturbingly, given the mayhem outside – encouraged me to execute handbrake turns and speed towards oncoming vehicles. I was – and am – heartily cheesed-off. I haven't succeeded in exploring too many pubs during the past six months; and today, when all was arranged to facilitate an expedition to one of the elite, I was stitched up left, right and centre. There is no justice.

Ignoring the deficit of pub visits and my failure to chalk up certain styles of frothy one – specifically Belgium's lambic ales, examples of which are skulking in the pantry in anticipation of my return to health – I regard my beer-hunting ventures thus far as a success; but today's travails have sounded one of the lowest notes of the year. The guilt lies not with **Pinkus Müller Pinkus Hefe Weizen,** a very light but fruity Weissbier, but with just about everything else. These things are sent to try us, I suppose.

Still, my reserves of optimism – effectively exhausted though they may be – allow me to fathom some contorted glee from this tissue-strewn mess: beer is off the menu, but whisky is very much on it. Lemsip, fruit juice and steaming cups of tea are all very well for replenishing vitamins, unclogging the snout and lubricating the throat; but no drink is more medicinal than a tot of Laphroaig, the most accosting of Islay's single malts. And I intend to prescribe myself a bloody large dose.

Pinkus Müller Pinkus Hefe Weizen (5.2 per cent ABV):   ★★★★

July 4

Nose unclogged and head devoid of aches, I am back. Although my taste-buds aren't operating at 100 per cent efficiency, it seemed churlish to deny myself any longer: with the weather joining me in perking up, it was obviously time to get quaffing again. I must say that my absence from the realm of frothy ones was not the baleful ordeal I feared; but then shunning beers is far from arduous when you know you honestly can't appreciate them.

The severest examination of my willpower came in mid-week – by which juncture the worst of my symptoms were receding – when Stuart and I dined at a Chinese restaurant in Sutton Coldfield, near Birmingham. The place had served Holsten Pils for as long as I could remember, so I anticipated no drain on my aptitude for abstinence; but I arrived to discover that, with strange yet almost soul-destroying inevitability, it now sold Tsingtao, the enticingly floral lager from the Chinese town of the same name. Not only did it sell Tsingtao – for that I might have been able to accept – but it sold it in bottles, virtually a singular treat when cans of the stuff have become alarmingly prolific during the past couple of years.

"Are you having one?" Stuart asked, immediately espying my covetous glance when the waiter delivered our drinks. "No," I said, though my resolve was already weakening. "Lemonade for me." Stuart poured a half-pint. "Sure you don't want some?" "Nah. Well, maybe I'll have one with the main course. No, I won't. Yeah, go on, then. No, no. Yes. No. No."

That sorry episode aside, my dry run has been something of a cinch; with Guillo in Nice, Eugene busy in Manchester and just about everyone thoroughly cheesed-off with the rain, perhaps it was never going to be anything but. Cinch or otherwise, however, what better way to mark its conclusion than by whipping out that model of patience, my lone bottle of **Richmodis Kölsch?** I reasoned that I might as well return to the fray in dramatic mode; and the Richmodis, set aside for a momentous occurrence, appeared ready-made to celebrate the happy event.

Kölsch may be the most delicate style of beer there is; indeed, ironically enough, its delicateness is probably its most distinctive aspect. Only breweries in Köln – which has more than any city in the world – and the surrounding area can use the "Kölsch" designation, which is rigorously and jealously protected. Kölsch beers are light-bodied, easy-drinking ales of Pilsner-like paleness; they are moderately fruity and beautifully soft; and they are invariably sampled in plain, cylindrical glasses of terrifying fragility (similar to Düsseldorf's stubby Altbekers but taller and thinner). It is initially difficult to discern the subtle disparities between each brewery's contribution, but seasoned devotees harbour strong convictions about which Kölsch is the best: I was once dumbfounded to hear Uncle Henny and another German relative viciously denounce Küppers, the most widely-exported brand, as essentially undrinkable – which, given the minuscule contrasts between one Kölsch and another, remains to this day a mind-boggling assertion.

Früh had always been my own favourite, but its reputation took a slight battering when my Bro' and I checked out the source

170

and departed somewhat disgruntled; now my allegiance is to Richmodis, impressive quantities of which were downed at Uncle Henny's home within hours of our trudging out of the Früh tavern. The real measure of Richmodis, I think, is that my ardour for it that evening was such that when Henny's wife presented us with a huge bowl of potato salad – which, to be blunt, I detest with a vengeance – I scarcely blinked at the horror of my gastronomic predicament, instead merely consoling myself with my frothy one and chomping away with nary a betraying grimace. Yummy.

The wait from then until tonight was made more than worthwhile by the first sip – a sip which metamorphosed into a less-than-respectful slurp and then several glass-emptying gulps. The same fate befell the next glass. I demonstrated commendable restraint come the third. I volunteer no apologies for my greedy approach, for I sincerely doubt there is another style of beer boasting such eminent drinkability. Magnificent.

I was briefly – *very* briefly – wracked by anxiety that a beer so delicate, so curiously unassuming, might not have a legitimate claim to top-10 status; but that, I have decided, was a false argument. My heart tells me Richmodis should be there. Besides, any misguided anguish over its stake to a slot on the list of honour was comprehensively dismissed when, literally seconds after I opened the bottle, the TV screened a trailer for a new series of *Columbo:* such miraculous influence cannot be disregarded. All in all, the evidence is overwhelming.

Richmodis Kölsch (4.8 per cent ABV): ★★★★★★★

July 6

My enthusiasm for frothy ones, refreshed barely 48 hours ago, has already been dented by an abysmal development: my Bro', it transpires, will be in England for only two weeks – and those

171

two weeks are the most inconvenient imaginable. My supremo is away on holiday during the first, so I shall be roped to my desk; and my Mum's glass-bearing chum is visiting during the second, when I shall have to fulfil my promise to chauffeur them around the Lake District, the Peak District, Oxfordshire and the rest. The chances of the brothers Robinson descending upon Antwerp or Munich are consequently looking disconcertingly slim. Some Summer Ale and a small pile of *Bilko*s are suddenly the zenith of our pragmatic ambitions.

I have, needless to say, formulated a cunning plan – although I don't for one instant dream that it will work. Could my Bro' and I not split the chauffeuring duties, dumping the old dears at sites of scenic importance and then scooting off to satisfy our own cravings at the nearest picturesque hostelry? This crafty scheme would leave everyone contented: the ladies would get to see some splendid countryside, and my Bro' and I would get to search for agreeable ales in unspoiled environs. I shall ponder my brainchild further, despite being nagged by the sensation that all but my humblest hopes are doomed.

Thus dejected, I conducted today's imbibing in an aimless and careless fashion. There was no theme to my choices, no basis for comparison, not even an assiduous yearning for the hop. Keen at lunchtime, I selected **Devil Mountain Devil's Brew Porter**; losing interest thereafter, it was another five hours before I uncorked some **Liefmans Goudenband**. The beers were sound (the Liefmans, in fact, was considerably more than that); it was I who was lousy.

I flirted with the pros and cons of marrying the Devil's Brew with the men's singles at Wimbledon, but the unerring ability of Pete Sampras to drill a ball past his bemused foe was not the sort of tedious spectacle likely to brighten my humour. I do not dispute that Sampras is a genius, but even acts of genius can appear monotonous to the non-fan – much as millions of dolts were bored by the driving of Ayrton Senna, dolefully commenting: "He just goes round and round." The cricket, complete with an embarrassing capitulation from England, made for more entertaining and appropriate viewing: the opposing bowlers were certainly too devilish for our batsmen.

Devil's Brew, from Benicia, California, is a rather mellow-tasting porter, more soothing than Satanic. Dark, smooth and roasted, with a very dry finish, it is peculiarly understated. Like all Devil Mountain beers – at least in my experience – its most amusing idiosyncrasy is its stupendous carbonation: even those with the steadiest hand would do well to decant a bottle without being panicked by the rapid up-rush of a foaming head, and arrogant oafs who dare turn their backs on a glass do so at the risk of having their tablecloths soaked by an unforeseen overflow.

Liefmans Goudenband, as I mentioned last month, is the king of brown ales. When I tout it as such to would-be disciples, unintentionally (or maybe, when I'm feeling a tad devious, intentionally) causing them to prepare for something akin to a Newcastle Brown, they are startled by its sourness and dryness; yet, although some express astonishment, few express disappointment. The normal Liefmans is matured for four months, but the vintage-dated Goudenband (Golden Band) is a blend of the basic beer and one which has been matured for up to twice as long. Goudenband – like Liefmans Kriek (brown ale with cherries) and Liefmans Frambozen (brown ale with raspberries) – is sold in corked, tissue-wrapped bottles, so from the earliest stage it is clear to the customer that this is a glorious beer.

The brewery, one of a number in Oudenaarde specializing in brown ales, is currently controlled by the Riva group. It is debatable whether meddling from above is responsible for the gradual climb in Goudenband's ABV – not so long ago it was less than 6 per cent, now it is 8 per cent – but I detect no adverse effects. And if Riva's commercial acumen can assist in bringing Liefmans to the attention of an even larger audience – while maintaining the integrity of the beers, of course – then one cannot complain.

173

Alas, this talk of Liefmans has reminded me of the various Goudenband-based carbonades flamandes my Bro' and I have tucked into both at home and in Belgium. Our cock-up on the calendar front haunts me again. I shall now bugger off and sulk.

Devil Mountain Devil's Brew Porter (5.4 per cent ABV):	★★★★
Liefmans Goudenband (8 per cent ABV):	★★★★★★

July 10

A conference with my pensions man this evening has left me hungering for retirement. I am budgeting to enter a life of peace and relaxation at the age of 55, which, depending on my mood-swings, is either dozens of years (sigh) or approximately 5,000 frothy ones (hurrah) away. Most folk want to travel when they are freed from the chains of labour, and I am no different; let's face it, the way things are going this year, I definitely couldn't do any less travelling than I do now.

I tackled my first lambic beer of the year while poring over the ins and outs of my financial plight. I must admit forthwith that lambic is far from being my preferred type of frothy one – there are numerous reasons for this, not least the fact that many lambics are tongue-shrivellingly awful – but the style is perhaps the most remarkable in the beer world, so I sporadically inflict an exemplar upon myself to ensure I retain a modicum of admiration for an imperilled art. Truly authentic lambics are rare finds in blighty, but **Timmermans Gueuze** is among the better commercial interpretations afforded the occasional inch of shelf-space.

Lambic ale, the production of which is nowadays confined to the Payottenland region of Belgium, is the result of spontaneous fermentation. Wild airborne yeasts plunge through slats in the brewhouse roof, just as they did more than 400 years ago, in a fabulously bucolic method of brewing. Newcomers think the idea of spontaneous fermentation off-putting enough, but the process which follows is guaranteed to deter the wary: the beer is allowed to mature for months in oak, a procedure so critical that the brewer will not even disturb the spider-infested cobwebs which eventually come to cloak the casks.

"What, there are creepy-crawlies all over it?" inquire the unenlightened.

"Yes," I say, a wicked glint in my eye.

An old lambic is mixed with a younger lambic to make gueuze; extra candy sugar is added to a lambic to make faro; and there are fruit lambics aplenty, though countless hardly qualify as bad jokes. Traditional lambic, frequently served in a champagne bottle bereft of even a label, is sour, musty and spritzy (and, to the novice, more than a touch appalling). Those from Cantillon, of Anderlecht, Frank Boon (pronounced "Bone"), of Lembeek, and Drie Fonteinen, of Beersel, are outstanding examples. At the nasty end of the scale are some of the mass-produced beers which masquerade as lambic but are actually sickly-sweet travesties trading on the name. Too many of the commercial efforts, notably those from the likes of Belle Vue (until consumer outrage sparked a rethink on Interbrew's part), Lindemans and even Mort Subite are so unbearably saccharine that you can almost sense your teeth rotting. Adapting to this most challenging of styles is made no easier by the likelihood of stumbling upon an absolute shocker in a deceptively appealing gold-foiled bottle.

Timmermans, of Itterbeek, near Brussels, is a purveyor of snazzy foils in miscellaneous hues, but its beers succeed in preserving a semblance of genuineness. The gueuze is perfectly tolerable, despite being sweetened and filtered, and represents a fitting introduction for beginners: it sits snugly between the fraudulent and the fierce. Conquer the Timmermans portfolio and you are ready to advance to the sublime Frank Boon Mariage Parfait and the shatteringly dry Cantillon Kriek.

My Bro' adores lambic beers and always seeks them out in Belgium. He had his first at the Mort Subite in Brussels (before we cottoned on to the despicable gueuze-agitating antics therein) and very soon was trying some of the masterpieces on the menu at the Brugs Beertje. I feel a trifle overshadowed when he orders a Frank Boon and I order a Hoegaarden or a Westmalle — not because the Boon is a superior beer, I hasten to stress, but because a foreigner who demands an esteemed lambic cuts a supremely knowledgeable dash in a specialist café. The staff issue the usual warnings — "I think you will not like it" — before he wins them over with a calm reassurance that he knows precisely what to expect. I suspect an affinity for wine — a trait I do not share with him — has something to do with it.

It was during one of his gueuze-guzzling nights at the Brugs Beertje that I last encountered the ales from Achouffe, an enterprising micro-brewery in Belgium's Luxembourg province. Achouffe's kruidenbiers — spiced beers — are almost uniformly excellent, its marvellous Lowie Kators a borderline top-tenner. Tonight's **Achouffe La Chouffe** started as an uplifting discovery at the Bottle Store but finished as an anti-climax: the brewery's "everyday" amber beer, it is irrefutably spicy but less multi-layered than Lowie Kators and the comparably elaborate McChouffe.

Whenever I drink Achouffe I cannot help but recall the aforesaid night at the Brugs Beertje, which was distinguished not only by the gallant stance of my Bro' but by the conduct of a mob of elderly British tourists. We were nestling in the back bar when they bundled in, clobbering chairs with their baggage and taking an age to seat themselves in an arrangement amenable to all members of the party. Credit to them for tracking down the Brugs Beertje, but our toes curled when they quickly fired off an excruciating barrage of inquiries directed at the waitress who had so adroitly catered to our whims throughout the evening.

"How many beers have you got here, then?"

"About 250."

"Oo, 250… Is that a lot, then?"

"Quite a lot, yes."

"What are they like?"

My Bro' and I swiftly adjourned to the front bar, telling the waitress when she asked why we were abandoning her: "Too many English people." Half an hour later, looking flustered and utterly fed-up, she paused while whistling past our table and said simply: "God, I miss you guys."

**Timmermans Gueuze
(5 per cent ABV):** ★★★★

**Achouffe La Chouffe
(8 per cent ABV):** ★★★★

July 13

Having sworn never again to subject myself to its iniquities, where did I find myself today? None other than the Babington Arms. I was invited for a snack, and common decency dictated that I could not refuse. The prospect of having to resort to a bottle of Beck's filled me with dismay; but then I dazzled even myself with an inspired burst of ingenuity.

A sneaky notion struck me when I spotted row upon row of **Newcastle Brown Ale** in the fridge behind the bar. More often than not it would have been chilled to the point of insipidness, but today the weather was scorchingly hot. I figured that the fridge would be fighting a losing battle in the blistering heat: with a speck of luck, the beer would therefore be served at something like the correct temperature. My lunch partner's mouth nearly hit the floor when I requested a Newcastle Brown – he is aware of my dismal opinion of the pub's ale-nurturing capabilities and was banking on my choosing a Beck's – but my hypothesis proved accurate: the temperature was bang-on. A triumph against the odds, then, but a Pyrrhic victory: a fluke bottle of brown ale will not compel me to boost the profits of the Babington Arms again.

As a Burtonian, I shouldn't really rave about Newcastle Brown: after all, it spearheaded the north-eastern counter-attack against pale ales. But parochial incorrigibility must give way to perception of merit, and Newcastle Brown's merit cannot be ignored. The beer, created 70 years ago by the incongruously-named Colonel Porter, is made from a blend of the low-gravity Newcastle Amber and a dark ale which is not available to the public. Teasingly fruity, vaguely roasted and pleasingly dry, it is Britain's biggest-selling bottled ale, exported to 40-plus countries and considered the embodiment of chic in the US and a cult drink in Russia. The most obdurate Burtonian would struggle to contest its worth (although I still favour Samuel Smith's Nut Brown Ale – and not just because it emanates from Britain's other capital of pale ales, Tadcaster).

I was enormously cheered by the possibility that a dodgy fridge might give rise to my relishing a Newcastle Brown in other establishments where frothy ones would otherwise be a no-no. The Spot-On and JD Wetherspoons across the nation took on a more alluring edge as the thrilling contrariness slowly dawned on me. But this fanciful sentiment became increasingly obfuscated as the day, courtesy of some mediocre beers, went downhill.

It is said that there are no desperate situations, only desperate men; and, with my pantry barren, I was a man desperate for a beer – perhaps *too* desperate. A predictably futile call at the Wine Rack yielded nothing more than a pair of lagers: **Lion Nathan Steinlager**, an award-winning (unbelievably) concoction from New Zealand, and **Vratislavice Pivovar**, a quasi-Budweiser from the Czech Republic. Did I sincerely want what I ultimately bought? My haul's value, I confess, lay purely in the fact that I had already tasted everything else remotely tempting.

According to its labelling, Steinlager, from Auckland's Lion

Nathan brewery, was "voted the world's best lager" at a beer exhibition in the '80s. I know they made for a wretched decade, but surely the '80s weren't *that* disastrous? Which other giants were in the running at said exhibition? Skol? Carling Black Label? A test-brew of Asahi Super Dry? Steinlager is mildly hoppy but pitifully unexceptional, as are most mainstream New Zealand beers. My Bro' once happened upon a NZ brewery which produced a Burton Ale – the brewer was cock-a-hoop at being showered with approbation by a Burtonian – but my scope for encouragement where the Kiwi scene is concerned has been limited to reading *Microbreweries of New Zealand*.

Pivovar's drab packaging belies a rather nice frothy one. The label notes are depressingly elementary ("well-balanced", "full-bodied", "the finest natural ingredients" etcetera), and everything seems a smidgen too nebulous; but, as Staromost before it illustrated, this appears to be à la mode for Czech lagers. As are many of these somewhat esoteric beers, Pivovar is like Budvar but without the panache: less golden, less flowery, lacking the richness of malt and the refined hint of vanilla. Tremendous in the wake of a Steinlager – which is to damn it with faint praise – but outclassed, I would imagine, in the wake of a Budvar.

Hmmm. So the day peaked at the Babington Arms, the pub of my nightmares. I shall endeavour not to dwell upon this. It is a bloody frightening state of affairs.

Newcastle Brown Ale (4.7 per cent ABV):	★★★★★
Lion Nathan Steinlager (5 per cent ABV):	★★
Vratislavice Pivovar (5 per cent ABV):	★★★★

July 14

My friend Kel – he who recently aroused my envy by staggering around Dublin in a Guinness-induced daze – has upped sticks to Birmingham, which is not a city for which I have any particular warmth. My doctor pal Tim once took me to a smashing boozer on the outskirts, but finding it again would tax my navigational nous to the utmost – a shame, since its combination of Holts Entire and a peerless mixed grill remains one I would dearly like to feast upon again. Kel's flat backs on to a canal running parallel to Broad Street, a haven of bars and eateries with pathetic American or Australian themes: all would be well if beers such as Anchor or Cooper's were featured, but – why does this fail to amaze me? – Budweiser and Foster's are the contemptible norm.

To my immense relief, we spared ourselves a tiresome session of bottle-clasping by tracing a tranquil Tap & Spile in a sidestreet just off the main drag. The Tap & Spile chain, which aims to provide conventional alehouses with expansive arrays of guest beers, is highly reliable; and this outpost, a discordant note in Broad Street's insensate symphony, was nothing short of a godsend. Modestly furnished and totally unpretentious, it contained a captivating surprise and a rank calamity – both from the Burton Bridge, no less.

I managed to resist the Bridge's presence at first, opting instead for a **Black Sheep Riggwelter**. Black Sheep was set up in 1992 by Paul Theakston, who left his family company when the Theakston brewery was taken over by Scottish & Newcastle, a mammoth group renowned for gobbling up and spitting out its acquisitions; now Black Sheep and Theakston stand side-by-side in Masham, North Yorkshire. Riggwelter is dark, fruity, soft and creamy. A rival to Theakston's famous Old Peculier? Arguably; but not as consummate.

The surprise was **Burton Bridge XL Dark Mild**, a caramelized version of XL designed to seduce the mild-lovers of the West Midlands. It is indicative of the geographical rigidity of many drinkers' attitudes that a beer which tickles fancies in one town or city is anathema to fancies in another but 30 minutes' horn-tooting away. Burtonians want pale ales; Brummies want milds; and buffoons want Budweiser and Foster's. A mild need not be dark, despite popular misconceptions, nor need it be low in alcohol: its determining characteristic should be a paucity of hoppiness and bitterness. Much as he might frown upon a brown ale, a staunch Burtonian might bristle at the concept of tinkering with a Burton bitter to render it more appetizing to a bunch of blokes 25 miles down the A38; but XL Dark Mild is an intriguing beer, if a mite thin.

And the calamity? Burton Bridge Summer Ale, the keeping of which evidently defeats cellarmen across the land. Gruesome ones have now been chalked up in Leicestershire (by Guillo), Nottinghamshire (by NG) and the West Midlands (by Kel). The fault is not the brewery's, against whom I will not hear a disparaging word; it is unfortunate, though, that some could mistake the ineptitude of the seller for an inadequacy on the part of the supplier.

We wound up in a Chinese restaurant, where, conscious of the drive home, I was once more forced to nurse a lemonade while enduring the dastardly sight of Tsingtao-savouring diners. This torture has now afflicted me twice in a month, and I will go crazy if I permit it to do so again. Tsingtao is duly promoted to the top of my beery agenda: irrespective of how many crispy aromatic ducks I have to ram down my throat, regardless of how many Peking ribs I must devour, I shall attain my goal.

Black Sheep Riggwelter (5.9 per cent ABV): ★★★★

Burton Bridge XL Dark Mild (4 per cent ABV): ★★★★

July 19

To some degree, if I am to be brutally frank, I brought today's painful events upon myself. As I cautioned at the commencement of this quest, there will be times when the spirited pursuit of frothy ones leads to an experience which transcends mere chagrin and encapsulates something between despair and disgust. One of today's beers was horrendous – not in an Asahi Super Dry vein but in a spluttering "What the hell is that?" vein. I do not hesitate in blaming the Wallersteiner brewery for my tribulation; but I also know that I was part-author of my own torment.

The ill-starred tale began last night at the Bottle Store. I had braved the M1 – again omitting to pause in Kegworth, somehow unwilling to prolong my agony – in a bid to obtain some liquid accompaniment for rounds three and four of a golf championship. It was only when I was trundling home that I realized 85 per cent of my buys, most of which were sedimented Belgian ales, would still be too unsettled for consumption when the trophy was being hoisted aloft. My gormlessness had been such that only two purchases, **Wallersteiner Classic** and **Wallersteiner Fürsten Weiße**, would be eligible for depletion come the weekend: a schoolboy error.

I was furious, but even the would-be ruination of my sport-watching could not persuade me to plod back to Leicester; and so I elected to polish off the Wallersteiner duo today and delve into my stocks of malt whisky – as befits golf, I reckon – tomorrow. Never, however, has a tournament been so cruelly marred by a dreadful beer: I shall now forever remember it not for a princely 64 by Tiger Woods but for the deeply nauseating growth – for I can conjure up no more expedient word – which I found bobbing on the surface of my German lager.

There can be only one fate worse than noticing such a body before you start supping: noticing it *after* you start supping. Worryingly, I was halfway down the glass when I finally deduced that what I had assumed was the last vestige of a near-non-existent head was in fact a splodge of slime-cum-scum. I did not probe it or pontificate as to its origins; I can only report that it looked monumentally repellent when I chucked it down the plughole. Did I warrant quite such hideous treatment for my faux pas at the Bottle Store? An unspectacular frothy one would have been ample punishment: the inhabitation of my pint by alien life-forms was, I felt, a fraction harsh.

I am confident that not every bottle of Wallersteiner Classic – which, judging by its 5.5 per cent ABV but not much else, is an Export-type beer – comes with this enchanting addendum. Yet, since this is the sole bottle I have ever had the misfortune to open (a position I do not envisage altering in the foreseeable future), I can only slap it with a one-star rating. It would be stretching credibility to suggest that any German beer is as dire as Asahi Super Dry; but, at least for now, that is Wallersteiner Classic's humiliating claim to infamy.

Who could criticize me for subsequently approaching the Fürsten Weiße with molar-chattering trepidation rather than unbridled rapture? It was, though, a fair Weizen: not as pale as some, turbid, the incipient onslaught of heavy carbonation fading after a couple of minutes. I believe I ought to grant it, too, a second chance, because the evils of the Classic had undoubtedly coloured my objectivity. If ever there was an afternoon of frothy ones to make me grateful for a Lagavulin or two, however, this was it.

**Wallersteiner Classic
(5.5 per cent ABV):** ★

**Wallersteiner Fürsten Weiße
(5.2 per cent ABV):** ★★★

July 21

The problem of how to show someone a grand time in Burton is one which has dogged me for innumerable years. The

Stapenhill Gardens are rather pretty. The Sainsbury's is intriguing in a semi-cubist kinda way. There's the Marmite factory. Oh, let's be honest: although tourism chiefs are paid to trumpet otherwise, anyone untroubled by a profound partiality to frothy ones is unlikely to tumble head-over-heels for the place. Strangers who subscribe to the Robinson Tour are bombarded with beer, boozers and breweries. Aside from the ale trail, I can think of nowt with which to wow out-of-towners.

My Bro' and I once escorted an American mucker of his around the Bass Museum, the Burton Bridge (which was closed), the Horseshoe in Tatenhill (in its pre-horsebrasses-with-everything days) and the Bridge Inn. He cherished each minute of his day-long stay — but then he *was* a Bass fanatic, the brewery's bottled products apparently the pinnacle of trendiness in his own community. I would be insulted by insinuations that he was easily pleased, even if he was the only Beatles buff in history who was satisfied with being photographed crossing an Abbey Road on an industrial estate just off the M1.

When Eugene arrived out of the blue this evening with Lisa, his girlfriend, I was in grave danger of drawing an inauspicious blank sightseeing-wise: a lady — a *pregnant* lady — would not, I mused, want to twiddle her thumbs while Henderson and I exercised our elbows (a fascinating display of athleticism though that is). But what else could we do? Should I have concealed the true Burton from her? Should I have manufactured a cosy fantasy? No. So we went to the Burton Bridge.

While Lisa was gregarious enough to have a half of Summer, I was traitorous enough to have a **Brakspear Special**. Brakspear, of Henley-on-Thames, Oxfordshire, makes a handful of very respected ales; its Special — tawny, sweet and malty, with a dry and bitter finish — had been the Bridge's Sunday-night guest beer, and the leftovers were still on tap (delaying, to my fleeting annoyance, the advent of Burton Bridge Battle Brew). My first Brakspear for three or four years, it was no letdown; but I switched to **Burton Bridge**

Bridge Bitter thereafter, keen that a pertinent prop should enhance my role as the native guide.

Lisa had kindly branded the Bridge "cute"; but even cuter, it occurred to me, was the Thomas Sykes Inn, a pub converted from the erstwhile wagon-sheds and stables at the defunct Thomas Sykes brewery (axed by Leicester-based Everard's in 1991). It is more quaint than cute, I would submit, with scant concessions to modern comforts; but why be pernickety? Stone-floored and high-ceilinged, with a tiny bar and no frills, it has beers from all the Burton breweries; and its **Draught Bass** is about as palatable as this once-illustrious bitter now gets.

To be charitable, I will acknowledge that Draught Bass can still be illustrious; but, without wishing to sound too pious, I would not counsel hazarding any at a venue too far outside Burton – except, of course, for a venue well-versed in the expertise required to look after this notoriously tricky beer. It is habitually served too "green", and its quality – and qualities – can vary insanely from pub to pub. Catch it at its best and it is malty, dry, quietly fruity (apples, like Pedigree), not too hoppy, with the sulphur aroma which the gypsum in Burton's soil imparts to the town's beers; catch it at its worst and it is… well, garbage.

Bass itself must shoulder a chunk of the culpability for its flagship's dubious rep, for Draught Bass was unequivocally robbed of some of its intricacies when the brewery jettisoned the "union room" system of fermentation for more contemporary (and, crucially, more frugal) methods. Marston's alone has persevered with the unions, complicated 19th-century contraptions famed for removing yeast from beer with brilliant effectiveness: it was afraid its ales would suffer if it relinquished its archaic apparatus – and the decline of Draught Bass, which has been fermented in open vessels since the early '80s, has verified as much. Who needs tradition and a world-class frothy one when there's a few quid to be saved?

Eugene, bless him, did his own bit for Burton by telling Lisa she would "love" the Bass Museum: "It's got horses!" She did not dissent, so a second trip to our metropolis is on the cards. I am convinced she is but a single black-pudding sandwich away from being smitten.

Brakspear Special **(4.3 per cent ABV):**	
Burton Bridge Bridge Bitter: **see January 16**	
Draught Bass **(4.4 per cent ABV):**	★★★★★

July 22

The ancient Chinese philosopher Lao-tzu, with his customary sagacity, observed that "a journey of a thousand miles begins under one's feet". It sounds as though, like me, he was having a spot of bother getting hold of a Tsingtao Beer. I might not have clocked up a thousand miles, but I have probably scoffed a thousand prawn crackers while being thwarted in my attempts to reacquaint myself with China's most prominent frothy one. Tonight, however, my journey reached its finale; and I must admit that it wasn't worth even taking that first step.

The Tsingtao brewery was founded late in the 19th century – several hundred years after Lao-tzu's reserves of wisdom had been exhausted, incidentally, so maybe his "journey of a thousand miles" nugget had wider implications than beer-hunting – when Germans came to the Shantung peninsula. Although it thus has its roots in Teutonic technology, Tsingtao utilizes China's own hops and barley; and these are not as consistent as some. The capricious nature of the local harvest may explain why Tsingtao, an ultrapale Pilsner, is sometimes pleasantly hoppy and sometimes numbingly dull.

Tonight's – during a carnival of abject gluttony with Stuart and Eugene at a Cantonese restaurant in Derby – was in the latter category, and this is often the case with beer: those you recollect fondly are wont to have deceived, especially when recollections have grown distant. Years have passed since I drank Wieckse Witte, the witbier from Heineken's De Ridder subsidiary, or Timothy Taylor Ram Tam, Landlord's dark cousin; and, although I would leap at the opportunity to rediscover either, I would be astounded if they were quite as phenomenal as my recondite powers of recall would have me think.

Lao-tzu also spouted the following pearl: "The great Tao flows everywhere. It fulfils its purpose silently and makes no claim. It does not show greatness and is therefore truly great." Close, Lao; but the last five words, it is now plain to me, are off-target.

Tsingtao Beer
(5.2 per cent ABV): ★★★

July 23

Celebrity is mine. Some time, somewhere, a diminutive band of dedicated couch-tatties will click on their TVs in the early hours of the morning, idly meddle with their zappers, locate an obscure cable channel and be greeted by the image of N Robinson at the bar of the Fat Cat, Sheffield, home of the Kelham Island brewery. And how will the insomniac population recognize me? How is the door to stardom and untold riches to be kicked off its hinges? Well, viewers, I'll be the fellow feigning jubilation at the pulling of a Bulmers Cider. Cheers.

I might have been denied this crushing indignity if the day had gone to schedule, but my escape was not to be. Due to meet Eugene and Stuart for lunch at 1pm, I rolled up 90 minutes late after Ayrton overheated in Derby and constrained me to crawl home to fetch the drearier but healthier Escort. My associates welcomed me by bragging that a crew assembling a documentary on Britain's premier pubs had filmed their clash at dominoes; but little did I know that I would be charged with dramatizing an infinitely more exacting spiel.

Before the lens beckoned, though, I allayed my nerves – beastly things, these screen debuts – with a **Kelham Island Best Bitter**. It must be nigh on three years since I was at the Fat Cat, an intimidatingly sturdy building whose interior is awash with breweriana, and the beers are as delectable as ever. The Kelham Island brewery – christened after the preserved industrial zone in which the pub stands – was established in 1990 and produces a broad range of ales, including English renditions of Bavarian Weizen. Best Bitter is hoppy, bitter and then arrestingly (but not offensively) sweet; it is also, lest anyone should be at all confused, rather better than Bulmers.

When I was summoned to do my thang – "Can we borrow you for a shot?" – I never guessed I would be treading the boards alongside a cider (and a cruddy one at that). Appetizing frothy ones, among them Belgian goodies like De Koninck, littered the bar; yet the only pump which sated the cameraman's desire for an attractive angle dispensed Bulmers. My heart sank when I was informed I would have to hover in the background and wait – as though interested – for "my" pint. I did make one stipulation, however: "I'm not drinking it."

For take one – as we say in the trade, like – I adopted a bastardized "method" technique, silently telling myself while it was being sploshed into the glass that Bulmers wasn't so rotten. I might have looked credible, then, but we shall never know: the director consigned my turn to the cutting-room floor by insisting we reshoot, now with the supplementary pressure of my having to grab the Bulmers and stroll back to my seat.

Take two proceeded amid much mocking from my alleged

mates. I adopted a "This is getting on my wick" technique. The landlord, who was as irritated as I, pulled another pint under my pseudo-appreciative gaze; I seized it, manfully striving to disguise my disdain, and marched back to my tittering companions. I was congratulating myself on my professionalism when some merciless tyrant declared that the host had gawped straight into the camera and another take was necessary.

I adopted the seldom-seen "I've had enough of this" technique for take three. Slumped across the counter and unable to bring myself to ogle the spattering of yet another Bulmers, I stared into space while being heckled by Eugene and Stuart, squeezed out a curt nod upon receiving a third unwanted pint and then shambled back to my stool, lingering listlessly until a "Cut!"-like proclamation authorized me to slink back to the bar and plonk my glorified apple-juice next to its predecessors. It was a performance pitched somewhere between Robert De Niro's Travis Bickle (the homicidal cabbie in Martin Scorcese's *Taxi Driver*) and Vincent Price's Fortunata Lucresi (the haughty wine-taster in *Tales of Terror*, Roger Corman's wonderfully camp and tacky Edgar Allen Poe compilation); and it was, thank God, a "wrap".

Obviously moved by the emotion and passion inherent in my artistry, the landlord proffered "a proper pint" – gratis: I chose **Kelham Island Pale Rider**, the house pale ale. Despite its tragic Ayrton Senna connotations – germane, I suppose, in light of my own Ayrton's demise today – it is a beer in which I always delight. Uncannily light and quenching for a British ale of its strength, it is extraordinarily tangy and moreish. I could not appease my lust for a second – even though my talent in the glare of the spotlight justified a gallon – for I had to get behind the wheel; but it can only be a matter of weeks before a multi-million-dollar contract from Hollywood liberates me from the burden of not having a chauffeur to ferry me from pub to pub.

Aye, I can picture it now...

"Warner Brothers are on the cellular phone, Mr Robinson."

"Not now, man! Onwards to the Burton Bridge!"

**Kelham Island Best Bitter
(3.8 per cent ABV):** ★★★★

**Kelham Island Pale Rider
(5.2 per cent ABV):** ★★★★★

July 25

My visit earlier this week to the Thomas Sykes rekindled an affection for a gem I had too long neglected. I shall not forsake it again, because it is a belter. In this era of alcopops and potato-skins, cold-filtered lagers and boil-in-the-bag baltis, Irish bars and assorted other rake-it-in-while-the-novelty-lasts fads, anywhere with fine beer and unadulterated grub (ah, the piggish pomp of *real* pork scratchings – bulky buggers from a butcher, not some ersatz fare in a miniature crisp-packet) should be prized.

In bygone days the Thomas Sykes sold ales from casks, an imposing queue of which stood along the back wall, and one night Gary sought to "go along the barrels". Whether he accomplished the feat is lost in the mists of time, but the reverential hush which attended the tapping of his Thomas Sykes Old Ale – the awesome (10 per cent ABV) winter beer which was once brewed on the site – is hard to forget. We had a chuckle about that when we returned tonight; but the evening stirred other memories, too.

Morland Old Speckled Hen was the frothy one I picked to commemorate taking delivery of Ayrton in 1994. I did not – and do not – rate it highly; but it was launched to mark the 50th anniversary of MG (which was based, like the brewery, in Abingdon, Oxfordshire) and derived its mysterious title from a Mogster with flamboyant paintwork, so I meekly fell prey to witlessness while preoccupied with insurance quotations and the quirks of a gearbox with no synchromesh on first. Tawny, hoppy, sweet, roasted and dry, it has never won me over (perhaps because I connect it with my Roadster and all the concomitant mechanical mishaps which have plagued me since that day in '94); yet others speak glowingly of it, and I accept I am in the minority.

More significant, though, was my bolder-than-bold decision to have a **Marston's Owd Rodger**. It was my first rendezvous in almost a decade with the frothy one which shaped not only my youth but my girth, and it was very much an impulsive act. For years I had fooled myself into presuming that even short-lived exposure to it would have me heaving uncontrollably, cursed by the thought of past superfluities, but tonight I told myself that, though it might have constituted lunacy in the late '80s, a 7.6 per cent beer was nowt from which to flee in the late '90s: in Belgium, after all, it would be pigeonholed as of average potency, dwarfed by Rochefort 10°, Westvleteren Abt, Bush Beer and a throng of other big-hitters.

It was blissful: dark red, massively fruity, malty, rich and smooth. Whereas once I had sipped it in a manner which surpassed veneration and nudged pusillanimity, I was able to swill it with revelational nonchalance – although the former tactic is more advisable with barley wines, which are generally England's mightiest ales. Separation had done us good: Marston's oft-overlooked heavyweight seemed better than ever. Just as Gary's days of going along the barrels are behind him, however, so I was not tempted to emulate the three-pints-and-a-duck-curry escapades of yesteryear: the Thomas Sykes and Owd

Rodger are manifestly not among them, but certain things are best left in the past.

Morland Old Speckled Hen **(5.2 per cent ABV):**	★★★
Marston's Owd Rodger **(7.6 per cent ABV):**	★★★★★

July 31

The competent pouring of a sedimented ale is fundamental to the enjoyment of beer. There is nothing more demoralizing than a dose of yeast plopping into your hitherto-flawless frothy one a nanosecond before you were poised to execute a clarity-sustaining flick of the wrist. The requisite dexterity must be cultivated over the course of hundreds of beers, and only then will clumsy consternation blossom into unruffled equanimity; and there is a deal more to learn after that, too.

My young buddies and I got to grips with the basics circa 1988 via Worthington White Shield, the bottle-conditioned kin of Draught Bass, which we gambled upon once in a while in pubs whose handpumped wares we did not trust. One of the chaps said he had been versed in the secrets by his grandad, and he would ostentatiously wave away barmen whose trembling betrayed their incapacity for the task; but howls of derision would ensue when he messed it up, which the poor soul did with opprobrious regularity. The axiom was that the bottle should be held at eye-level and the beer poured slowly down the side of a sloping glass: it sounded simple, but it was an irksome intrusion for sozzled teenagers.

Now, scores of Orvals later, I am – if I say so myself – a virtuoso, often cocksure enough to deposit the contents of a Belgian bottle from a height and into the centre of a waiting ballon, bolleke or kelk. I do this not out of a woeful fervour to mimic the stars of *Cocktail* (an execrable movie) but to generate the head vital to the presentation of most Belgian beers. Some ales (Orval, Hoegaarden Grand Cru, Dolle Brouwers Arabier) throw a gigantic crown without prompting, and these must still be released from their slumbers with prudence; others (Rochefort 10°, Verboden Vrucht, Gouden Carolus) benefit from adept urging – although I would never countenance the Mort Subite bent for whisking the beer in the glass to induce a thick cap of foam, for such skullduggery is daft rather than deft. Proficiency comes only with practice, but the gratification upon achieving mastery is sufficient reward in itself; and then there is the perverse bonus of obliterating your work.

How much beer you waste in guarding against catastrophe is influenced by a number of factors, not least your own courage. Even staff in Belgian cafés will leave one or two centimetres' worth in the bottle, so there is no point in trying to be *too* clever. The key is to keep the bottle horizontal during decanting, which enables you to monitor the sediment as it slides inexorably towards the neck; and you cannot have another stab once you have stopped, because the residue will have been irredeemably discomposed.

Tonight my own adroitness was laid open to the sternest scrutiny by a slippery trio: **Moortgat Duvel**, whose sediment is practically impalpable; **Van Eecke Poperinges Hommelbier**, whose sediment is gargantuan; and **Van Steenberge Gulden Draak**, whose sediment may not even exist but would be hidden by the frivolous whitewashed bottle if it did. My job on the Duvel was beyond reproach; I made rather a hash of the Hommelbier (hey, it happens); and – depending on whether it did indeed carry a sediment – I was either charmed, skilled or none of the above when it came to the Gulden Draak.

Duvel – so-called, legend has it, because a brewery employee hailed it as "a Devil of a beer" (which makes me seriously wonder about Van Steenberge's Bonk, but there you go) – deserves the impeccable, as it is incontrovertibly one of the greats. Moortgat, of Breendonk, near Brussels, introduced it in dark form before the Second World War; its current incarnation, the original "strong golden" ale, only emerged in 1968 in response to the Pilsner-galvanized leaning towards pale beers. Although it is top-fermented, it is routinely offered at a temperature more suited to bottom-fermented beers (around 8°C). There can be no ale of analogous muscle – a lethally deceptive 8.5 per cent ABV – which is so drinkable: Eugene's record, for some reason yet to be certified by the men from the *Guinness Book*, is nine.

Duvel's success was such that imitators, each with its own devilish or roguish tag, have been popping up ever since. Three or four – such as Lucifer, from Riva, of Dentergem, and Judas, from the Union branch of the Alken-Maes conglomerate – capture its essence, yet none is its match. They are all straw-coloured and usually intensely hoppy, but Duvel's complexities – its stunning bouquet, its incredible smoothness, its perfumed finish – set it apart from the chasing pack.

The Van Eecke brewery is in Watou, a hop-growing area near Poperinge, West Flanders: hence Poperinges Hommelbier – hop beer from Poperinge. A pale ale almost as perfidious as Duvel, Hommelbier is indeed crammed with hops; but it is also crammed with sediment, a sizeable helping of which I emptied into my glass. My cretinous bottle-handling led only to cosmetic defects, I am glad to say, and could not detract from the vigorous hoppiness. The luminary among Van Eecke's output is not Hommelbier, though, but Watou's Witbier, a Hoegaarden-pulping wit with a fantastic lemoniness; I shall be extremely upset if I have not ferreted some out by the end of the year.

Gulden Draak is gorgeous to behold in its Duvel-ish ballon: dark and contemplative, topped with a cream-tinged head, it has a beguiling air. It is a very herbal beer, like a medicinal Verboden Vrucht, and is ideal for a game of *Scrabble* in front of a roaring fire. The bottle is just stupid, of course, and if there is a sediment in there somewhere then the brewery should have its knuckles rapped; but then where would the fun be if we wizards of the pouring world were not tested every now and then?

Moortgat Duvel (8.5 per cent ABV):	★★★★★★
Van Eecke Poperinges Hommelbier (7.5 per cent ABV):	★★★★
Van Steenberge Gulden Draak (10.5 per cent ABV):	★★★★★

August 1

Many years ago, during a weekend in the Lake District, I visited a pub near the banks of Windermere and was shocked to find on my table a notice declaring that vinegar was not allowed with the food: a sprinkling of Sarson's, claimed the management, encouraged misguided customers to moan about their beer. I had never known the like. Had it not been for my feeble English restraint-cum-cowardice, I might have launched into a verbal volley – something along the lines of "Listen, I'm from Burton – that's where beer comes from, like – and I've never seen owt as ridiculous there, so you'd better fetch me some vinegar for my steak!" – but instead I simply mumbled into my pint of Jennings, from Cockermouth, Cumbria, and accorded myself an extra ton of salt by way of compensation. I did not comprehend my own ignorance.

The reality is that the owners of that secluded boozer had a point: vinegar with beer can be utterly ruinous. This is not resolutely the case – there are, for instance, numerous respected alehouses which sell pickled eggs without accumulating any complaints – but an horrific ordeal last year with a portion of fish and chips and a glass of Westmalle Dubbel, the latter of which was wrecked even though I consumed it two hours after my well-soaked cod, has left me deeply wary. My loose rule now is that the risk is not warranted.

Tonight, however, I not only took the risk but got away it – although whether the frothy one concerned necessitated my valour is a matter for debate. Around two-and-a-half hours and a couple of mouth-rinsing fruit juices separated vinegar from **Villers Triple**; perhaps I should not have exercised even those moderate precautions, because this desperately dry and somewhat uninspiring tripel – from a brewery in Liezele, between Antwerp and Brussels, renowned for the distinctive (to use a courteous word) nature of its products – might have benefited from whatever flavour input it could get.

Villers Triple is by no means awful; but it is scarcely an exemplary tripel if, to apply a rigid rule of thumb, Westmalle's is taken as the model. It is more orangey in colour than most and visually appealing for it, yet it is let down by a weird paucity of hoppiness and a curious thinness. I could not help coveting Stuart's Hoegaarden Grand Cru as I pecked away with ever-diminishing zeal, but then jealousy is bound to result when a big-hearted chap such as myself gives the best beers to his chums and grants himself an unknown quantity in a bid to further his experience: just as I once paid the penalty for my ignorance, from time to time I must pay the penalty for my willingness to explore.

**Villers Triple
(8 per cent ABV):   ★★★**

August 3

Calamity. I have committed a terrible sin, albeit in all innocence. Only today was the error of my ways disclosed to me, and the revelation cut me to the quick. Last month I reflected that the **Tsingtao Beer** at a restaurant in Derby was a trifle dull, possibly because the batch from which it emanated had not enjoyed the pick of China's harvest; but today I learned that, though the standard of hops and barley may indeed have played a role, there was an altogether more straightforward explanation for its relative lousiness. Forgive me, for I have drunk canned beer.

I uncovered the horrible truth when I peeked at the shelves under the bar while settling the bill for my buffet lunch, which – with the notable exception of another lacklustre Tsingtao – had been outstanding. There was a satisfying element of "I thought as much"; yet there was also an infuriating element of "I don't bloody believe it", because I abhor tinned frothy ones and garner no pleasure whatsoever from imbibing them. Some tinnies (as the Australians dub them) are worse than others, naturally, but there isn't a single effort which succeeds in crawling out of the swamp of the merely acceptable. Even if I were marooned on a desert island and had for sustenance only a selection of canned beers – say, for the sake of argument, Pedigree, Draught Bass (a disgraceful misnomer) and Becker's, all of which are available in that form – I would have to think long and hard before tugging a ring-pull. No more Tsingtao for me, ta very much.

Almost as disagreeable, though for completely different reasons, is the silly pottery-crock bottle which holds **Sterkens Poorter**. Bottles which conceal their contents are preposterous beyond redemption: Poorter, Gulden Draak, Sainsbury's Trappist Ale – all are damned by an ill-conceived marketing ploy. That alone ought to have been sufficient to dissuade me from parting with my cash in Leicester last month, and the fact that Poorter is practically identical to Sterkens St Paul Double (which I tried in June) should have dispelled any lingering reservations and sealed its fate as a no-no; but, susceptible so-and-so that I am, I fell for the concomitant glass and ended up buying the whole ensemble.

Poorter, as I have mentioned previously, has nothing to do with porter, the two barely sharing more than top-fermentation and a dark hue: it means "Freeman of the Borough", the beer having been created in 1985 to commemorate the 775th anniversary of Hoogstraten, the municipality in which Sterkens' home village of Meer is located. Poorter is unmistakably similar to St Paul Double, but I consider it a smidgen more noble: smoother yet more pronounced (if you'll pardon the awkward contradiction in terms), with a hint of roastedness. Shame it has to be presented in something resembling a chimney.

I don't know. Cans and crocks... what next? McDonald's-style cartons, no doubt.

Tsingtao Beer:
see July 22

Sterkens Poorter
(6.5 per cent ABV):

August 10

As we journalists are wont to write when we are at our most eloquent: "Wotta scorcha!" A remorselessly muggy week, replete with the sort of stewingly oppressive temperatures which sporadically blight British summers, has been enough to sap anyone's zest for all but the most refreshingly light beers. My stocks of frothy ones during the ongoing heatwave have consisted almost entirely of Trappist ales, and it is difficult to imagine a more inappropriate genre of frothy one for a thermometer-popping climate; and that is why I have endured a dry spell.

Tonight, despite the persistence of sweltering conditions, I could resist no longer and, discarding my Chimay and Rochefort as hopelessly incongruous, seized upon the two non-Trappist options at my disposal: **Unibroue La Maudite**, a spicy ale from one of Canada's most dedicated breweries, and **Cooper's Sparkling Ale**, a rare classic from Australia. Neither country has earned even a perfunctory esteem for its frothy ones, but both of these beers would stand comparison with exalted emissaries from any land.

Only last night I watched *The Entertainer*, in which Laurence Olivier delivers a barnstorming performance as music-hall has-been and chronic ale-guzzler Archie Rice. A washed-up comedian with womanizing tendencies, Rice has an opportunity to leave behind his mounting debts and his end-of-the-pier subsistence when a relative offers him the chance to run an hotel in Ottawa; but − notwithstanding the grimness of his predicament − he bluntly dismisses the suggestion thus: "I think it's a bloody pointless idea. Anyway, you can't get Draught Bass in Canada." The film was made in 1960, since when Canada − beleaguered by insipid drivel like Molson Dry and Labatt Ice − has not exactly enhanced the brewing reputation of which Rice thought so little; yet there is a pocket of superior producers, and one of them is Unibroue, of Chambly, Montreal.

I first sampled its range in 1994, having never even heard of it until then, when the ever-generous Guillo brought back from a holiday in Quebec four huge bottles: two of Blanche de Chambly, the brewery's witbier, and one apiece of La Maudite and the tripel-ish La Fin du Monde (End of the World). These came equipped with a superb leaflet which dealt with such details as which glasses assisted in expressing the beers' qualities and how to pour the sedimented ales so as to generate a handsome head and not dislodge their yeast deposits: this, needless to say, was a document after my own heart. I remember that Eugene and I polished off every bottle after adjourning to the patio on an evening whose weather was much like today's; the next morning my neighbours, in whose garden each of the four corks had landed after opening, wildly speculated that I had been sipping champagne.

My latest La Maudite was again a gift from Guillo, who nabbed a six-pack at the airport as he prepared to fly back from his break in Nice. Although understandably less fluffy than its predecessor − ales often develop a softer edge in corked bottles

199

– it boasted the marvellous spiciness I recalled from my last Unibroue session. La Maudite – whose name is a tribute to the French-Canadian legend of a flying canoe (and why not?) – is copper-toned, thoroughly delicious and very probably the finest Canadian frothy one I have ever encountered (challenged by Blanche de Chambly alone); and I do not intend that final assertion to be construed as meagre acclaim.

If Canada's beers are typically deemed abysmal then what can be said about those of Australia, the nation which inflicted Castlemaine XXXX and Victoria Bitter upon unsuspecting drinkers across the globe? Few countries are so readily associated with the Cold & Tasteless school of brewing; and, as I discovered when I spent a month in Sydney in 1991, there is an enormous amount of dross. It is easy to reject Oz beer altogether on the evidence of its high-profile brands, yet there are actually some decent breweries and brews: the Pumphouse, Sydney, with its English-influenced bitters; Cascade, of Hobart, with its urbane Premium Lager; and Cooper's, of Adelaide, with its velvety Stout and its majestic Sparkling Ale.

Cooper's was established in 1862 by Yorkshireman Thomas Cooper, who had emigrated to Australia a decade earlier, and it is controlled by his family to this day. It flirted with oblivion by continuing to churn out ales when lager was sweeping all before it, but now its products have attained the ubiquitous recognition they deserve. Sparkling Ale – a queer appellation, as the beer contains a heavy sediment which invariably tumbles into the glass (with a consequence which is anything but detrimental, I must confess) – is massively fruity, hoppy and quenching; my pal Stotty, who has lived in Oz for the past several months, slipped into the laudable habit of supping nothing else after I recommended it to him when he rued the lack of virtuous frothy ones in Melbourne.

Incidentally, although there is conspicuous latitude for metaphor and analogy, I do not care to direct attention to England's cricketing fortunes against Australia. When the

200

Canadians thrash us at cricket – and, given our current plight, who would dare estimate how soon that might be? – I shall, of course, succumb to the inevitable.

Unibroue La Maudite (8 per cent ABV):	★★★★★
Cooper's Sparkling Ale (5.8 per cent ABV):	★★★★★★

August 14

It is not unfair to expect someone infatuated with frothy ones to cram their every sentient hour with trips to pubs, festivals, breweries and assorted beery happenings. For me, though, there is a tiny problem: my job. Without wishing to sound too pitiful (as Basil Fawlty once sneered: "Do I detect the smell of burning martyr?"), I have to say that the unpredictable flexibility of my hours limits my scope for such luxuries: although my schemes are not destroyed with any outlandish regularity, the threat of terminal disruption is always but a beeping pager away.

Take two nights ago: I was relaxing after a meal with Gary in Leicester when I was abruptly dispatched to the Derbyshire village of Lower Pilsley. I won't bore you with the background, but what should have been an evening of idle repose became 10 hours of through-the-night lunacy. I told myself that a nocturnal stint of "doorstepping" would at least be more tolerable in the Escort than in the reviled Punto, whose unfeasibly firm seats would have rendered the task yet gloomier; but that was my sole consolation as I resigned myself to a period of extraordinary bleakness.

As it turned out, the good people of Lower Pilsley – well, two of them – could not bear to witness a hapless hack suffer so cruelly. At 2.30am, with my will to survive ebbing away, a gentleman with a torch ambled across to the car, tapped on the window and, to my astonishment, inquired: "Do you want a coffee?" So I came to keep be slouched in the lounge of the wonderful Tom and Gladys, who amazed me with not only their kindness (how many members of the public, after all, would welcome a skulking reporter into their house in the wee hours?) but their down-to-earth wisdom.

And it wasn't just coffee which was served up for this solitary scribbler: Tom brought out his home-made wines, and what an intriguing bunch they were. One of them was so splutteringly dry that Cantillon Kriek would have appeared puny in its wake; another, the proffering of which was attended by conspiratorial chuckling from my host, was the most chest-scorchingly alcoholic concoction I have ever braved. They reminded me of the theory espoused by Leon Brand, patron of the Netherlands' Christoffel brewery, who proudly retorted when questioned about the intense bitterness of his famous Pilsner: "I am not trying to brew for everyone. Plenty of brewers already do that." I will concede that I would have preferred a Pils to a Pilsley, but Tom's inventions were nonetheless fascinating.

Tonight's **Lefèbvre Barbar** could have been a non-event after such striking fare, but it is not a beer which is easily eclipsed. Tripel-like in strength and (as the labelling never tires of stressing) made with honey, it is arrestingly sweet but not repulsively so; it has the approximate shade of its much-vaunted ingredient, although the Barbar glass is a rather showy frosted mug which obscures the genuine tint. Ales brewed with honey are not uncommon, but examples made with such accomplished flair are far from abundant.

My most memorable Barbar came at the Brugs Beertje, where owner Jan de Bruin bewitched me with an enigmatic observation worthy of Lao-tzu. I was trading Travis Bickle monologues with local businessman Patrick Meersman (with whom I was engrossed in a rambling discussion about the movies of Martin Scorcese and Francis Ford Coppola) when Jan, spotting my choice of frothy one, gestured towards his statue of the Bruges Bear and, with a conspiratorial chuckle to equal Tom's, drew upon his mastery of

English to advise me: "The bear – he likes the honey." The conversation faltered a tad thereafter, and precisely what he was babbling on about I still don't know; but I was honoured to be addressed, however eccentrically, by one of the leading figures in the Belgian beer revival.

By the way, that was back in the days when I went on holiday. And yes: you *do* detect the smell of burning martyr.

**Lefèbvre Barbar
(8 per cent ABV):**

August 17

My Bro' has arrived from Singapore, signalling the commencement of what should have been the most spectacular week's drinking of the year. I feel able to say "should have been" at this juncture, premature though it might seem, because we are well aware that the catastrophic constraints of our respective timetables will preclude our scaling dizzy heights. We peaked in '96, when we knocked the top off frothy ones in Brussels, Antwerp, Westmalle, Köln, Bonn and Hoegaarden; this week we will count ourselves outrageously fortunate to flee the environs of Burton. At the start of the year there was optimistic talk of a sojourn in the town of Rochefort, but we rapidly concluded that was the stuff of dreams; now we might manage a bottle of Rochefort between us, I suppose, yet that is as close to Belgium as we are likely to get. I have taken modest measures to ensure the restrictions imposed upon us do not totally rob us of non-British attractions, but it cannot disguise our tragic comedown.

Last week I faxed a list of desired goodies to Guillo, who works in Leicester, and when he duly handed it over at the Bottle Store the man behind the counter took one look at it and said: "Is this for the guy who has all the Belgian beer? Dark hair, glasses, tweed jacket?" Such celebrity is flattering (maybe he saw my star turn with the Bulmers at the Fat Cat), although the insinuation that I always wear my tweed jacket is a mite disturbing. Anyhow, the ever-benevolent Guillo procured the requested array of Anchor (Liberty Ale, Steam Beer and Porter), Hoegaarden (only the Wit, I'm afraid), Warsteiner (an above-average German Pils) et alia.

Shortly before lunchtime today, however, I began to panic about the dearth of lambic and charged to the Wine Rack, Derby, in an attempt to obtain some gueuze for my Bro'. To my surprise and delight, amid the rows of San Miguel and Heineken were **Timmermans Kriek** and **Timmermans Framboise**: in the absence of Cantillon and Frank Boon, which are like gold-dust on these shores, these represented a formidable catch. I was so chuffed to track down competent lambic in a run-of-the-mill shop that I graciously splashed out on some wine for Mum and Mrs Bro' (just the one bottle, obviously: I didn't want them to overdo things).

My Bro', still fighting off abiding traces of jet-lag, was not fit for too much other than unwinding; and the Timmermans, which he adored, definitely boosted his cause. Along with the brewery's gueuze, Timmermans Kriek and Framboise are irrefutably commercial in their underlying traits; but they could never be accused of being sickly, for their sweetness is balanced with a saving semblance of acidity. Like my Bro', I have long favoured Kriek over Framboise – possibly because I simply favour cherries over raspberries – but still I would not want to see the ABV of Timmermans Framboise plummet any further: it is now 4 per cent, compared to the Kriek's 5 per cent, and the beer could be in danger of becoming a low-alcohol joke of the ilk of many of its purported competitors.

By 9pm the battle against jet-lag had been lost: my Bro' was dozing in an armchair, and even the combination of *Bilko* and **Lefèbvre Student** could not stir him from his slumbers for more than the odd second of tortured blinking and brain-engaging. To sleep through a bottle of Student – a quaffable and fruity witbier, grainier and less delicately spiced than

Hoegaarden – is excusable, but to sleep through Bilko (and not any old *Bilko*, mark you, but the seminal *It's for the Birds* instalment, in which *Bilko* scoops the jackpot on *The $64,000 Question*) is indefensible. He retired to his hotel after somehow staying awake long enough to empty his glass.

After he had shuffled off into the night I helped myself to a **Marston's India Export Pale Ale**, but I swiftly found myself wishing I hadn't. Burton exported its ales to India in the days of the Empire, brewing them to high gravities so they could ferment during shipment; nowadays no India Pale Ale (IPA) has such potency, nor is any as heavily hopped as the originals. Marston's India Export Pale Ale has a divine bronze colour, but after this initial joy lies only disappointment: if a beer it to be so cloying then it might as well be imbued with all the clout of its illustrious ancestors rather than a tentative 5.5 per cent ABV. I have another bottle in the pantry, but I shall not foist it upon my Bro': he has already related the tale of a colleague who flew back to Singapore after an excursion to the UK and grumbled that Pedigree was "too creamy", and I cannot hazard adding to his nascent suspicion of Marston's before we embark upon our pilgrimage to the Bridge Inn.

Timmermans Kriek (5 per cent ABV):	★★★★
Timmermans Framboise (4 per cent ABV):	★★★
Lefèbvre Student (4.5 per cent ABV):	★★★★
Marston's India Export Pale Ale (5.5 per cent ABV):	★★★

August 18

There was a time when my Bro' would struggle to contemplate anything but Pedigree when it came to readjusting to British ale after a spell in foreign climes; now, thanks mostly to the expansion of his beery horizons but partly to my relentless scare-mongering about Marston's creamy leanings, he is able to cast his net that bit wider. Hence our expedition to the Bridge Inn was today put on hold: if he is to stride in and find the barrels discarded and a cream-flow pump in their place, crushing his spirit and devastating our week, he might as well do so later rather than sooner. His Pedi-lust will become voracious anon, but tonight the supremely reliable Burton Bridge won the nod.

The notion of being denied draught British frothy ones for a year fills me with dread, but there is another side to such ghastly deprivation: just cogitate the unadulterated rhapsody of that "comeback" pint. Absolutely fantastic, isn't it? My Bro', the lucky beast, opened his account with Summer Ale (it did not last long, and who can blame him for his blatant alacrity?) and moved on to Bridge Bitter; I defied the blazing sun and chose the vaguely autumnal **Burton Bridge Battle Brew**, which is stronger, darker and maltier than Bridge Bitter and, arguably because of as much, not as amusing.

My Bro' told me a sorry story about his gallant but ultimately futile endeavours to administer an education in beer to some American cohorts who visited Singapore. He dragged them to the bar where he had slurped Belgian and German greats, ordered a round of Leffe Radieuse and Hoegaarden Grand Cru and invited them to tuck in, assuring them they would not have been confronted by the like in the US. One of his guests prattled on about America's micro-breweries, although when pressed on the subject he could only cite Pete's; another commented that the Grand Cru was "like honey" before effectively spurning it and vowing to purchase some "real beer" when it was his round. My Bro' was subsequently supplied with a glass of Miller Lite by those

he had sought to enlighten: I'd wager that even a cream-flow
Pedi would cheer him after that.

**Burton Bridge Battle Brew
(5 per cent ABV):**   ★★★★

August 19

Talk about a faith-restoring episode. My Bro', loath to delay
the moment any longer, insisted upon a reintroduction to the
ecstasies — or, as I warned him, the potential evils — of
Marston's Pedigree; and, to our relief, the Bridge Inn did
not disenchant. I can honestly say that we revelled in the
most sublime Pedi it has been my privilege to drink in many
a year. I cannot gloss over the fact that a dodgy version is
being dispensed elsewhere in the Marston's kingdom, but
the Pedigree at my local, the birthplace of my Dad, remains
magnificent; and for that I am truly grateful.

Its brilliance was clear from the instant the tray
carrying our pints emerged from the cellar. The beer
almost glowed with gloriousness, exuding class; and it
had a comely, light, domed head — not a dollop of
whipped cream lumped on top by the invisible tentacles
of a marketing division's money-grabbers. It tasted as
stunning as it looked, and it really did leave me
extremely content and strangely proud; my Bro',
meanwhile, ran out of superlatives in showering lavish
praise upon it. Not even a promotional poster depicting
a thick-collared specimen of its iniquitous off-shoot could
dampen our mood (well, not much).

Having enjoyed the best of British, we undertook to
bestow an Antipodean angle upon the proceedings by
staging a barbecue. My Bro' has become a veritable
virtuoso with the charcoal chunks after six years in Australia
and New Zealand (and grilling alfresco is jolly hip in
Singapore, too, he says), so he conducted me around B&Q and
Sainsbury's and gave me a crash-course in the fundamentals of

burger-mixing and rib-flipping. Amassing a suitable spread of meats was a doddle; but what of the beer? In Oz we usually gulped the home-grown Power's Big Red, essentially because it was no worse freezing-cold than it was at what I would regard as a correct temperature. A bang-on accomplice, I thought, would be Aecht Schlenkerla Rauchbier, but I had none. With the advantage of hindsight, I realize I should have hauled out the Anchor Porter. I could now kick myself for the wretched poverty of innovation I exhibited in selecting **Warsteiner Pilsener** as an accompaniment.

Although not barbecue-fodder, Warsteiner is a commendable beer – the beer, indeed, on which I got stupendously sloshed at Nienburg's Hotel am Posthof in 1991. My appetite for its elegant dryness that night was such that it took the barman longer to pull a glass's worth than it did me to neck it, prompting my astounded (or was he appalled?) Uncle Henny to exclaim: "Mensch, das habe ich nie gesehen!" It is not in the loftiest echelon of Rhineland Pilseners – it is dwarfed by the likes of König – but it has its merits, albeit not as a partner for a beefburger-and-black-pudding bap.

Rain was hammering down by 10pm, yet my Bro' and I toughed it out on the patio by sheltering beneath a parasol with some Trappist ales and a box of Belgian chocolates. We had once done so on the Grand' Place in Brussels, we mused, so why should we not do so in Burton (even if, as we were forced to accept, the vista was a touch less breathtaking)? To sit there in the downpour with our Rochefort and Chimay, chomping on our choccies and watching the embers dying in the barbecue, may not have been as indelible as loafing on the Grand' Place or as beguiling as a stop at Westmalle; but in the humble circumstances, all things considered, it was pretty magical.

My Bro' tackled a Rochefort 8°, which occupies the middle-ground of the abbey's three-beer line-up, while I nursed a **Chimay White**, which does the same in Chimay's range. The

Chimay ales are produced at the Abbaye de Notre Dame de Scourmont, near the Ardennes hamlet of Forges, and are the most popular of the Trappist beers; they were the first in Belgium to be sold commercially and the first to employ the designation "Trappist Beer". While some of their rivals, as perhaps befits the Trappist tag, can be teasingly elusive or downright anonymous – Westvleteren, with its minuscule yield and its prohibitively parochial points of sale, is the most unfamiliar of the group – the Chimay wares jostle with Pilsners, bitters and (in a grotesque meeting of the holy and the infernal) even alcopops in supermarkets, city stores and pubs: this is indubitably a basis for jubilation, although it is often distressing to see a tremendous beer surrounded by garbage which has no right to lurk in the shadow of a giant – particularly when morons just buy the garbage.

Chimay's dubbel-ish Red and mighty, complex Blue are dark and sweet, leaving the White – the beer they flank – as something of an exception to Chimay's general character. The White is amber-coloured, hoppier, firmer and drier – a tripel, to all intents and purposes, but a profoundly singular one. It is the Chimay ale I most admire, and I used tonight's to christen the gold-rimmed kelk John brought me from France in April (which reminds me, to my infinite guilt, that I still haven't given him the standard Chimay glass I pledged in return).

Rochefort's ales, unlike Chimay's, are not frequently found on supermarket shelves – or any shelves at all – which is sad, for the beers from this most reserved of abbeys, again situated in the Ardennes, should have a broader audience. Their subtle but recurring character – especially in the awesome **Rochefort 10°**, which weighs in at a meditative (if you have but one) or sedative (if you have two) 11.3 per cent ABV – is one of chocolate, which is why my Bro' and I were munching away at exotic nibbles twixt our appreciative nips. All three beers – 6°, 8° and 10°, their names derived from a redundant Belgian system of original gravity – are dark and delicious. I am eternally poised to confer top-10 status upon the 10°, and I reckon the exclusive reason for my not doing so is that I am always bedevilled by an abominable hangover the morning after raving over it: that same reason, I believe, was behind the decision by my Bro' to swap his 10° for a less lethal Chimay Blue, the spineless chicken.

I had been hoarding all of these Trappist ales in readiness for my viewing of the escapades of Brother Cadfael, TV's one and only crime-busting monk, but this will now have to wait until time permits. When it comes to choosing someone with whom to share a Chimay or a Rochefort, quite frankly, there can be no contest between Brother and Bro'.

Marston's Pedigree: **see February 3**	
Warsteiner Pilsener **(4.8 per cent ABV):**	★★★★
Chimay White **(8 per cent ABV):**	★★★★★★
Rochefort 10° **(11.3 per cent ABV):**	★★★★★★

August 20

He's hooked.

We are falling into a routine: I get in from work, my Bro' and I loiter for a polite half-hour to appease our loved ones, and then we bugger off to the Bridge Inn with thinly-veiled haste. It will be another year before he can once more slap his paws on anything as exquisite as prime Pedigree, so who can begrudge him his thrills? To his credit, though, he is not reluctant to experiment: tonight he briefly shunned Pedi to join me in evaluating Marston's foray into the Weizen scene, **Marston's August Wheat** – although we both came to wonder why we bothered.

Marston's operates a policy of brewing occasional beers and then assessing the reaction of the punters for a month or so: those creations which are well-received will be brewed again, those which are scorned will vanish. It is a cracking idea, but some of the beers have been monumental duffers.

My Bro' bragged that he could perceive a dash of lemon in his August Wheat, and I gladly bowed to his palate (it has always been twice as sharp as my own); but the word "bandwagon" unavoidably sprang to mind. A British Weizen such as Salopian Jigsaw, from Shrewsbury, Shropshire, humiliates August Wheat, which doesn't even possess the guts to be cloudy.

My Bro' immediately reverted to Pedigree, but I rocked him on his heels by demanding a **Banks's Mild**. I protested that I had Pedi seeping out of my ears and was keen to try something else, yet still he slowly shook his head as he walked to the bar. He was justified in his dismay, I think, for I ought to have postponed this radical plea until I found myself in a pub whose Pedigree was inadequate; but the deed has been done now, so I can only grovel for absolution. Banks's Mild, from Wolverhampton, is deep amber, malty and roasted and can stake a near-indisputable claim to being the classic West Midlands mild; but I wouldn't sacrifice a Pedigree for it again, especially when my Bro' is drilling holes in me with his contemptuous glare. Addiction is a frightening affliction.

Marston's August Wheat (5.5 per cent ABV):	★★★
Banks's Mild (3.5 per cent ABV):	★★★★

August 21

And that, lamentably, is that. After a few days, a few
Pedigrees, a few lambics, a few Trappist ales, our time is up:
tomorrow my Bro' departs for London, Preston and –
somewhat more enticingly – Singapore. He will call in on
the 24th while en route from The Smoke, but, because of the
miles he'll be covering at the wheel, our scope for frothy ones
will be in the region of zero; and so our glass-clunking has
reached its denouement. It has not been a vintage year (how
dismal it is that our "year" must be condensed into less than a
week), yet our straitjacket-like schedules were guaranteed to
inhibit us. We did the best we could; but there is no
substitute for Belgium.

Before our farewell pints – which came this evening at
the Burton Bridge – I had the bonus of a mid-afternoon
tipple with Phil, who moseyed over to Derby out of ennui.
Both of us would have been more partial to a La Trappe
Tripel, an Orval or a Pilsner Urquell; but, short of
screaming to Leicester and swigging away on the
pavement outside the Bottle Store (a state to which I
have not yet been reduced), something handpumped and
British was ineluctable. The ancient puzzle of where to
bag a satisfactory drop between 3pm and 6pm was solved
by a trek to the Brunswick Inn, which, with its ever-
changing roster of beers and its own brewery, is
traditionally touted as the city's pre-eminent outlet for
real ale; my allegiance was always to the adjacent
Alexandra Hotel, but the Brunswick is open all day.

One of Britain's elite breweries, in my opinion, is
Bateman's, which is based in the charming village of
Wainfleet, near Skegness, Lincolnshire. It is to my perpetual
shame that during my innumerable sorties to Skeggy in the
late '80s and early '90s I never once paused in Wainfleet for a
Bateman's from the source, instead charging along the A52 to
hit the coast ASAP; but if there was one thing I relished more

than beer back then it was shoving coins into *Space Invaders* machines. Among Bateman's "good, honest ales" (to quote the brewery's motif) are its hoppy bitter, XB; the fruity and divertingly perilous XXXB; the luscious Salem Porter; and the delectable **Bateman's Dark Mild**, which may be the champion of the lot.

Dark Mild is almost black, full of roasted-malt and biscuity flavours, with some hoppiness and bitterness in the finish. I know of no better mild; Sarah Hughes Dark Ruby Mild is as impressive, but it is twice as powerful and therefore not an authentic contender. I swear that I shall detour through Wainfleet on my next journey to Skegness, for expedient homage must be paid to this splendid beer.

Since it is my goal to whisk Mum and Margret, her German friend, to the Falkland Arms in Great Tew next week – how selfless I am – I could also take a long-overdue detour through Hook Norton, near Banbury. The eponymous brewery, like Bateman's, has a much-prized portfolio – including the tawny Old Hooky, of which I was very fond some years ago. The golden **Hook Norton Best Bitter** – malty at first, with a wisp of sweetness, then dry and hoppy – has been my customary pick at the Falkland Arms, but I could not dally until next week when I noticed it was chalked up on the Brunswick's blackboard.

Having reacquainted myself with a pair of old mates, I had a final frothy one with my oldest mate of all: my Bro'. It was **Burton Bridge Summer Ale** for me (I must have have consumed more Summer Ale than I have anything else this year) and Porter for him. A Leong's ensued, followed by some single malts and a smattering of *Bilko*s. As if to torment me after he had gone, however, he revealed that he had lunched in a Derby pub where one Pedigree pump offered the proper variation (hurrah) and the other offered a creamy interpretation (hiss); and the one for which everyone was clamouring, of course, was the latter. Cheers, Bro'. This I did not want to hear.

**Bateman's Dark Mild
(3 per cent ABV):** ★★★★★★
**Hook Norton Best Bitter
(3.4 per cent ABV):** ★★★★
**Burton Bridge Summer Ale:
see April 24**

August 23

I fear I am in for a sensational seven days.

Margret, beer-glass benefactor and die-hard devotee of Altbier, touched down at 9 o'clock, unpacked my Pinkus Müller flute at 9.45 and was sitting down to a frothy one with me by 9.50. And that's 9.50*am*, folks. Only Eugene, with his 9am can of Stella Artois on the Eurostar to Brussels, has displayed more determination in knocking the top off one. This is not a sign of being a lush: this is a sign of an infectious yen to have a fabulous week. Margret has never before visited Mum in England and – just to add to the fun – will celebrate her 70th birthday on the 27th, so why should we waste time with morning tea? Prosit!

Her enthusiasm, though, caught me on the hop (a pathetic pun, yes, but such is my schtick). I presented her with a Weizen – a Bavarian breakfast, although she lives near Düsseldorf – and scrabbled around in the fridge and pantry before making do with a leftover **Anchor Steam Beer**: it was far from ideal, but being sociable took precedence over my personal caprices. It quickly occurred to me that an emergency dart to the Bottle Store was vital, so this evening I raced up the M1 in search of Teutonic treats.

The assignment was no breeze, as the shop was devoid of

Altbier (save for St Stan's, which I shall submit for Margret's expert inspection) and Kölsch (will poor Leong ever get his Küppers?), but I secured a cluster of Weizen, Pils and Schwarzbier. To my smirking glee, Wallersteiner Classic – the lager in which I last month came across a substance whose genealogy I still cannot bring myself to ponder – was the subject of a "Buy four and get a free glass" promo: the glass was a beauty, but even I would not jeopardize a kindly pensioner's nerves for that.

Anchor Steam Beer: see March 22

August 24

My Bro', as promised, popped in this afternoon to say hello and goodbye. As I had envisaged, frothy ones were off his menu: he faced navigating the carnage of the M6 to Preston and was already half-knackered after negotiating the M1 from London. While his driving duties compelled him to heave out the coffee cups, even fraternal solidarity could not prevent me from having a **Pete's Wicked Honey Wheat**; but he did not need to be envious, for this "wheat-beer brewed and flavoured with honey" would have been an unworthy send-off for him.

A brewery can produce too many beers. Pete's first two, Wicked Ale and Wicked Lager, are excellent; a significant number of those which have appeared since are nowhere near. Marston's now spews forth a stream of numbingly mediocre ales. Some new enterprises, perhaps within the space of as little as 12 months, parade three times as many beers as Chimay has trotted out in more than 130 years. Might there be a lesson to be learned somewhere? It is doubtless tempting for the brewer to have a stab at every style on the planet, yet those who foot the bill should be just as tempted to urge that he masters one before moving on to another dozen.

There are breweries which have shown themselves to be all-round achievers – Anchor, Burton Bridge, Samuel Smith's, Timothy Taylor – but, although I do not imply that the exercise provides concrete proof, it is interesting to study the output of some of the breweries responsible for acknowledged classics. How many beers does Orval make? How many beers does Westmalle make? How many beers does Rodenbach make? How many beers does Schneider make? How many beers does PJ Früh make? How many beers does Heller make? How many beers does Rauchenfelser make? How many beers does Cooper's make?

Well, enough sermonizing: now I must steel myself for a week of chauffeuring the ladies around this green and pleasant land. Lincoln beckons in two days: should I expose Margret to the backstreet bliss of a bacon buttie and a Landlord at the Victoria?

**Pete's Wicked Honey Wheat
(4.8 per cent ABV):   ★★★**

August 26

Ah, Lincoln: captivating, enthralling, architecturally arousing – and that's just the Vic. Untold moons ago, when I was commanded to spend two or three weeks at the Lincoln office, this sturdy pub alone made the abject misery of the daily 90-minute slog from Burton worthwhile. For all my wizened associates' recollections of lying on the lawns outside the castle courthouse and lazily penning their prose, the things I really savoured during my stints in the city were my bacon butties and pints of **Timothy Taylor Landlord** at lunchtime. Yet when it came to the crunch today I refrained from granting Margret access to the Victoria, instead proposing that she and Mum hunt down one of Lincoln's legion of quaint restaurants.

I went to the Vic myself, naturally. It was much the same as ever: dreary on the outside, terrifically functional and snug on the inside – if less bustling than before. I sat down with my Landlord (which, I must say, was slightly off-key) and my buttie (which was as gorgeous as ever) and had a peaceful perusal of the sports pages, the tranquillity fleetingly shattered only by a grating American who noisily conveyed her bewilderment as the existence of Czechoslovakian lager (welcome to the real world, madam). The experience made for a nice blast from the past, and I was only frustrated that it couldn't last longer.

I think Margret would have liked it, actually. Certainly the last German tourist I took to Lincoln, my cousin Andreas, was a fan: although a staunch health-freak, he was so enamoured with his buttie and Landlord that he took more snapshots of the boozer than he did of the cathedral. But as I ruminated upon the pros and cons I could not forget the exchange I had with Mum when I once shepherded her into the Vic.

"Can't we go in the lounge?"

"Mum, we *are* in the lounge."

Anyway, the Damen dined in a tea-room – but Margret still had a frothy one. What a woman.

**Timothy Taylor Landlord:
see February 24**

August 27

Margret toasted her 70th birthday with an Oechsner Schwarzbier and then a nosh-up with Mum at another posh eatery. She opted for a frothy one there, too: wine apparently holds minimal appeal for her, and she will not compromise. She even persuaded Mum to risk a Hoegaarden yesterday, which was a sight to treasure, and it transpires that she is also prone to single malts: she thought my Lagavulin was "wunderbar".

Guillo and I toasted something else: European football nights are again upon us. But we must venture to enrich our beer intake before the season progresses: tonight's duo –

Kaiserdom Burgerbräu Pils and **Pete's Wicked Summer Brew** – was shabby. Soccer pundits may advocate getting the rotten performances out of the way in the preliminary rounds and sparing the best for the later phases; but what applies to footie does not apply to frothy ones. I want a Juventus of a beer with every game, and Burgerbräu and Summer Brew were more like Preston North End (whom I have chosen merely to annoy Eugene).

The Kaiserdom brewery is the largest in Bamberg, Rauchbier capital of the cosmos. I have never seen Kaiserdom Rauchbier, but its varieties of Weizen – now bearing the horrendously twee Weizenland label – are almost omnipresent. Burgerbräu Pils is malty and dry to a tongue-deadening degree, as are most of the Kaiserdom beers; depressingly, I have a pile of Kaiserdom Weizen in the pantry.

Pete's Wicked Summer Brew is described as a "pale ale with a hint of natural lemon". A sound concept, but the implementation is flawed: for "hint" read "heap". It is not revolting, and it might even tickle some twisted fancies (Guillo, the jammy sod, was wrapped up in his La Maudite and Anchor Liberty Ale, so I could not solicit a verdict from him); but, like Honey Wheat before it, it is far from the Pete's pinnacle.

No matter: if all goes to plan my next beer will come at the Falkland Arms. Unless Mum can be shoehorned into the MG's boot, alas, we shall have to take the Escort, which will remove some of the Englishness I had craved for the event; but I trust it will still be a momentous jaunt.

**Kaiserdom Burgerbräu Pils
(5 per cent ABV):** ★★★

**Pete's Wicked Summer Brew
(4.9 per cent ABV):** ★★★

August 29

I could lambaste England for hour after hour. There is, after all, much to deride: its cuisine (steak-and-kidney pie and the fry-up exempted), most of its cities, its weather, its asinine yearning to be a mini-USA. But when I'm at the Falkland Arms, Great Tew, with Oxford to the east and the Cotswolds to the west, with golden-stoned cottages and thatched roofs stretching down every narrow lane, with tankard-strewn beams above my head and a flagstone floor beneath my feet, the whining has to cease.

This is the England over which foreigners drool, the idyll unscarred by McDonald's drive-ins and rapacious pub-chains. Margret said her hols, which climax tomorrow, would have been the lesser for not seeing it; Mum was similarly agog. And if the village is a gem then the pub, which dates from the 16th century, could very well be peerless: oak panels, shuttered windows, oil lanterns, miscellaneous stools and settles, an inglenook fireplace, Doulton jugs, snuff, geese wandering around the garden, an affectionate cat – it has it all.

And the ale is no weak link. Hook Norton Best, brewed barely 10 miles away, is still there and found a fervent supporter in Margret (Mum let the side down by having a pineapple juice, but there is no teaching some), while beers from Wadworth, of Devizes, Wiltshire, now occupy the majority of the pumps (let us pray that Wadworth, to whom this jewel of a pub is now tied, doesn't do anything stupid to spoil its precious acquisition).

The copper-coloured **Wadworth 6X** is among the premier ales from the south of England and is one of those spellbinding beers which drink beyond their strength. Full-bodied, fruity and malty, it seems far bigger than its temperate 4.3 per cent ABV – and that sextet of Xs probably intensifies the illusion. It is often served directly from the barrel (although this is not the case at the Falkland Arms) and would unquestionably be slotted into my discerning northerner buddy's "pisswatter" file; I am not its most ardent buff, but I would rate it rather more positively than that.

If I had invested in eight pints of **Wadworth Henry's Original IPA** – well-balanced between malt and hops, with a vestige of acidity – I would have been entitled to a gratis ninth; but, though it is a session beer extraordinaire, I felt this might be to the detriment of my fellow road-users and thus confined myself to a pragmatic half. That's the drawback of the Falkland Arms: you have to drive to it, and its stature is such that you can only take drunken refuge in one of its rooms if you have booked around three months in advance.

We should book for Margret's next junket. Having said that, there is still much of Burton she has yet to behold: the Bridge Inn, the Burton Bridge, the Bass Museum... Oo, I'm excited already.

Wadworth 6X
(4.3 per cent ABV):   ★★★★

Wadworth Henry's Original IPA
(3.8 per cent ABV):   ★★★★

September 9

It troubles me to relate something so despicably doleful, but I get the impression that winter is lurking just around the bend. The last drops of summer ale, Burton Bridge or otherwise, will drip from the taps anon: the time for porter, stout and all things warming is virtually upon us. It's growing nippy at night; miserable, too. I take comfort only from the following: (1) a cornucopia of seasonal beers will start appearing in cosy pubs; (2) the pantry will be restored to its 13°C glory, liberating me from the inconvenience – nay, the ignominy – of cooling my top-fermented frothy ones in the fridge. It is niggling to note that my stocks consist almost entirely of Weizen as the frosty weather approaches, but I shall address this quandary when finances permit (and immediately herald a prolonged spell of blistering heat, obviously).

Portentous confirmation of winter's imminent onset was submitted when Eugene and I both opted for **Burton Bridge Burton Porter** as the accompaniment to our pork scratchings at the Burton Bridge. Moreover, even though it is due to vanish within weeks, I could not bring myself to select Summer Ale when I fancied a change, instead plumping for the oft-neglected (by me, that is, not the pub) **Burton Bridge Bridge Bitter**. All was so convivial and busy that I pictured snowfall outside. I regarded anything light and invigorating as far from appropriate.

Back home, with the Weizen and similarly sunny fare spread before me, the decision was trickier. Schneider Aventinus, as delectable in the depths of winter as it is at the height of summer, was a tempting possibility but not quite apposite; I am preserving my surviving supplies of La Maudite for Guillo, who has declared his admiration for it; and Chimay Red, although it would have done nicely, goes better with *Cadfael* than it does with *Columbo*, and I was geared up for the man in the crumpled mac. Curiously for one in search of the wintry, I ultimately settled for a taste of California: **St Stan's Amber Alt**, the conventional cousin of St Stan's Dark Alt.

Amber Alt does possess something of a wintry edge, in fact, for its ABV of 5.8 per cent is easily in excess of those of Germany's Altbier originals, which hover around the 4.5 mark. Although maltiness dominates, there are also faint winy notes: this may be why I find the Dark – which, a trifle ironically, is the stronger beer – the more drinkable of the duo. I have inferred that both Amber and Dark are more gratifying when served in an authentic Altbeker rather than in my St Stan's Red Sky Ale glass; I cannot begin to explain why that should be the case, but such trivial discoveries help me sleep sounder.

Now is the moment, I think, to compile a list of sturdy ales. I fear there are some long, black nights ahead.

Burton Bridge Burton Porter:
see February 17

Burton Bridge Bridge Bitter:
see January 16

St Stan's Amber Alt
(5.8 per cent ABV):　　★★★★

September 10

Yes, no sooner do I even *think* about purchasing a batch of potent beers than the country is basking in magnificent sunshine. What is this strange impact my choice of frothy ones has on the nation's climate? I buy a Rochefort – thermometers explode; I buy a Hoegaarden – an ice-age dawns. I am the stuff of a particularly bizarre *Twilight Zone*.

It was definitely **Burton Bridge Summer Ale** weather today – which was fair enough, because I made an impromptu visit to the Burton Bridge after learning the young chap who had come to our office for some "work experience" (which is invariably anything but) was a fan of real ale. He was not previously conversant with the Burton Bridge's delights, amazingly, but had only flattering words to say about Summer and Porter after an hour or so spent investigating them at the source. Maybe he was simply seeking to amuse me with a view to earning a complimentary reference; but surely that's an assumption too cynical even for one as hideously misanthropic as I.

To be truthful, I would offer him a job tomorrow if hiring and firing were within my scope. He likes Pedigree but complains that few landlords can maintain it to an acceptable standard; Samuel Smith's OBB was once his favourite pint; he speaks fondly of Bateman's Salem Porter, Hook Norton Old Hooky and Sarah Hughes Dark Ruby Mild; all the boozers he frequents are "proper" pubs; and he is even a talented writer (an ancillary bonus though that is). Okay, so he had never heard of Orval and admitted he knew bugger all about Belgian beers in general; but, a little spookily, he does like single malts – and, even more spookily, his number-one film is *The Hustler*.

My *Twilight Zone* theory gathers pace: I have stumbled upon my psychological doppelgänger. And, as if subconsciously eager to add to the pervading ambience of weirdness, I have said I will introduce him to the Yew Tree in Cauldon, Staffordshire, a remote and remarkable inn which would not be out of place in the most preposterous Rod Serling script; I must snap up a crate of Christmas beer to guarantee pleasant weather for the trip.

Burton Bridge Summer Ale: see April 24

September 11

My beer-hunting this month is not exactly setting the world alight. Nine days of naff all have been followed by a deluge of old hat: Burton Bridge, Burton Bridge... I wouldn't call it a rut, but the tyre-tracks are becoming distinctly well-worn. Tonight I again omitted to push back the frontiers, reverting to **Greene King Abbot Ale** while dining at the Royal Oak, Abbots Bromley. I do not mean to imply that the supping of Burton Porter or Abbot Ale constitutes sanity-threatening disillusionment – even when it is done for the umpteenth time – but I am nonetheless desperate for a new challenge.

And that's why I'm off to Belgium. Eugene, Stuart and I are jetting to Brussels on the 26th, and we don't care where we end up thereafter: Bruges, Antwerp, Ghent – nowhere is safe. No hotel has been booked. No motor has been hired. No plan has been formulated. Freedom is ours. It will all go abysmally awry, of course, but at least I have a purpose once more.

Greene King Abbot Ale: see February 5

September 16

Twice I have vowed never again to venture into the plastic palace that is the Babington Arms; and twice I have betrayed my vow. Aside from the nauseating decor and prevailing atmosphere of fakery, the foible which irks me more than any other when I am tugged therein is the infuriating inconsistency of the ale: one can be auspicious (April's Courage Directors), another can be scandalous (May's Hop Back Summer Lightning), one can be surprisingly accurate (today's **Hook Norton Generation**), another can be wildly erroneous (today's **Younger Scotch Bitter**). I hereby swear for a third time that I shall no longer subject myself to this menace of an establishment. It drives me potty.

An instant of misguided chutzpah was responsible for my doing battle with the Babington Arms' pumps. Resigned to giving the JD Wetherspoon empire my custom, I had cogitated a cop-out Beck's, a sneaky Newcastle Brown (on condition the fridges were felicitously off-kilter) or an utterly negative lemonade; but the galling paucity of experimentation so far this month motivated me to try my luck. I appreciated the perils inherent in my conduct but was provided with early grounds for encouragement when the Hook Norton emerged with a familiar maltiness/fruitiness; yet my fragile optimism was quickly shattered.

Just when I had been lulled into a false sense of security, just when an iota of faith had been replenished, I ordered what turned out to be a thoroughly appalling half of Younger Scotch.

The phrase "a tad cold" would be a ridiculously inadequate description: "freezing", probably prefixed by some manner of expletive, would be more germane. I sincerely doubt that its temperature was above 8°C: certainly I have encountered lagers which were less fang-chattering. Younger Scotch, from the Edinburgh subsidiary of the brewery-and-beer-wrecking Scottish & Newcastle, is hardly top-drawer when at its best; but this was execrable. I was forced to rub the glass with my hands in a totally futile, vaguely pathetic and somewhat idiotic attempt to instil its contents with a modicum of heat. Irredeemable junk; but my mercy is such that I shall award a score pertinent to a Younger Scotch which has not been damaged by the attentions of incompetents.

More reliable wares awaited at home, the problem of my intrinsic reluctance to trundle to Leicester and back having been solved by the wonderful expedient of requesting that Gary deliver a Bottle Store haul when he popped round last night. Talk about bringing the mountain to Mohammed. I had to pay for said haul, alas, but no-one ever suggested life was perfect. The assistant had again studied my demands before slipping into his "Is this for the guy who..." spiel; he still sent me the wrong kind of Rodenbach, though.

I split some **Lindeboom Pilsener** and **Oechsner Premium Pils** with a pal who a couple of days ago returned from a holiday in Turkey. Like Eugene before him, he brought me an Efes Pilsen glass (Eugene brought me two, actually, but I broke one of them while tramping from the office to my car – which, as Euge never tires of reminding me, represented criminal ineptitude in the wake of his warily conveying them across Europe); I shall never use it, since Efes is outstandingly dreadful, but it swells my collection and will therefore be cherished like any other.

Lindeboom Pilsener is often forgotten among the ranks of more well-known Dutch Pils, which is a terrible shame. Whether it has the measure of Grolsch Pilsener is debatable, and it is unquestionably humbled by Christoffel Bier (which is no disgrace); but it knocks spots off the likes of Oranjeboom, Amstel and Heineken. Its enduring head is gleaming white; its body is gentle yet crisp; and its finish is agreeably dry. The brewery, based in Neer, Limburg, also makes a decent Meibock.

Oechsner Premium Pils, the sampling of which completed my scrutinizing of the Oechsner line-up, is a deal maltier than Lindeboom Pilsener but not in the tiniest bit cloying. If anything, I believe, there is a vestige of fruitiness in it − a trait also manifest in its Heller Bock stablemate. None of the Oechsner beers, with the possible exception of the Schwarzbier, is thigh-slappingly superb; but what rejoicing there would if something of their honourable ilk cluttered the shelves of every JD Wetherspoon pub in the land.

Dream on.

Hook Norton Generation (4 per cent ABV):	★★★★
Younger Scotch Bitter (3.7 per cent ABV):	★★★
Lindeboom Pilsener (5 per cent ABV):	★★★★
Oechsner Premium Pils (4.9 per cent ABV):	★★★★

September 18

Once more Guillo and I were inexorably drawn to the Burton Bridge, my relentless patronage of which I have now become weary of excusing: if a pub this laudable is but three miles from my door then even I, despite my quest, cannot ignore its lure − especially when there is only time for a swift pint. Theoretically, it transpires, the Summer Ale could linger until late October, the end of BST, so I had no qualms about ceding to the dismal weather with a **Burton Bridge**

Burton Porter; with the rain pelting down, even Guillo graduated to a Bridge Bitter.

I paired with my Leong's a smashing example of Oriental brewing: **Boon Rawd Singha Lager**, which may just be the ace of Asia's beers. Named after a mythical beast resembling a lion, it is powerful, hoppy, bitter and beautifully floral. Like Tsingtao, the Boon Rawd brewery, of Bangkok, Thailand, was set up with German technology; but there can be no dispute about which has made better use of it.

Coincidentally, Guillo presented me with a Tsingtao this evening. It was one of a trio dispatched to him by his brother-in-law, a teacher in Hong Kong. Don't get excited, though: it's still in a bloody can.

Burton Bridge Burton Porter:
see February 17

**Boon Rawd Singha Lager
(6 per cent ABV):** ★★★★★

September 19

It is now around two years since I pledged to secure a crate of Kölsch for Leong; and don't imagine that he lets me forget this. That the stomach ailment which a bottle of Küppers temporarily quelled has long since been relieved by more mundane methods is immaterial; that his own son was in Köln on business and brought back nary a millilitre of beer is irrelevant; that Kölsch, be it from Küppers or any other brewery, does not feature on the Dram's inventory is a peripheral concern. I have failed him.

Yet if I could not take excellent beer to Leong, I pondered, I could accomplish the reverse; and so today I did so. Our destination was not Köln — if only — but Oxfordshire: to be precise, Great Tew and Oxford. Leong berated me for not giving Ayrton a blast down the M40 — this from the man who is perpetually urging me to sell my precious rag-top — and I must confess that barrelling along in the MG would have been lovely; but Ayrton's year is over, his battery sapped by inactivity and damp mornings. Arriving in Great Tew in a shabby Escort was no less unbecoming than it was last month, but then Leong could have tossed me the keys to his Merc if he wanted refinement into the bargain.

My inaugural excursion to Great Tew came in the early '90s – the specific year I cannot recollect – after Gary and I had spent a day flitting from pub to pub in Oxford. I was the designated wheelman (plus ça change...) and had exercised abstinence; Gary was nigh on legless. We had been to the Three Goats Heads (twice), the White Horse (Inspector Morse's favourite inn, someone informed me), the Eagle and Child (where Tolkein penned *Lord of the Rings* and – in a further slice of literary history, albeit one on which the premises have declined to trade – Tim once conferred upon me a copy of *Cookie Monster's Book of Cookie Shapes*), the Gardeners Arms (a noble backstreet hostelry, even if we did overhear the barman ask a kilt-wearing punter who ordered a whisky: "Scotch or Irish?") and a handful of others before scouring the fringes of the Cotswolds by moonlight. A gallon of ale had massacred Gary's map-reading abilities, and only after much aimless lane-pounding did we crest the hill which dips into Great Tew; but I knew at once that our circuitous sortie would not be in vain. Several years and several sojourns later, although the original beguilement cannot be matched, my fascination for the Falkland Arms has not diminished.

Leong, upon my recommendation, got to grips with some Hook Norton; I tucked into a **Hall & Woodhouse Badger Dorset Best**. The Badger brewery is in Blandford Forum, Dorset, and produces Tanglefoot, a fruity and hoppy premium ale reputed for its drinkability. NG, who often confronted them during his formative years in Wiltshire, tells me that Badger ales were traditionally referred to as "the black-and-white bastard", but that judgment is a touch harsh: the copper-coloured Dorset Best is marginally innocuous, but it is not an objectionable beer – and I certainly wouldn't query its parentage.

If the Falkland Arms' allure is eternal, however, Oxford has lost its shine. It is not a city with a capacity to boggle over and over again; and grey skies did nothing to aid its bid for my affections today. Leong loathed it, principally because he was unable to detect among the dreaming spires a bookie's where he could have a flutter on the 3.55 at Wolverhampton; nor did he like his frothy one at the Eagle and Child – although, perversely enough, the offending half was from Burton.

Why slog all the way to Oxford and then polish off an **Ind Coope Draught Burton Ale**, a beer brewed four miles from my front door? I cannot deny that it was goofy; yet time constraints limited us to a cursory pause at but one pub, and that pub's most appealing offering was DBA.

Now that Carlsberg-Tetley and Bass are bosom buddies as well as neighbours – and Ind Coope doesn't even exist per se – DBA is routinely touted as a future casualty of merger-mania. That would be an outrage, for it is an underrated beer – nowhere more so than in Burton, where it has long been third fiddle to Pedigree and Draught Bass. It is malty, hoppy, stunningly fruity and (as Leong moaned) rather sweet. Ind Coope's unofficial tap, the Roebuck, served me the most delicious I ever had.

Having plagued him for two years with an unfulfilled promise of Kölsch, then, I have now dragged Leong to a city he despised. And given him a beer he hated. And, to cap it all, the bet scuppered by Oxford's dearth of turf accountants would have scooped him a tidy sum. Hmmm. Better make that *two* crates of Küppers.

Hall & Woodhouse Badger Dorset Best (4.1 per cent ABV): ★★★

Ind Coope Draught Burton Ale (4.8 per cent ABV): ★★★★

September 21

I should have had a beer yesterday. That is not to say that today's **La Trappe Tripel** was disastrous, but yesterday was crammed with circumstances which begged the savouring of a frothy one. Why I resisted I do not know, but now I am nagged by the sensation that up to three marvellous opportunities were overlooked.

The first arose when I scanned my mail and found a postcard from Margret, Mum's Lagavulin-loving friend. I had presumed the missive would be from Mum herself – currently in the middle of a five-week stay with her sister in Nienburg – and was astonished when I read it. Margret triumphantly reported that she had obtained a Berliner Kindl Weisse glass for me during a break "at the seaside" (I could not discern the identity of the resort) and would be passing it on to Mum with all speed. What a woman: if she were 50 years younger I would marry her.

Kindl is not the most acidic Berliner Weisse, but it is still hugely arresting and has always struck me as a breakfast beer: it not only startles you into action but is very low in ABV (less than 3 per cent). Unless I am mistaken, I had a bottle of Schultheiss Berliner Weisse, which is even more lip-puckering, on Christmas morning in 1995; any sort of Berliner Weisse has been a rarity in blighty since, however, maybe because the acidity is too extreme for most palates here (indeed, even in Germany syrups are employed to subdue the tartness). It was 9.30am when I perused Margret's card, and I was fleetingly inspired to toy with the notion of getting the day underway with a "normal" Weizen; but the boring Brit in me persuaded me I should not ("The sun's not quite over the yard-arm yet, old man") – and thus the first opportunity was lost.

The second came when my Bro' telephoned me shortly before lunch and made a veiled stab at enticing me to Singapore with dizzying tales of food and drink. He bragged that he was en route to Wing Seong Fatty's, a peerless restaurant, for a portion of black-pepper crab or some such culinary masterpiece; I was poised to shove a steak-and-kidney pie in the microwave at that stage, so I cannot pretend I was spared a pang of jealousy.

"I'm going through the door now. Can you hear it? Listen! Oh, and there's Fatty Jnr…"

"Yes, well, I'd better get my chips out of the freezer," I sighed.

"And there's Fatty, the man himself, sitting outside…"

"This is making me incredibly grim, mate."

As if his running commentary had not imparted sufficient torture, he then callously revealed he had consumed merriment-inducing quantities of Erdinger Dunkel the preceding evening. His ploy worked, for Singapore seemed heavenly; but I was stuck at home with my pie and chips, so the inevitable result was a bout of depression. When I shambled back to my feeble feast I was gagging for a frothy one, anxious that my jet-setting Bro' should not leave me behind in the grub-and-beer stakes; yet I was so annoyed at not boasting a suitable pale ale among my provisions that I shunned the would-be substitutes and sulked instead – and thus the second opportunity was lost.

My final chance was to mark what had been a splendid display of pool-shooting. My endeavours on the green baize have been erratic of late, veering from the cultured to the cretinous with distressing regularity, but if my proficiency reached a trough two months ago when I narrowly missed potting a ball on table 12 – you might think this far from catastrophic, but I was playing on table 15 at the time – then new peaks of Mosconi-like magic were scaled last night. But where was Brooklyn Lager when I needed it? My hoard of Belgian ales would be felicitous if I had conquered the intricacies of three-cushion billiards, I thought, but they were not apropos to straight pool – and thus the third opportunity was lost.

Such farcical fastidiousness is woeful and counterproductive, but there could be no excruciating deliberation over tonight's preference: *Cadfael* was in the VCR, so

231

a Trappist beer was critical to the proceedings. Cadfael is not a Trappist – the show's dialogue would be a mite restricted if he were – but it is only right that something painstakingly crafted by monks should be imbibed as, robes and all, he quietly goes about his sleuthing. Even an abbey ale would be an insult, although the beers from the brewing monasteries of Germany and Austria – notably Ettal and Weltenburg – would qualify (if only I could locate them nowadays, confound it).

When I was scavenging in the bookshops of Bruges in 1995 I noticed that the *Cadfael* novels were all the rage in Belgium, yet it was the tripel from the Netherlands' Trappist brewery which I chose to raise to him tonight. This may have been a minor blunder, for La Trappe Tripel is a slight disappointment (that pesky Barneveld Effect again). Hoppy and bitter-sweet, more bronze than golden, it is by no means a poor beer – anything but – yet it is, if you'll forgive my tedious insistence upon the unavoidable comparison, a lot less sophisticated than Westmalle Tripel. The luscious La Trappe Dubbel would have been a more fitting option.

Blimey, I'm becoming a fussy git.

**La Trappe Tripel
(8 per cent ABV):** ★★★★

September 23

Another *Cadfael*, another Trappist ale. This time, though, I evaded the danger of a letdown by relishing a **Chimay Red** while our habit-clad hero, dispensing words of wisdom and flaunting an unrivalled and rather astounding grasp of forensic science, glided through assorted scenes of medieval mayhem. Brilliant.

The dark and red-brown Chimay Red was the founding Chimay beer. It is broadly in the style of a dubbel, just as the White is broadly in the style of a tripel; and it has a moderately sour character, balanced by a gorgeous softness and a delicate spiciness. Like the bigger-bodied Blue, it is at its finest at a temperature of between 15°C and 18°C; I once braved one which had been chilled well beyond the brink of calamity in a British pub, but – predictably, I suppose – my subsequent protests fell on deaf ears.

From La Trappe to Chimay, then; but whither now for a *Cadfael*-escorting Trappist ale? For the third and concluding yarn, methinks, it can only be Orval. The moronic scheduling by which the series has been cursed means a year or more is likely to have elapsed before the crime-busting Brother again graces our screens, so I am duty-bound to grant him the grandest of send-offs.

I must say, however, that Cadfael himself has demonstrated a disturbing indisposition when it comes to grabbing a frothy one. As his abbey's resident herbalist, he is not averse to one of his own concoctions now and then; but I have yet to espy him with his mitts wrapped around a foaming kelk of "liquid bread", and this worries me. In tonight's story, *St Peter's Fair,* his pursuit of a brutal murderer took him to the local tavern, yet still he spurned the prospect of blowing the top off one.

"Will you not stop for a drink, Brother?" the innkeeper asked him.

"Oh, thank-you," he replied. "No, I have some berries to gather."

With which to make a hearty framboise, I trust.

**Chimay Red
(7 per cent ABV):**

September 26

A 5am journey by taxi to Birmingham Airport really is no way to begin a day's boozing in Belgium. Not when you're a scaredy-cat who is refused his habitual nerve-steadying nip of Johnnie Walker Red Label (most passengers prefer coffee or orange juice with their in-flight breakfast, apparently) and is thereby robbed of a vital doze on the plane. It tends to catch up with you approximately 22 hours, a dozen beers and a double Irish later.

I was aware that the majority of the venues and frothy ones for the year's second Belgian crawl would be passé to Eugene and to me, and so it has proved thus far. No matter: the pleasure on this occasion will be – and already has been – derived from welcoming Stuart, a newcomer, to their charms.

By 10.15am we had descended the incline from Brussels railway station to the Bourse and were arranging ourselves around a table in Cirio, of which we were mighty proud to be the morning's keenest clients. We resolved, in a quasi-palliative gesture, to snub the St Feuillien Blond and relax with the more temperate **De Kluis Hoegaarden Wit** (vastly superior to the Falstaff's February effort) while grappling with the *Guardian* crossword. It was paradise. We briefly felt disconcerted, even embarrassed, as we surveyed a blossoming circle of tea-sippers; but then the OAP onslaught commenced, and Cirio was once again fabulously awash with silly hats and ballons of Duvel.

Afterwards we inadvertently hit the Pierre Celis trail, sliding into an anonymous bar near the Mannekin Pis to be greeted by **Celis White**. The witbier which the man from Hoegaarden created after emigrating to Texas, radically different from its predecessor it is not – a shade more lemon? – but it is none the worse for that. I seized upon the serendipity to regale the hapless Stuart with the Celis legend (Mr Party Animal rides again) before we adjourned for lunch at – grit teeth – the Falstaff.

I must concede that the Falstaff regained my respect today. It was packed, yet the waiters were in scintillating form and equal to the task; and to witness Stuart's exhilaration at experiencing the dignified bustle for the first time, to sit there with an ale and idly watch the world go by, was to wipe clean my own slate. Our carbonades flamandes were scrumptious, and even the **De Kluis Hoegaarden**

Speciale – though as lame and conceptually bankrupt as ever – could not be reproached too viciously.

Save for a superficial inspection for Stuart's benefit, the Grand' Place, with its exorbitant prices and mediocre beers, was boycotted. As per eight months ago, neon Leffe logos blazed in every window. Interbrew's coffers were clearly bulging: sod 'em. Antwerp beckoning, we sauntered back to the station and its concomitant chaos.

(It was directly outside Brussels railway station, incidentally, that my *Good Beer Guide to Belgium and Holland* recently suffered an horrific demise when Tim, to whom I had loaned the hallowed tome, selfishly used it to stem the flow of blood as the wound from a grisly operation on his neck suddenly reopened and showered terrified commuters with claret. Tim was hospitalized, the *Guide* was drenched, and the pavement was spattered – although any evidence of this tragedy [the ruining of the *Guide*, I mean] has since been scrubbed into oblivion.)

Sole erosion and good fortune saw us to a four-star hotel just off the main road leading from Antwerp's railway station to the city's historic centre. More economical than the Hilton and less dispiriting than the Hotel Tourist, it was ideal. Stuart and I shared a room whose lounge and sleeping areas were separated by a wall which turned at odd angles and was crowned with a tier of frosted glass lapsing four feet short of the ceiling: it was akin to an affluent version of Albert and Harold's polarized abode in the seminal *Divided We Stand* episode of *Steptoe,* and it provoked much mirth. We checked in at 4pm; Stuart flicked on the porn channel at 4.02pm, which, given the 90-second stroll from reception to room, was a pretty impressive performance.

Our enthusiasm was undimmed as a cab swept us to the Eleventh Commandment. Stuart and I were crowing that we would round off the fun by heaving a sofa on to our balcony and depleting the mini-bar while observing the nightlife. But our intake during the ensuing hours annihilated any hopes of nocturnal japery.

Stuart was dazed by the Eleventh Commandment. It is, as I said in February, visually extraordinary. The array of beers is weak – I nursed a **Haacht Haecht Witbier** while Stuart, armed with an abbey ale, groped for *Madonna with the Head of a Dog* amid the befogging assembly of icons – but no-one is bothered. Stuart also liked Paters' Vaetje (the Priests' Little Barrel), a cramped and mirror-dotted café 50 yards away: his 75cl bottle of Achouffe McChouffe dwarfed my **Palm** – Belgium's most popular pale ale, from the eponymous brewery in the village of Steenhuffel, Brabant – but he drained it with an insouciance bordering on the alarming.

Kulminator was almost empty when we wandered in, but Leen was typically gregarious; Dirk was dour, so we left him alone. Stuart hailed **De Kluis Benedict** as "the best beer I've ever tasted" and **Abbaye des Rocs** as an improvement on that – solid evaluations, I would say – and I reckon it's no exaggeration to speculate that I garnered greater satisfaction from his enjoyment than I have from any beer-drinking of my own this year. To behold a novice's education in such revered surroundings was enthralling indeed.

We perhaps should have quit there and then; but the bait of a vintage **Westvleteren Extra**, from the smallest of the Trappist breweries, pulled us into the mire. We were in that horrible state in which fatigue is confused with drunkenness and vice versa. Were we knackered or hammered? Were we ready for bed or past caring? Westvleteren Extra – dark, fruity, sour, intimidating, frighteningly uncompromising – was no beer for men in our condition.

On the trek back to the hotel we dashed into an undistinguished hovel to avail ourselves of its lavatory; I exited the loo to find Eugene leaning on the bar, large whiskeys prepared. There was no coming back from that, and Stuart's incomprehensible behaviour at the frittur – "Hiya, duck! Y'all right? Three bags of chips, please – one with curry, one with ketchup…" – sealed our suspicions that we were absolutely wasted.

The sofa never did make it to the balcony. I nodded off on it, fully-clothed, while ogling the porn channel.

De Kluis Hoegaarden Wit: **see February 1**	
Celis White **(5 per cent ABV):**	★★★★★
De Kluis Hoegaarden Speciale: **see February 28**	
Haacht Haecht Witbier: see March 1	
Palm **(5.2 per cent ABV):**	★★★★
De Kluis Benedict: see March 1 **Abbaye des Rocs: see March 1**	
Westvleteren Extra **(8.4 per cent ABV):**	★★★★

September 27

Yesterday's vim had spectacularly evaporated this morning. Dishevelled and disorientated, I awoke from my post-Kulminator slumbers at 4.30am – by which juncture even the porn channel's dynamic dignitaries were taking a breather – and clattered into bed after undressing with intoxicated abandon. Sleep was fitful and infested by a throbbing bonce and a bubbling gut. A punitively arctic shower was prescribed at 10am, but lamentable lassitude persisted as we bade a bleary farewell to the Steptoe suite. Damn you, Westvleteren Extra.

We discussed our next move over coffee at a swish bistro close to the hotel, and all concurred that a fresh locale was required. I mooted Köln, but Amsterdam eventually won the vote: I knew it well from when my Bro' was there, we mused, and three hours on a train would afford us ample latitude to extend our recovery period. In retrospect, I should have exhibited more commitment to Köln's cause: Amsterdam was a shock.

What has happened to this city? In 1988 or thereabouts, when my Bro' lived in luxury by the Singel, it was phenomenal: teeming with quality bars and restaurants, warm-natured, exuberant and unmenacing even in the dingiest corners of the red-light district (of which I had a merely transitory knowledge, naturally). By 1992 a layer or two of its lustre had gone, as if the city's squalid and sordid aspects were at last floating to the surface. Now it's ghastly: filthy, vexatious, swarming with crooks and imbeciles, the red-light district transformed into a salacious cancer nourished chiefly by drug-peddling and supplemented by crime. Maybe it's society which has mutated, or maybe I'm getting old; but today we walked through parts of Amsterdam in which – even shielded by the towering Stuart and Eugene – I found myself uncommonly apprehensive.

Our hotel, to which the Tourist Information bureau graciously steered us, was an unmitigated dump. I have seen more elegant accommodation on North Sea ferries. It had plainly been furnished by *Rising Damp*'s Rigsby, with rickety chairs, drab duvets and a telly from the Chocolate Fireguard School of Usefulness. Across the street was a grotesquely pink building adorned with banners trumpeting "Gay Gang-Bang Night", an extravaganza we determined to accord a wide berth. How déclassé. Only our continuing poverty of pep prevented us from vacating the premises.

Consolation hid in the mid-afternoon peace of a nearby Irish bar. Flanked by decaying flats in a grimy terrace, it was the antithesis of the sanitized and shamrock-shrouded abominations which masquerade as Irish bars in England: intimate, functional and blessed with an all-enveloping stench of Guinness (of the **Guinness Export Draught** variety, I guess). The barman advised us to seat ourselves while he filled our gills, and five sedulous minutes later I was treated to a supremely bitter and dry stout – as morale-boosting a ration of hair-of-the-dog as one could contemplate.

A **Palm Steendonk** in a rowdy and congested hole choked with TVs screening a Blackburn Rovers match tipped the scales back towards the bleak; but a meal at the Café de Klos, a snug cellar-bar illuminated by a roaring charcoal grill, cured all ills. Uniquely, the Klos didn't seem to have altered a jot since my Bro' and I last chomped its incomparable racks of ribs. Everything from the owner to the Barry White and Tom Jones tapes was as per the '80s; even the beer repertoire had remained constant, as Eugene discovered.

"And to drink, sir?"

"What beers have you got?"

"We have **Amstel Bier**."

"And?"

Silence.

"I'll have an Amstel."

Billiards guru Robert Byrne once acclaimed pool as "a game as thrilling as skydiving but cheaper and not so hard on the joints" – a summary I considered wholly credible until I shot some after dinner stick tonight at the Prix d'Ami. In happier times I reeled off frame after frame while downing Heineken; now the tables are in terminal disrepair and the lager has been superseded by unorthodox cigarettes. To engage one of the in-house hooligans in a wager was to invite compound fractures, and thudding a misshapen cueball around dead cushions made for a gruesome nadir.

Valour soon deferred to discretion, but Café Belgique – a beer oasis in one of Amsterdam's cruder and more labyrinthian quarters – had the necessary pick-me-up: **St Christoffel Christoffel Bier**, the ultra-bitter Pilsner I mentioned last month in detailing the searingly unyielding wines engineered by Tom, my saviour in Lower Pilsley. St Christoffel, of Roermond, Dutch Limburg, is run by the singular Leo Brand, whose fierce defences of his primary product are as stirring as they are valid: "I am not brewing to please everyone!" Christoffel Bier kicks off with an immense

239

hoppiness and progresses to a long, dry, wickedly bitter finish; it is unpasteurized. We tried this tremendous beer while chatting to two British couples who were uncannily undeterred by (1) our devotion to frothy ones and (2) our being scummy journalists: folk usually flee upon ascertaining one or the other, and those who condone both are positively dodo-like in number.

What a nightcap before retiring to our stockade and the distant howls of Gay Gang-Bang Night: **De Ridder Wieckse Witte**, the Maastricht wheat-beer after which I had hankered for years. Tart, lemony and with hints of toffee, it was as spicy and as tangy as I recalled; but even its potential for energizing could not conceal the sombre reality of an early train to Brussels and a midday flight to Birmingham.

An exhausting, sporadically traumatic but essentially sound two days, then. Antwerp rules; Amsterdam rankles but has thrown up Christoffel Bier and Wieckse Witte and so can't be all bad. I have snored on a sofa in a four-star hotel and played pool on a table which would have defeated Mosconi himself. I have expanded the Abbaye des Rocs Supporters' Club and risked Westvleteren Extra for the first and last time. A rich tapestry. We're pooped, but so what? And – ah, yes – there's still tomorrow's Johnnie Walker to come.

Guinness Export Draught
(5 per cent ABV): ★★★★★

Palm Steendonk: see March 1

Amstel Bier: see March 16

St Christoffel Christoffel Bier
(5.1 per cent ABV): ★★★★★★

De Ridder Wieckse Witte
(5 per cent ABV): ★★★★★

October 5

Another week's sobriety painlessly negotiated. To be honest, it came as a welcome relief: it was born not out of the usual perverted blast of self-denial but out of a genuine need to lay off the sauce.

Tonight Eugene was present as my quest resumed with **Straffe Hendrik**, which now smacks of being almost pedestrian in the wake of its Brune counterpart (upon which I so propitiously stumbled in May) but is still a splendid ale. It is as pungent and as hoppy as ever; and it is also a trifle stronger than previously, although this is apparent only on the label rather than in the taste. On the negative side, the experience of rediscovering it after a year or so left me momentarily pining for Bruges; but a speedy review of recent superfluities rapidly squashed that sentiment.

We adjourned to the computer for a round at New Laphroaig GC, steadying our nerves with some Weizen while brawling over the awesome jackpot figure of £5. As has become traditional, I accorded my guest a model of top-flight brewing – Schneider Aventinus – and condemned myself to less exalted efforts. I detest the infantile daftness of the Disney-ish "Weizenland" concept, which is more Fantasia than it is Franconia – "Hey, kids, why don't we go to Weizenland this weekend?" – but I swallowed my resentment with commendable aplomb and had a **Kaiserdom Weizenland Hefetrüb** and a **Kaiserdom Weizenland Dunkel**.

Cloudy, yellow-orange and thick-headed, Hefetrüb has the air of an archetypal Weizen, as though it were ripped from a brewery's promotional poster, and is blessed with the apple-and-cloves aroma and sour finish of some of the Weizen greats; only Kaiserdom's penchant for underlying dullness weakens it. Its dark sibling, however, is abysmal: thin, too dry, too malty, devoid of character, almost obnoxious.

I stung Henderson for £1.98. This will hardly recover my expenses for Belgium and Holland, but a replacement bottle of Aventinus is within my grasp.

Straffe Hendrik (6 per cent ABV):	★★★★★
Kaiserdom Weizenland Hefetrüb (5.3 per cent ABV):	★★★★
Kaiserdom Weizenland Dunkel (5.3 per cent ABV):	★★

October 8

JD Wetherspoon (whoever you may be), why do you torment me so? No sooner do I have every reason to believe I will never again set foot in the Babington Arms than I am bundled into another outpost of your empire; and no sooner do I have every reason to believe you incapable of serving an acceptable ale than you stagger me with a beauty. What is the motivation behind your evil chicanery? It has to stop: the uncertainty of it all is too much to take.

I was to dine at Chai Yo, a Thai restaurant in Derby, but en route – to my will-sapping dismay, although I concealed it handsomely – it was proposed that my colleagues and I pop into the Standing Order, a Wetherspoon outlet "sympathetically" transformed from a one-time bank into a soulless, high-ceilinged, bookcase-bedecked lookalike. Wine and McEwan's C&T were available, so my colleagues were catered for in style; but I had to suck in many a deep breath before I felt brave enough to gamble with a half of **Cotleigh Old Buzzard**.

I reckoned the odds of my being furnished with a cultured drop of Cotleigh – from Wiveliscombe, Somerset – in a Wetherspoon boozer in Derby were ludicrously slim; but it was absolutely, gobsmackingly, presumption-shatteringly spot-on. I am not one to withhold praise when it is due, so I conveyed my astonishment to my associates – who, after all, are familiar with my opinions apropos Wetherspoon establishments and must have been oppugning my level of merriment as we hunted for a spare table amid the lofty stools and velour banquettes. Old Buzzard is a strongish ale, ruby-black, coffeeish, intensely roasted and affably smooth; and this was a faultless specimen. The C&T was also reported to be in optimum nick, so there could be no complaints.

There was additional joy at the superb Chai Yo, where the uninitiated were introduced – and converted – to the delights of **Boon Rawd Singha**. It was proffered in Singha glasses identical to the example I number in own collection, so I was even spared the ordeal of begging for one or – heaven forbid – surreptitiously slipping one into the sleeve of my jacket (do not infer from this any degree of proficiency or experience).

All things considered, an uplifting – if moderately bemusing – outing. I shall definitely go back to Chai Yo; whether my confidence has been sufficiently bolstered to warrant another trek to the Standing Order remains a topic for debate.

Cotleigh Old Buzzard (4.8 per cent ABV): ★★★★

Boon Rawd Singha: see September 18

October 9

Mum flew home from Germany yesterday, gallantly lugging with her an impressive array of glassware. From Margret came two snazzy Berliner Weisse goblets, one of them Kindl and the other Schultheiss; from cousin Andreas came a ridiculously enormous Spaten Krug (the sort of leviathan which is brandished with ease by Oktoberfest waitresses but will probably prompt the collapse of my shelves) and an equally sturdy Aotai Pure Draft Beer mug (snatched while he was in China, such is his dedication to my cause); and from assorted kith and kin came various other bits and bobs, all of them greedily embraced. Although it is a minor concern, I have no idea where to put them all (I could always use the Krug as a walk-in wardrobe, I suppose); and Mum is off to Germany again next month, so a crisis point might have been reached by the end of the year if this tide of generosity does not recede.

This afternoon I journeyed to the Dram, keen to inaugurate my gifts by tracking down some Berliner Weisse or Spaten Märzen. Neither was there, but there were plenty of other goodies by way of atonement: Hofbräu Schwarze Weisse, Erdinger Pikantus, Riva Dentergems Wit, a glut of stuff from US micro-breweries. By far the most gratifying find was Küppers, which has finally fallen into my mitts just days after I endowed Leong with meagre compensation for his unfulfilled Kölsch-lust: kismet?

My other incentive for travelling to South Yorkshire was to meet the ale-supping, whisky-sipping young chap who last month spent a week marvelling at our journalistic savvy (i.e. gazing in despair as we slobbed around the office). Spurred by our mastery, he is studying the secrets of the Fourth Estate at a college near Sheffield; but he is oblivious to the city's premier pubs, so – awkward memories of *Neil Does Bulmer's* notwithstanding – I thought I would show him the Fat Cat. Alas, our scope for a pleasant pint was severely restricted by the fact that we had arranged a post-3pm rendezvous: with the Fat Cat closed, we were forced to extend our search for an accommodating hostelry into the wilds of Derbyshire.

We began by driving to Bretton for a recce of the Barrel, an isolated yet hospitable white-washed inn perched atop a hill affording an expansive vista of the surrounding countryside (apart from today, of course, when the panorama was blanketed in rain and mist): it was shut. Onwards, then, to the nearby Three Stags Heads, Wardlow Mires: it, too, was shut. Running out of candidates – not to mention patience and petrol –

I headed for Beeley, a pretty village a mile from Chatsworth House, and the Devonshire Arms: it was, thank gawd, open.

Oak-beamed and multi-roomed, this 18th-century inn immediately struck us as an intriguing place – not least because of its devotion to beers from both Theakston and Black Sheep, the disparate camps of a brewing family split by a controversial takeover. I unerringly favour the latter, for it is nowadays impossible to discern before consumption whether a Theakston ale has been fashioned in Masham or knocked up in Newcastle; but after trying a **Black Sheep Best Bitter** – faintly fruity and hoppy but unspectacular – I was unable to rebuff the renowned **Theakston Old Peculier**, which is among Britain's most cherished "old" ales.

I know folk who swear by OP, which became one of the best-loved beers in the land during the '70s real-ale revival. I have never been as wowed by it as some, but its calibre – though it might not be as incontrovertible as in the past – is difficult to deny. Old Peculier – the misspelling is intentional – is near-black, rich, fruity, winy, roasted and assertive, with a warming finish; it is one of those quaint British beers which Americans, usually with predictably horrific but nonetheless entertaining consequences, yearn to chuck down their throats when they tour these shores.

Tomorrow I shall shower Leong – who would, I imagine, regard OP with the same underwhelming zest he reserved for DBA – with his Küppers. It should prove to be a momentous event.

Black Sheep Best Bitter (3.8 per cent ABV):	★★★
Theakston Old Peculier (5.7 per cent ABV):	★★★★

October 10

"Why didn't you get a crate?"

Thus spake Leong upon receiving his seven bottles of Küppers. Bearing in mind the interminable delay he has endured, he is entitled to query my wisdom in purchasing a mere septet: who is to say it will not be another couple of years before Kölsch once more graces the Dram? The problem, I told him, had been that my wallet was not equipped for the shock when I strolled in and espied those distinctive green-and-yellow labels: a grand total of eight bottles – I nabbed one for myself – was all I could handle.

Leong briefly pondered this pathetic plea for mercy and then dismissed it: "What about your credit card?" I took comfort from his jovial demeanour and his obvious affection for a distinguished frothy one. I trust that, having at last taken delivery, he will not dally before resurrecting his appreciation of Kölsch's delicate charms.

My lone half-litre will have to wait: tonight was a Burton Bridge night, and I was chuffed to observe that the autumnal **Burton Bridge Staffordshire Knot Brown Ale** was taking its seasonal turn as Guillo and I sought shelter from the wind and rain. Unlike summer itself, any lingering traces of which have been vanquished by gusting gales and depressing downpours, Summer Ale is hanging around; but it lacks the robustness to compliment (or even combat) weather as ghastly as tonight's. The malty Knot Brown, which lies somewhere between Bridge Bitter and Battle Brew not only in ABV but in characteristics and body, is perfect for these gloomy evenings.

This is more than can be said for **Faxe Premium**, the tedious Danish lager I chose to accompany my takeaway. If why I selected it tonight constitutes a mystery, though, why I even bought it earlier this week is utterly unfathomable: maybe I was simply reluctant to depart Morrisons without a frothy one in my basket ("Beer and cat-food – all the ingredients for a sound meal, eh?" I said to the check-out girl, on whom any

stab at humour [however limp] was sadly lost). I have owned a
Faxe Krug for several years – a dubious privilege – and never
in that period have I slurped from it; and I saw no basis for
precedent tonight, since I would have needed to decant my
330ml of Premium from the summit of a step-ladder to
generate the 670ml of head necessary to fill a receptacle of
such absurd dimensions.

Faxe, of Fakse, south of Copenhagen, has an adequate
reputation, yet I deemed its Premium so dreary – not
abominable, granted, but nor what I would strictly term
"decent" – that I flirted with the notion of necking my
Küppers to get over it. I quickly concluded that such rashness
would be unjustifiable: Kölsch is a rare treat and should not
to be squandered – as Leong would no doubt confirm.

Burton Bridge Staffordshire Knot Brown Ale (4.8 per cent ABV):	★★★★
Faxe Premium (5 per cent ABV):	★★

October 11

A dilatory evening in front of the TV brought a trio of
excellent programmes and a trio of middling beers. To
be truthful, prior encounters with two of said frothy
ones meant I was steeled for scant dividend; but I had
hoped for more from the third. Two of the programmes
were American and the other Chinese, while two of the
beers were German and the other Belgian: at least the
roles were not reversed, for my humble knowledge of
German and Belgian TV puts it very much on a par with
Bud Lite and canned Tsingtao.

I started with *King of the Hill* and **Waitrose Bavarian
Wheat-Beer**, a Weizen produced for the Waitrose
delicatessen chain by a brewery which – as per the originator of

Sainsbury's Hefe Weissbier – is kept shrouded in secrecy by infuriating labelling. The minimal notes say "brewed near the town of Plattling", but my cursory examination of a map of Bavaria threw up numerous could-bes and no concrete clues. Like scores of other nondescript wheat-beers, Waitrose's is yellowy, turbid and slightly sour: full marks for appearance, not a lot for anything else. Incidentally, the animated protagonists of *King of the Hill* – a more naturalistic version of *The Simpsons* – idle away the bulk of their time by resting on their ride-on lawnmowers and guzzling tins of beer: the identity of their preferred brand is not disclosed, but, since they are Texans, I assume it is the dry and drab Lone Star – an appropriate designation, for that is precisely the score I would be tempted to award if any should ever come my way.

Next came *Frasier* and **Riva Dentergems Wit**, a popular yet somewhat trite wheat-beer from Belgium. The ever-distending Riva group, based in Dentergem, on the border of East and West Flanders, has gained a foothold in the wit market with 'Gems, but I shall forever remember how the waitress at the Brugs Beertje (she of "I miss you guys" fame) cautioned against it when I mooted one: "It's not good," she counselled solemnly, and I had to concur. Tonight's was not as lustreless as some I can recall, being somehow softer and less conspicuously grainy than its forebears; but Hoegaarden, Brugs Tarwebier and the superlative Van Eecke Watou's Witbier have oodles more panache.

I rounded off the night by relaxing with a frothy one and a Bruce Lee kung fu extravaganza. To my sadistic rapture, *The Big Boss* did not divert from the uniform plot of Bruce's early works: Bruce is dispatched to act as nursemaid to relatives in foreign parts (here it was Thailand, in *Way of the Dragon* it was Italy, and so on); he exercises commendable restraint while the baddies do their iniquitous deeds; his restraint exhausted by their persistent malfeasance, he pummels the baddies; with the agility of a cat, the brawn of a rhino and the vocal dexterity of a demented Chihuahua, he inflicts a humiliating scudding upon the chief villain; the chief villain, recognizing he is outclassed, arms himself with deadly blades; and Bruce, by now a mite miffed, kills the chief villain with bone-crunching abandon. I cannot sit through a Bruce Lee movie without exclaiming expletives in bedazzled admiration; but the expletives mumbled in response to **Dortmunder Union Brinkhoff's N° 1**, a bland lager from Dortmund's largest brewery, were in anything but an admiring vein.

How often must the message be hammered home? Dortmund's Export beers are among the sublimest of bottom-fermented fare, and yet its breweries insist on showcasing their lesser wares. Brinkhoff's N° 1 – named after a founding brewer at the Dortmunder Union Brauerei – is passable, but it is to DUB's Export what Jean-Claude Van Damme is to Bruce: an uncouth pretender. No wonder I neglected to debut the enchanting Dortmunder Union mug which Margret sent me a few months ago.

Three three-star beers on the bounce; and a two-star stinker before them, damn it. I am on a poor run. This cannot continue.

Waitrose Bavarian Wheat-Beer (5.3 per cent ABV):	★★★
Riva Dentergems Wit (5 per cent ABV):	★★★
Dortmunder Union Brinkhoff's N° 1 (5 per cent ABV):	★★★

October 14

His philosophizing was not at its most sagacious when I was last propping up his bar ("The bear – he likes the honey"), but supremely wise words from Brugs Beertje proprietor Jan de Bruin adorn the title page of the *Good Beer Guide to Belgium and Holland:* "Life is too short and the liver too brittle," he declares, "to bother oneself with second-rate drink." I think it is time I heeded this judicious advice.

Why, if my ambition is to sample as many different beers as possible, do I regress to frothy ones which I know to be medial, questionable or just plain awful? There can sometimes be mitigating circumstances (an Oranjeboom has to suffice when the Wine Rack has no other answer to your desperation; and when you're shoved into a Wetherspoon pub you have to seize upon whatever scraps you can), but I have been guilty of some disgracefully senseless buys this year. To saunter out of the Dram with Dentergems Wit and Brinkhoff's N° 1 was asinine in the extreme: I was well aware of their dowdiness, so where was the merit in my actions? Last month I moronically augmented the Kaiserdom coffers, irrespective of my long-held contempt for Weizenland Dunkel. In July I even stooped so low as to snap up a bottle of Steinlager, a concoction of brain-boggling banality which I shouldn't have contemplated in my most febrile dreams. Such conduct is irredeemably silly, and it has to cease.

The year would not be complete without an Orval, a Pedigree, a Summer Ale, a Schneiderweisse, a Landlord, a Liberty Ale and myriad others which I am glad to imbibe over and over again; but I must endeavour not to fritter away my time, money and energy in pursuit of reacquainting myself with dross. If I come across dross in the course of experimentation then so be it; and if a benevolent chum foists dross upon me and then declines to bugger off, thereby robbing me of the opportunity to empty his or her gratuity down the plughole or fob it off on an innocent fool, that's okay; but my own witless slackness shall not be tolerated in future. This is a formative lesson which I must learn; indeed, I should have learned it ages ago.

All of this weighed heavily on my conscience when I approached tonight's **Hofbräu Schwarze Weisse**. I had never had it before, and it promised much: Hofbräu, of Munich, with its cavernous beer-hall, its royal connections, its haughty "HB" labels and its seminal Maibock, is a brewery of no mean import. But – as I perhaps should have prophesied, given my hapless plight of late – Schwarze Weisse was a disappointment: dense-headed and vaguely toasted, yes, but bereft of any great individuality and an eternity from the black hue its eye-catching tag evokes (it is certainly a Dunkel but nothing like a Schwarzen, so congratulations to the spin-doctors in Hofbräu's marketing section).

On goes the three-star parade, then. I have mentally chalked up another decent but mundane beer with which I should tangle again only in emergencies. As if to highlight the breadth of my frustration, the Schwarze Weisse came between the knackering of my leading computer and the hair-tearing irritation of struggling through two hours of *Arsenic and Old Lace* before the video-tape expired five minutes ahead of the film's climax. Hurrah.

When will it all end?

Hofbräu Schwarze Weisse (5.1 per cent ABV): ★★★

October 15

I stopped the rot this evening. Only by effectively cheating, though; and by the end of the night the rot had set in again.

There were roughly three options at my disposal when I pondered how to restore some dignity to my quaffing: (1) to wander far and wide and investigate every frothy one I found; (2) to sneak into the pantry and help myself to a Chimay Blue or a Rodenbach Alexander; (3) to go to the Burton Bridge. Both 2 and 3 were scandalous cop-outs, yet 1 was too fanciful; and so I went for 3, trundling to the BB with Guillo. With Summer Ale's stint over, **Burton Bridge Staffordshire Knot Brown Ale** had the honour of pulling me out of the three-star ooze. To take indolent refuge in a tried-and-tested beer represented a hollow victory; but these are desolate days, make no mistake, and better a hollow victory than another dismal defeat.

It was fun while it lasted, but I was dragged back into the mire of mediocrity just two hours later by **Het Anker Tripel Toison d'Or**. The weak link in Het Anker's range – Gouden Carolus is a terrific beer, and the bitter-sweet Mechselen Bruynen is almost as delicious – Toison d'Or is grainy to the virtual exclusion of any other trait. Whether it is an authentic tripel or nothing more than a pale ale of some fortitude is disputable: it is as much a sub-standard Hoegaarden Julius as it is a sub-standard Westmalle. Monumentally ordinary.

I blame Eugene for my being cast back into the realms of the excruciatingly conventional, as it was he who brought the Toison d'Or back from the Dram a fortnight ago. Still, to harangue him would only invite the retort that a Belgian ale offered infinitely superior potential than did Brinkhoff's N° 1. It looks as though I am not alone in labouring to locate laudable frothy ones this month.

**Burton Bridge Staffordshire
Knot Brown Ale: see October 9**

**Het Anker Tripel Toison d'Or
(7.6 per cent ABV):   ★★★**

October 16

Oh, come on. This is getting beyond a bloody joke now.

Wasn't I asking for it, though? I remorselessly moan and gripe about the absence of above-average beers, yet what did I turn to tonight for a change in fortunes? **Kaiserdom Weizenland Kristallklar**. Talk about wishful thinking: even in the whimsical kingdom of Weizenland, where all is happy and frolicsome and twee, miracles are a tall order.

I am not one to heed health-freaks' calls to shun meat and eat piles of fruit and vegetables, but I cannot dissent from the view of young Germans that cloudy wheat-beer is the epitome of wholesome well-being. It is probably nothing of the sort, quite frankly, but the allegation is a reassuring one for those Bavarians who swig Hefeweizen twixt copious chunks of pig's trotter. Kristallklar wheat-beer, on the other hand, is a dim alternative, and it is tough to nominate any which has garnered too many plaudits: Weihenstephan's is one of the best, but the majority – even those from specialists like Erdinger – suffer horribly by comparison with their sedimented stablemates. A Kristallklar cannot match the apples-and-cloves aroma or sour finish of a cloudy Weizen, and the attraction of the style really is rather limited.

So why was I messing around with Kaiserdom's lame, lifeless, listless interpretation? Because it was in the pantry. Because it had been in the pantry for some time and was annoying me. Because I am a romantic. Because I am an optimist. Because I am a prat.

Kaiserdom Weizenland Kristallklar (5.3 per cent ABV): ★★

October 19

<u>American cities I would like to visit – and why</u>

(1) New York – because the Brooklyn Brewery is there; and because Zip City, a brewpub noted for its sparkling cuisine à la bière, is also there.

(2) San Francisco – because the Anchor Brewery is there; and because I could hire a '67 Mustang fastback and recreate the chase sequence from *Bullitt*.

(3) Chicago – because it is the pool-hustling Mecca (if not literally then mythically), and I harbour a warped hankering to risk my thumbs by engaging some of the more colourful locals in a bout of straights; and because I could hire a bashed-up Dodge Sedan and recreate the chase sequence from *The Blues Brothers*.

Although its beery allure is the broadest, I would generally relegate New York to third; and yet tonight has persuaded me that its frothy ones might just have the edge over emulating Steve McQueen's tyre-smoking antics on the streets of 'Cisco or having a Balabushka cracked over my knuckles in one of the dingier corners of the Windy City. The beer which has provoked this rethink is the New-York-brewed **Neptune ACME**, a find so outstanding that it must rank alongside Straffe Hendrik Brune as the surprise of the year so far.

Unless my recollection of cartoon history is erroneous, ACME – the fictitious firm whose idiotic devices (rocket-powered rollerskates, for instance) consistently failed Wile E Coyote, the Road Runner's perpetually doomed stalker – was conjured up when Warner Brothers wanted "A Company Making Everything" to feature in its animations. Neptune must therefore have substantial faith in its product, since anything cursed with ACME's signature is bound to invoke thoughts of incompetence and ineptitude: my first reaction upon seeing it at the Dram was mentally to picture Wile E plummeting from a cliff, his impact with terra firma announced only by a muffled thud and a cloud of dust. Not satisfied with the cretinous connotations of the name, Neptune supplements the ruse by dressing ACME in a label boasting a calculated elementariness: predominantly off-white, it sheepishly proclaims that ACME is "an okay bottle of beer". If the daftness of Wile E's supplier lives on, though, quality control is evidently on the up-and-up.

ACME is much more than "an okay bottle of beer" (as if Neptune didn't know): copper-bronze and enticingly fruity, with a dry finish and a distant tang of lemon, it is surely a wanna-be Anchor Liberty Ale – and an amazingly proficient one, too. All of which illustrates that when I was cogitating how to escape my three-star rut I was wrong to be lily-livered and decide upon the go-for-what-you-know recourse: happening upon a gem after a spell of exasperation was, I have to say, twice as rewarding as what amounted to a spineless surrender at the Burton Bridge four days ago.

254

There was more encouragement in the form of **Smuttynose Shoals Pale Ale**, another morale-booster from a US micro. Brewed in Portsmouth, New Hampshire, it is a darker shade of bronze than ACME – maybe with blushing tinges, like Samuel Smith Old Brewery Pale Ale – and is dry and quite bitter. Like ACME, it is bottle-conditioned; and, like ACME, it has cheered me up no end.

My Stateside-inspired bliss is such that I could almost write "God bless America"; but let us not forget that amid the ACMEs, the Balabushkas and the '67 Mustangs lurk Miller Lite, Michelob Dry and Bud. No point in getting carried away.

Neptune ACME (5 per cent ABV):	★★★★★
Smuttynose Shoals Pale Ale (5.3 per cent ABV):	★★★★

October 21

My beer calendar appears to have gone out of the window this year. To adhere to it is no picnic, and – as I stressed at the beginning of the crusade – to try to be its slave is self-destructive; but I cannot avoid the fact that I have made a particularly talentless hash of it. No Easter beer; no Maibock in May; a pantry crammed with ales in the summer; a fridge overflowing with lagers in the winter; and this month, with the frost biting in earnest and no Oktoberfestbier on the horizon, a flood of German wheat-beers – Kaiserdom, Waitrose, Hofbräu and, joining the Weizen cavalcade tonight, **Erdinger Pikantus**.

All is not irrevocably disastrous, however: although Weizen is essentially a summer beer, Erdinger Pikantus – like the peerless Schneider Aventinus – is a Weizenbock and thus an exquisite tipple for nippy nights. Weizenbocks are not exactly multitudinous – I know of only four or five, though there may be

scores of them when the villages of Bavaria are buried in snow –
but none of the very few I have managed to enjoy has been
anything but lovely. To sit by a roaring fire with a thick-headed
Weissbier bubbling in a towering glass (there is a less
ostentatious Pikantus goblet, but it is fundamentally flawed: too
small to accommodate the contents of the bottle) is initially
incongruous; but to warm to the task is not inconceivable.

Every Weizenbock is judged against Schneider Aventinus,
and Erdinger Pikantus measures up to it in much the same way
that Erdinger Weißbier stacks up against Schneiderweisse: it is
so close to excellence that it hurts, a solid performer but a
smidgen less consummate than the exemplar in its category.
Pikantus is tawny, with hints of chocolate and raisins; it is
malty, fruity and dry but not as full-bodied as might be
expected. Unlike other Erdinger beers, which are a little
softer, it has a sorry tendency to fizzle out and lose its head;
but don't we all from time to time?

Anyway, that's enough Weizen – normal, Bock,
Doppelbock or otherwise – for this month. I state here
and now that October (which, to be blunt, has already
been something of a mini-catastrophe) shall go down in
the annals as rivalling the reviled January if my Spaten
Krug has not been slopped out with Oktoberfestbier
come the 31st.

Erdinger Pikantus
(7.3 per cent ABV):   ★★★★

October 23

Having made our customary stops at the Burton Bridge
(*Burton Bridge Burton Porter* for me, Bridge Bitter for him)
and Leong's (Kölsch hoard terminally depleted: "I don't
drink a lot, but I like to have one every day," he explained),
Guillo and I settled down for the year's zillionth European
football night. How monotonous, you might say; but the off-
pitch activity was acutely significant.

Wallersteiner Landsknecht Bier, a dark lager from the brewery responsible for the infamously sludge-plagued Classic, had loitered on the "not just yet" list for some time while I strived to shake off the abiding turpitude of its predecessor; but tonight, imbued with humanity and benevolence, I was prepared to give it a whirl. A rich and creamy Dunkel with a bitter-dry finish, it convinced me that the Wallersteiner Classic I was luckless enough to pluck from all the Wallersteiner Classics in the world was nowt but a rogue duffer: I really ought to invest in a second and grade it anew.

Meanwhile, Eugene is bidding to wangle for us a freebie jaunt to Iceland. He would pen an article for his latest paymaster; I would audaciously masquerade as his photographer, à la Bruges. Having consulted a guidebook, though, I face the sombre chore of informing him that Iceland has one brewery and, because of alcohol laws which make Norway's look stupendously liberal, is vexed with some of the puniest beers anywhere; then again, although lagers of 2.5 per cent might not thrill us as profoundly as Abbaye des Rocs or De Kluis Benedict, the idea of boozing all night and never once having to worry about getting sloshed – especially after last month's heroics – has an obvious appeal.

**Burton Bridge Burton Porter:
see February 17**

**Wallersteiner Landsknecht Bier
(5.2 per cent ABV):   ★★★★**

October 26

I have always maintained that Formula One has never been the same since Ayrton was killed, but there is one amusing Senna-like aspect which survives: the determining of championships by means of ramming one's opponent off the track.

My fellow retina-burner Tim and I used to play a computer game in which two bi-planes whizzed around the screen and strafed each other with gunfire, the conqueror being the first to down its adversary 15 times. If the pair were involved in a mid-air collision then each was awarded a point: hence the player who had racked up a score of 14 would promptly disregard his weaponry and merely fly a suicide mission into his foe, thereby accruing the crucial last point in numbingly cynical fashion. Our kamikaze tactics were fondly referred to as "doing an Ayrton", and today I kept watch for such twisted ruses while lazily monitoring the Grand Prix with a **Peroni Nastro Azzurro**.

Peroni, of Rome, is the biggest brewer in a nation whose young drinkers are rejecting wine for frothy ones in the belief that the hop is healthier than the grape (ah, the perspicacity of youth). Yet why anyone should envision the likes of Nastro Azzurro (Blue Riband) to be of benefit to his or her constitution is baffling: it is a crisp and well-balanced Pilsener but − like the preponderance of its compatriots − so pitiably light that there is a grave danger it might simply float away. Loath though I am to inveigh the brewing industry of an entire nation with one sweeping denunciation, it could be contended that there is not a single Italian beer capable of triggering excitement: a handful are interesting, but none threatens to bedevil the directors at Pilsner Urquell with sleepless nights.

As sour as Ayrton's notorious Prost-pummelling ploy of 1990 was my **Rodenbach Alexander**, the least acerbic incarnation of the most arresting ale on the planet. Michael Jackson once remarked that "the unimaginative are apt to consider Rodenbach's beers undrinkable", but it must be accepted that the stance of these blinkered blockheads is forgivable: Rodenbach is, to be fair, stern work. The brewery, in Roeselare, West Flanders, produces the archetypal aged, sour, red ale indigenous to the region, maturing its beer in colossal oak tuns for between 18 months and two years; there are many imitators, but a serious challenger to Rodenbach's paradigm has yet to come forward. "Neat" Rodenbach is sold as Rodenbach Grand Cru and, though an alarming prospect for the layman, is a classic; less devastatingly uncompromising, with a diminished tartness, is the beer known only as Rodenbach, a blend of young (around five weeks old) and 18-month-old brews; and Alexander – christened after the brewery's founder – is a kriek variation of Grand Cru, sweetened with cherry essence.

Rodenbach's ales are strange things. Extraordinarily sour, vastly complex and arguably more refreshing than any lager or wheat-beer, they are so stunningly incomparable that they almost defy subjectivity: if a connoisseur had warned me they were fantastically dreadful I might well have agreed. The Grand Cru is undoubtedly beyond the resilience of the average palate; moreover, to compound the confusion, it fascinates some sceptics who detest frothy ones. Despite a frenzy of lip-puckering, I have grown to respect these beers; and respect, above anything else, is what they deserve.

Respect is also due to whoever came up with the monicker of the third member of today's irreconcilable triumvirate: **Brewer's Cave Black Roasted Barley Ale**. Catchy – not. I had envisaged this to be the pride of my US crop from the Dram (which incorporated last week's ACME and Shoals Pale Ale), but – as if to yet again underline that a snazzy label is no indication of substance – it was the shoddiest: uncannily thin and humdrum for an ale trading (rather clumsily, as though targeting the hard of understanding) on its use of black and roasted barley.

Brewer's Cave is made by the Minnesota Brewing Company, an eminent contract-brewer whose clients have included Pete's, but I recommend that Minnesota ditch it and concentrate instead on inventing a beer to commemorate the achievements of a sportsman who could have taught dear old Ayrton a thing or two about losing with grace. Ladies and gentlemen, I give you America's favourite low-calorie beer... Minnesota Fats. Oh, sod you, then.

Peroni Nastro Azzurro (5.2 per cent ABV):	★★★
Rodenbach Alexander (6 per cent ABV):	★★★★★
Brewer's Cave Black Roasted Barley Ale (5.1 per cent ABV):	★★★

October 27

It is always nice to have something to toast, and tonight Eugene and I had a smashing occurrence to celebrate with our frothy ones: Henderson has become a father. Shame, then, that my pint of **Burton Bridge XL** was somehow off-key: it wasn't brackish or in any way disgusting – just a tad anomalous.

I made amends back at the ranch by uncorking some **Chimay Grand Réserve**, the large-bottled edition of Chimay Blue. Whether Chimay Grand Réserve and Chimay Blue are one and the same is a matter of neither science nor semantics: it is, if anything, a matter of mood. Each of the 33cl Chimay ales has a 75cl brother – the Red has Première, the White has Cinq Cents – and the differences between them are probably confined solely to the softer texture of the 75cl beers. How magnificently hypocritical: if an everyday brewery released its beer in a Bordeaux bottle and under a flamboyant alias – Grand Cru, Cuvée, Speciale – I would be among those queuing up to slate it, yet when Chimay seemingly perpetrates such a crime I start scrabbling around for excuses.

Grand Réserve's attributes are frequently likened to those of a port. Fruity and smooth, with a huge depth of flavour, it is vintage-dated and often laid down for years by its enthusiasts (mine languished in the pantry for a somewhat lamentable 27 days, but I would cite impatience rather than lack of reverence as the grounds for its fleeting respite). It is a beer for reflection; and Eugene, with the spectre of nappies and potty-training looming before him, suddenly has much upon which to reflect.

He and Lisa have called their son Jim. Very conventional; but then Eugene would not listen to my suggestion. I admit that it is cruel to saddle one's offspring with the name of a soccer team or a car, but who would not want to sail through life as Mr Orval Henderson?

Burton Bridge XL: see May 22

Chimay Grand Réserve (9 per cent ABV): ★★★★★★

October 29

I seldom indulge in a frothy one at other people's homes: not because I am an unsociable git, I should add, but because there is usually nothing worthy of indulgence. Such an inflexible attitude more than qualifies me as the unsociable git I protest I am not, you may claim; but would a gastronome rejoice at the adducing of a tin of spam? One long-standing mucker habitually tenders cans of Stella Artois; only last night another dared to urge that I revel in a bottle of American Budweiser (minus glass, naturally). I don't count on having a 1989 Westvleteren Dubbel thrust into my paw when I bang on the door, but would it hurt to keep a four-pack of Hoegaarden around the house? Blimey, even something as ignoble as Beck's would do the trick.

This evening saw the exception to the rule: Phil, a clear winner in the hosting stakes, served me **Rodenbach Grand Cru** and **Orval**. He said the former would be wasted on him, which translated as: "I'm not having any of *that*." He treated himself to Westmalle Tripel, a massive consignment of which he secured during a day-trip to France: I fought to hide a speck of jealousy while the Grand Cru shredded my salivary glands, but even the finest tripel in the world could not sway me from my Orval.

It hasn't been a memorable year Orval-wise, for I have savoured just three: two at the Spinnekopke, Brussels, and tonight's. Phil's was the pick, since the Spinnekopke has a knack of over-chilling Orval and so obliterating its subtleties (why such a tremendous restaurant permits this aberration I do not know); but, as ever, there is room for further improvement. Which reminds me: the third episode of *Cadfael* still awaits. It's about time I went to the Bottle Store.

Rodenbach Grand Cru
(6.5 per cent ABV):   ★★★★★★
Orval: see February 28

October 31

The month has not been as atrocious as I regularly had cause to fear while the past weeks' trials and tribulations unfolded, but – save for two or three – the beers which have induced the toothiest grins have been old hat. Dramatic discoveries would have been more desirable than the well-worn wiles of Straffe Hendrik, Rodenbach, Chimay and even Orval. So it was again tonight, with **Marston's Pedigree** and **Draught Bass** providing inured virtue but leaving me with no real sense of satisfaction.

My plans for an expedition to the Bottle Store were cancelled when Gary said he would obtain my requirements and come to Burton for a pint and a takeaway. When he submitted my list – from which I inadvertently omitted Orval, such is my dimwittedness – the assistant inquired if Gary was procuring for "Mr Tweedy-Jacket"; Gary said he was my butler. Unfortunately, the only Oktoberfestbier in stock was Löwenbräu's: I wanted Spaten's (he wailed), and I had no passion for waving goodbye to the month with a cloying lager which, though expedient, would only have heaped extra woe upon October's litany of letdowns.

The Bridge Inn's Pedigree was typically luscious, but the night's genuine pleasure was neither the Pedi nor the Bass but my return to the impeccable Coopers Tavern. When I last visited – perhaps six or seven years ago, which is a frightening thought – this backstreet jewel was the unofficial tap for the Bass brewery, in whose giant shadow it cowers. In a move of phenomenal crassness, a piece of business acumen akin to flogging drainpipe trousers to Regan and Carter or peddling Lamborghinis in Maranello, Bass sold this unprepossessing treasure to Hardys and Hansons, of Kimberley, Nottingham, as soon as legislation obligated it to off-load a percentage of its tied houses; but local outrage guaranteed that Draught Bass duly regained its position in the row of casks – albeit alongside Kimberley Classic.

What an entrancing pub. The tiny tap-room itself is as bustling as the lounge is tranquil and snug; once a taste for it has been acquired, the gravity-dispensed Bass is glorious; and the pork scratchings – fist-sized beasts in cellophane bags – are the tops. It's one of a dying breed, and I'll be back there next month if – as I suspect – the quest for new sensations flounders afresh.

Come on, November. Do your worst.

**Marston's Pedigree:
see February 3**

Draught Bass: see July 21

November 6

The month did not start with the brightest of omens. Having intimated that I would revert to the Coopers Tavern for some **Draught Bass** in the event of drawing a blank in my hunt for fresh challenges, where and with which beer did I get November underway? Cooper's Tavern; Draught Bass. Still, it *was* lovely; and Guillo was impressed.

I arranged something moderately less familiar for home, although it was by no means a first: **Bateman's XXXB**. I was persuaded to order some from the Bottle Store last week after NG brought me a pair of Bateman's glasses from his local pub, the landlord of which had intended to raffle them off until he learned of my sad obsession (a charity's loss is my gain, then; I did contribute to the town's hospice by way of a thank-you, though, so my conscience is clear). Many a year has passed since I last slurped XXXB, and its character has not diminished in the interim: it remains as hoppy and as malty as ever, even in this pasteurized incarnation, with an underlying fruitiness and a well-rounded finish. It is an outstanding premium bitter, as multiple awards have illustrated.

After Guillo's departure I grew uncommonly reckless, helping myself to an **Abbaye des Rocs La Montagnarde** and an **Abbaye des Rocs Blanche des Honnelles**. As I am perpetually eager to divulge to all and sundry, the eponymous ale from Abbaye des Rocs is arguably the beer I most adore; yet La Montagnarde and Blanche des Honelles, though not as breathtaking (apart from Orval, what is?), should not be be dismissed.

Brewed from five cereals (and do not be perturbed by that, unappetizing though it might sound), La Montagnarde lacks the massive complexities and supreme nuances of Abbaye des Rocs; but it is just as dark, just as strong and just as warming, with an intriguing burntness in its finish. Its dedicated goblet is lamentable – the bottle accommodates 330ml, the glass roughly 275ml – but this is, I must concede, a petty gripe.

The flute purportedly designed for Blanche des Honnelles is even worse; more importantly, the beer is not quite as distinguished as its fellow Abbaye des Rocs ales. It is pale, light and very dry – the type of beer which is revered in Wallonia and reviled in Flanders. There is nothing awry with it per se, but Abbaye des Rocs and La Montagnarde are far smarter bets.

No fresh challenges, then. But – perhaps unsurprisingly – I do feel pretty damned cheery. Ah, mustn't grumble.

Draught Bass: see July 22	
Bateman's XXXB (5 per cent ABV):	★★★★★
Abbaye des Rocs La Montagnarde (9 per cent ABV):	★★★★★
Abbaye des Rocs Blanche des Honnelles (6 per cent ABV):	★★★★

November 8

Ever the tragic figure, I held my own one-man Oktoberfest tonight. Better late than never; or maybe, come to think of it, better never. More than five-million litres of beer are consumed at Munich's Oktoberfest, the mother of all booze-ups, which actually kicks off in the second half of September; a grand total of one litre, made up of the two bottles of **Löwenbräu Oktoberfestbier** I was reluctant to risk at the tail-end of last month, was consumed at mine. Much as thousands of the lunatics who take on the real festival conclude their orgy of imbibing with the hunch that they have overindulged on an apocalyptic scale, my single Krug's worth of super-malty and sickly-sweet lager was more than enough for me: I still cannot grasp how some folk guzzle paunch-swelling quantities of the overwhelming brews trotted out by Löwenbräu and Paulaner.

The ordeal, I am dejected to report, has convinced me I would face abject humiliation at an Oktoberfest. On the evidence of tonight's maiden battle with what neophytes insist on branding a Stein, suddenly the notion of having a litre mug plonked down in front of me fills me with dismay: there is not only the terror of failing to empty it but the terror that I might topple into it and drown. While the seasoned

265

sloshers of Bavaria and the have-a-go heroes from Australia and New Zealand would dispatch litre after litre with casual aplomb, I would labour pathetically over my first and gawp in crushed consternation at its successor. Conversation would cease. The Lederhosen-clad oompah band would fall silent. Every pair of eyes in the 5,000-seat Mathäser would focus on the slender Englishman and his never-dwindling measure of Märzen.

I can hear the whispers now: "Der Englander kann sein Bier nicht trinken! Mensch, vielleicht sollt er Lemonade trinken!" "Yeah?" I would reply. "Right, Fritz, let's see you cope with a pint of Pedi!" But it would be a token retort, especially if it came as I was being stretchered away to the nearest stomach-pump.

And my minimal capacity for cloying frothy ones would not provide the only embarrassment: my inept handling of the Krug would also yield shame. Now I understand why Germany always seems to foster medal-scooping shot-putters: spend a fortnight every year at the Oktoberfest and you're ready for a world-record bid. Drink the stuff? I could hardly *lift* the bugger.

Löwenbräu Oktoberfestbier
(6 per cent ABV): ★★★

November 13

Hmmm, isn't this where we came in? **Burton Bridge Top Dog Stout**: "an ideal match for a chat and a bag of pork scratchings on a bone-chilling January night", as I recall. My beer calendar has roughly seven weeks left to run, but the Burton Bridge's has gone full circle. It is November rather than January, the weather may be a fraction less bone-chilling, and I'm trying to eschew pork scratchings for a while (the Coopers Tavern's beauties have attained heights which others cannot rival), but otherwise what applied at the commencement of this quest applies now: Top Dog – dry, bitter and magnificently roasted – is still an exquisite ale.

I was reminded of just how exquisite, though, only when I furthered my stout intake at home with **Samuel Smith's Oatmeal Stout** and **Samuel Smith's Imperial Stout**. I had feared the Tadcaster duo would outshine Burton's sole contender, but – and I trust parochial bias is not responsible for my inference – it had the edge over the former and was arguably as compelling as the latter. The exercise made for a revealing night's quaffing, although in hindsight it is important to remember that each is from a different "school" of stout and thus not strictly comparable to the others: dry stouts like Top Dog are deeply roasted and bitter; oatmeal stouts evolved out of the fad for sweet and allegedly nutritious interpretations and are smoother, less uncompromising; and imperial stouts – burnt, powerful and warming – hark back to the days when Britain exported dark beers to the Baltic, strengthening them for the voyage in much the same way that IPAs were fortified for the passage to India.

I buy Samuel Smith's Oatmeal Stout on a regular basis, for it is my Gran's favourite tipple; but it must be 13 or 14 months since I last had any myself. It is not produced with a huge amount of oatmeal, yet its chocolatey silkiness speaks volumes. Tonight's struck me as a trifle less distinctive than previous examples, and it now occurs to me that I might have been better advised to approach the evening's beers in order of ascending intensity; but then I feel my fervour for frothy ones will have reached a level warranting psychiatric attention when I am prepared to knock back an Oatmeal in the comfort of my living-room, dash to the Burton Bridge for a Top Dog and then whizz home again to polish off an Imperial.

The epic tale of what is now known as imperial or Russian stout encompasses thousands of miles, and to plot its route on a map of the world would be to perpetrate a Pythagorean nightmare. Samuel Smith's Imperial Stout adds a few extra miles to the story, as (like Oatmeal) it was originally created for – would you credit it? – the brewery's American disciples. It is curious, considering the style's London connotations and its spread across the Baltic, that perhaps the two leading imperial/Russian stouts are fashioned in Tadcaster: Samuel Smith's neighbouring brewery is John Smith's (Sam and John were brothers), which makes the vintage-dated Courage Imperial Russian Stout for the Surrey-based Courage group.

Three fine beers, then, but the night was not without disappointment: Guillo, who only minutes earlier had been extolling the virtues of the Burton Bridge above those of all other hostelries, was furnished with a below-par pint of XL. He was supremely distressed, speculating that he had become a victim of idol-with-feet-of-clay syndrome. What he should have done, of course, was deliver the offending drop back to the bar, thereby sparing himself torture by tartness and warning the staff that the bottom of the barrel was being plumbed; instead he soldiered on, no assistance forthcoming from yours truly. Most upsetting.

We were both at fault. Guillo once scolded a Leicestershire pub for its woefully-kept Summer Ale, yet tonight he was either too nervous or too incredulous to express his reservations about a beer at the source; and I, lest we forget, am the coward who lacked the guts to complain about a shocking Hop Back Summer Lightning at the Babington Arms, so stirring up a fuss at the BB was always going to be beyond my timid scope. Whether I am compounding my own pluck deficiency by even now refusing to disparage the Bridge for an oversight which has earned lesser inns a vicious rebuke is, I'm afraid, something I am unwilling to discuss.

Burton Bridge Top Dog Stout: see January 6	
Samuel Smith's Oatmeal Stout (5 per cent ABV):	★★★★
Samuel Smith's Imperial Stout (7 per cent ABV):	★★★★★

November 14

With a bloated belly and a castigated constitution to show for last night's banquet of stout and takeaway food, I resolved that today's menu would be limited to a couple of sandwiches from Marks & Spencer and absolutely no frothy ones whatsoever. How typical, then, that John – still crowning my roster of people waiting for a Chimay kelk, the poor fool – telephoned and suggested we adjourn for lunch at Chai Yo at the very instant I tossed my depleted sarnie-box into the bin.

Heavy of heart but heavier of tummy, I decided to err on the side of discretion; yet the prospect of a beer – inevitably, I suppose – was tougher to resist, and John and I were soon contemplating our options for a decent pint. When your host has at his disposal an expense account of mammoth proportions it is sorely tempting to nominate the priciest haunt available; but the priciest haunt seldom boasts the nicest frothy ones, and this tends to sway my deliberations. Time and traffic cones notwithstanding, I reasoned that Burton afforded opportunities superior to Derby's; and, because I had introduced him to the Bridge Brewery and was keen to unveil another treasure, the Coopers Tavern and the Bass Museum emerged as the most enticing candidates for our custom.

"We're passing a lot of pubs, Robbo," he remarked as we crawled through the villages between Derby and Burton.

"Yes," I sighed, painfully aware that the tedium of the journey was threatening to wreck the jaunt, "but they're all crap."

And so they were – at least by the standards of the Bass Museum, the venue upon which we finally settled ("I went to a museum today," he crowed; "Oo, you must be clever," gasped everyone). If the Coopers Tavern was once Bass's unofficial tap – and is now, courtesy of the brewery's lamentable myopia, a bastardized echo of such – then the pub at the hub of

the Bass Museum is its officially-sanctioned heir: certainly it
would be difficult to track down a more delectable specimen
of **Draught Bass** (even if the gratis half-pint – *half*-pint! –
accorded every museum-goer represents the epitome of
predictably wretched stinginess). The museum itself –
whose exhibits include locomotives, a bottle-shaped lorry
and the famous Bass Shires – is jolly entertaining, but the
biggest lures are of the liquid variety and are found midst the
breweriana and oak beams of the bar; and that was where John
and I headed with almost impudent haste.

My lingering tumescence and John's continuing diet meant
neither of us could feast on the charmingly-christened
Cholesterol Timebomb, a vast bap crammed with bacon,
sausage, black pudding and "lashings of full-fat butter"; but I
was consoled by prior cognizance of this culinary masterpiece
(my Bro' and I encountered it 18 months ago, and I have just
about digested it now) and by the mellow **Bass N° 6 Mild**.
The museum is an appropriate spot in which to revel in
sporadic offerings like N° 6, for many are imitations –
some vague, some veracious – of Bass beers of the past: a
quaint and extremely commendable idea. N° 6's ABV is
lofty for a mild's, while its colour is a shade darker than
that of the red-bronze mild made in the West Midlands
town of Walsall by the Bass-controlled Highgate Brewery;
it is very soft and smooth and, like all quality milds,
marvellously drinkable – the perfect lunchtime ale.

Our cultural mission climaxed on something of a
clanging note, though, when John sought to employ his
tabloid skills in signing the museum's guestbook.
Thoroughly captivated by his surroundings, he wanted to
sum up his sentiments with a line of *Sun*-like snappiness.
It has since dawned on me that a witty morsel of *Times*-
like wordplay might have been built around N° 6 Mild and
a *Prisoner* reference (although I still can't think of anything),
but in the heat of the moment John's inherent craving for a
jovial pun could muster only a snippet which, bonce in hands,
I immediately lambasted as monumentally insulting: "Gone for
a Burton!"

"Do you know what 'Gone for a Burton' means, John?" I asked.

"What?"

"It means 'Gone for a Burton Ale'. As in 'Gone for a Draught Burton Ale'. As in 'Gone for an *Ind Coope* Draught Burton Ale'. As in 'Thanks, Bass, but I don't like your beer'."

"Oh."

**Draught Bass:
see July 22**

**Bass Nº 6 Mild
(3.9 per cent ABV):**

November 20

Even though a ludicrous assignment for a national newspaper once dictated that I undergo an uncannily accurate reading by a fortune-teller in Skegness (don't ask), I have never placed too much stock in astrology. Nonetheless, I could not deny a pang of excitement when practically every Sunday supplement's star-gazer presaged a November of extraordinary prosperity and happiness for Capricorns: their confidence in my impending rapture was such that I half-expected Orval to relocate its brewhouse in my back garden.

No wonder, then, that this has been one of the dreariest, bleakest, most miserable and boring months I have ever endured. I was banking on free trips to Bamberg, a Lotus Seven, a mountain of unprecedented frothy ones, maybe a Lottery jackpot; but no. The weather has been unspeakably dank and filthy, casting a cloak of grimness over the country; my days in the office have been tiresome, while my evenings have been blighted by work-related interruptions (murders, abductions – the usual depressing fare); and, worst of all, I've enjoyed precious little beer. So much for those assertions that Saturn was poised to forge

271

a beneficial link with Mars: I suspect Uranus is my dominant
planet, because this has been a complete arsehole of a month.

If I am unable to improve the climate or prevent killing
and kidnapping, though, I can still have a bearing on my
choice of frothy ones. Recently I have relied on Guillo and
Gary to pop into the Bottle Store for me, and this has been
part of the problem: convenient though it is for them to slap
in my requests – and I am eternally grateful for their efforts –
I can only summon the beers which I know will be there, and
so any new arrivals which might occupy the shelves are
doomed to slip through my net. Last night, observing that
drastic action was necessary, I shook myself out of my
November malaise and at last cut a swathe along the Derby
Southern Bypass, storming to the Bottle Store in a whisker
under 35 minutes.

My burst of zest was rewarded – but only just. The thrill
of flinging open the door and beholding hundreds and
hundreds of beers is often tempered by the realization that
I have experienced virtually every last one of them, from
Abbaye des Rocs to Zámek, from Asahi Super Dry to...
er... some other beer whose name begins with Z; and so
it was on this occasion. There were bonuses here and
there (the lagers from Rothenburger, of Reichelshofen,
near Nürnberg; a trio of American ales; a seasonal
witbier from Huyghe, of Melle, Ghent), but the
excursion was not among those visits when I peruse the
supplies with an ever-widening smile and flee with an
axle-straining batch.

There had been the chance of a boost from a bizarre
quarter, my boss having announced last week that an
independent off-licence near his preferred boozer
harboured a vast assortment which might tickle my fancy. I
thought this implausible, not only because his affinity for
frothy ones grinds to a shuddering halt at C&T but because
any establishment in the proximity of the aforementioned
boozer – a dive so unfathomably abysmal that it elicits
withering ridicule even from its loyal clientele – would be prone
to degeneration by osmosis. Despite my doubts, I lumbered him

with a list of brazenly esoteric requirements which would test the most amenable emporium: Andechs Doppelbock, Frank Boon Kriek Mariage Parfait, Van Eecke Watou's Witbier, Cooper's Stout etcetera. I was less than amazed when he declared yesterday that closer inspection had exposed the "vast assortment" as row upon row of Hoegaarden and not a great deal else.

Desperate situations call for desperate acts; and so tonight I strived to alleviate the all-pervading gloom by permitting myself that rarest of treats, Kölsch. This was not Richmodis Kölsch, however, but **Küppers Kölsch** – the lone bottle I had purloined from Leong's consignment, to be precise – and it was, I must concede, not up to the job. Last year I was flabbergasted when Uncle Henny launched into his scathing vilification of Küppers: he did not bellow the oft-proffered criticisms of its pre-eminent position in the sales stakes – Küppers, a modern brewery, has enraged traditionalists with its commercial acumen – but simply slated the beer itself, dismissing it as disgusting hangover-fodder. Well, I should not have questioned Henny's wisdom: Küppers, if Früh and Richmodis are prized as models, is indeed a ropey Kölsch.

As I stressed after savouring a Richmodis in July, Kölsch is such a delicate ale that the contrasts between brands are far from blindingly conspicuous; then again, class will always shine through – and Küppers, to be blunt, isn't exactly radiant. It is soft and sweet but irredeemably bereft of charisma: the term "functional" springs to mind. I would still gladly drink it by the bucketful, for I adore Kölsch and have yet to come across a "bad" one; moreover, I would never in a million moons attack it as furiously as Henny did (although he is infinitely more qualified than I to do so); but I readily admit that it lies several echelons below the elite. It is to Richmodis what La Trappe Enkel is to Orval, what Sainsbury's Hefe Weissbier is to Schneiderweisse.

Which brings me (rather too felicitously, cynics might claim) to the dark Weizen from Erdinger, a brewery which shares

Küppers' status as the largest producer in its field. The nearly-black **Erdinger Dunkel** is rich, chocolatey, moreish and deliciously smooth; it is let down by its finish, which is a mite fleeting, but is nevertheless a splendidly soothing beer.

I relaxed with one while watching *Key Largo,* and for a while it seemed Erdinger and Edward G Robinson would succeed where Küppers had flunked; but then the dreaded pager bleeped, heralding a premature end to my repose.

The message, needless to say, did not inform me of a jackpot win. Russell Grant and Mystic Meg, kindly explain yourselves.

Küppers Kölsch (4.8 per cent ABV):	★★★
Erdinger Dunkel (5.6 per cent ABV):	★★★★

November 22

At around 8.30pm, with Gurminder a handful of points ahead and one gruesome shot after another flowing from my cue, the spectre of defeat was hanging over my dingy corner next to table 15 at the Spot-On. Which beer, I quietly mused, could possibly compensate for my losing at straight pool? I would be the first to toast Gurminder's accomplishment, but the frothy one I raised would have to reflect his momentous achievement *and* console me in my hour of ruination.

The quandary, fortunately, never presented itself. My estimable adversary abruptly fell prey to his C&T and, like Fast Eddie before him, was rendered a shambling shadow of the player who had promised so much; I seized upon his decline and pulled myself together, and by 9.30pm I was gently rolling the three into the side pocket to record a 100-57 drubbing. Gurminder accepted his loss with his habitual grace, and I drove home in the knowledge that any old beer could now be dragged out of the pantry to round off the day.

The pantry, in fact, was slightly bare. It mostly contained ales bought at the Bottle Store in mid-week, and this gave rise to a quandary of another sort: would their sediment have recovered from the trauma of the mad thrash along the A50 from Leicester to Burton? Some might think it a farcically superfluous refinement, but I normally allow my bottle-conditioned ales seven days in which to regain their equilibrium: those in the pantry had been granted only four days' respite, so there was a danger of cloudy frustration if I proceeded.

To my relief, the **Golden Pacific Golden Gate Original Ale** was crystal-clear; and it was a good beer, too. Golden Pacific, of Berkeley, California, entered life as a lager brewery, and Golden Gate Ale – which is more blushing than golden – is as clean-tasting as many a Pils or Export. The sceptic in me pondered whether it might be bottom-fermented, but the realist in me rejected such conjecture as preposterous.

My luck on the sediment front persisted with **St Stan's Whistle Stop Pale Ale**, a stab at diversification by the Californian Altbier brewery of which I am so fond. Transparent or muddied, though, Whistle Stop is rather dispiriting: pale in colour and dull in character, it is ruled by a nasty, disturbingly fake bitterness. The hideous label appears to have been inspired by Chelsea's away kit, an unwitting sin which comes within a grain of condemning Whistle Stop to two-star disrepute. Stick to Altbier, St Stan's.

Proof that you can never be too careful ultimately came in the form of **Ipswich Dark Ale**, which emanates not from Suffolk but from Massachusetts, New England. It was as murky as the weather, and I berated myself for succumbing to my own impatience. The sediment could not have been more displaced if I had battered the bottle against the floor – which, to be honest, was a manifestation of pique which appealed to me enormously. Idiot. Ho-hum: another lesson learned.

The label notes for Ipswich Dark Ale equate its joys to those of chocolate cake, and it would definitely go well with a thousand-calorie pud (although Rochefort 10° is the exemplar for such a deleterious duet); yet it is more coffeeish than chocolatey. The effect is not an instantaneous one, but a roastedness of awesome profundity slowly develops in the long, dry finish. The Indian Monsooned Malabar of beer (dregs optional)?

None of these frothy ones would have fulfilled my criteria if I had staggered out of the Spot-On a broken man; and yet only now is it obvious to me that they would have been inadequate not because they were insufficiently agreeable but because they were insufficiently rotten. I should not salute a Gurminder victory with a classic: I should salute it with an utter stinker. If I vow to greet a trouncing by ceremoniously necking a pint of Carling Black Label, the very concept of which makes me nauseous, then my mental fortitude should double automatically when I am faced with a debacle on the green baize.

As Eddie said: "How can I lose?"

Golden Pacific Golden Gate Original Ale (5.7 per cent ABV): ★★★★

St Stan's Whistle Stop Pale Ale (4.6 per cent ABV): ★★★

Ipswich Dark Ale (5 per cent ABV): ★★★★

November 26

The members of Spinal Tap once boasted that they had toured "the world and elsewhere", but the spectacularly restless Eugene could give them a run for their money. After his short-lived expedition to Hong Kong – which cost me, as I am wont to whine, a "farewell" Abbaye des Rocs ballon – he is now setting a course for that remotest of lands, that most forbidding and forsaken of outposts, Scotland. Another callous desertion of his beer-divvying duties; he'll do well to get a glass from me this time, the git.

Not that our imminent separation is without its advantages. Having been cursed by disaster in my endeavours to cross the border – my Bro' and I had booked a cottage in Dunbar when Aunt Brunhild's `death precipitated a rapid switch in destination – I now have no excuse not to pamper myself with a multitude of weekend breaks. Eugene's patch will be either Edinburgh or Glasgow, both of which have their attractions: Edinburgh is enveloped by some of the most hallowed golfing turf on Earth (to soak up the majesty of the Old Course at St Andrews is one of my ambitions), while Glasgow is enveloped by some of the most hallowed distilleries on Earth (to soak up a tot of Lagavulin at its Islay distillery is another of my ambitions [Islay is an irksome odyssey by ferry from Glasgow, to be fair, but this matters not]). Although I never honoured my pledge to zip to his current abode in Warrington – I blame the troublesome Ayrton, in whom I had lost any semblance of faith by August – I swear I shall frequent McHenderson's Scottish residence. To say so might sound brutal, but I can scarcely wait until he abandons Cheshire.

Furthermore, as Eugene has already astutely identified, an approximate halfway point between Burton and Edinburgh/Glasgow is Cumbria; and within Cumbria is Cartmel Fell; and at Cartmel Fell is the enterprising Masons Arms, where we could meet for an overnight session of examining an extensive hodgepodge of frothy ones from around the globe. As if to practise for that very event, we supped our way through a microcosmic assembly tonight – albeit in the less bucolic environs of Burton and with a bill of fare restricted to English and Belgian ales.

Eugene had nipped into the Dram. His spree was not distinguished by anything startling, but he picked up some Leffe Radieuse and Tripel. His most alarming buy was Wallersteiner Classic, the resurfacing of which has instilled in me a

queasy cocktail of anticipation and tribulation; he also secured
for me a bottle of Wallersteiner Hochzeits Pils and – just
when the Abbaye des Rocs controversy was about to to be
resurrected – an elegant Wallersteiner glass. His lousiest buy
(how was he to know?) was the awfully thin Villers Triple,
which I neglected to urge him to take home to Warrington;
I shouldn't really moan, though, since I also neglected to pay
him for anything.

Before we turned to our Belgian crop – consisting not of
Henderson's haphazard haul but of more dependable wares
amassed during the month – I took Euge to the Coopers
Tavern: as well as acquainting him with its **Draught Bass**, I
had been charged with the task of obtaining a bag of its pork
scratchings for a connoisseur of porcine haute cuisine. The
pub was at its backstreet best: crowded, convivial,
reverberating with banter. I dared to moot a Kimberley
Classic, conscious of having so far studiously ignored it, but
Eugene heaped scorn upon my twisted whim: to nurse a
Kimberley when mere yards from the Bass fermenters, he
cautioned, was tantamount to sacrilege.

To the Belgian array, then, and the chestnut-hued
Riva Vondel. From the producer of last month's
Dentergems Wit, Vondel is a brown ale whose suave
packaging has surely shifted thousands of units. It suffered
through Riva's dithering when it was ditched in 1991
before being revived two years later; now it appears to be
the target of a marketing push. Its preponderant sweetness
is similar to that which afflicts Riva Christmas, the
kindred winter ale by which I was seriously unmoved last
year, and I imagine it has a latent ability to irritate.

Almost as sweet but thrice as downable was my dessert
beer, **Huyghe Blanche des Neiges** (students of French
may be interested to hear that the label is blessedly devoid of
the Seven Dwarves). Hoegaarden-like but softer and less
impressive, it is one of the more rational ales in Huyghe's
brain-boggling jumble; a hit amid a scatter-gun blitz of gallant
tries and wild misses. Among Huyghe's outrageously expansive
range are the tripel-strength La Guillotine (I kid you not), whose

crockery bottle is the bane of pourers everywhere; the equally potent Delirium Tremens (still I kid you not), a spiced ale which is routinely served in a glass decorated with pink elephants (I have often teetered on the brink of purchasing said lunatic receptacle at the Horseshoe, Bruges, before coming to my senses); and the lurid Minty, a liquefied Polo which I have avoided like the plague since the *Good Beer Guide to Belgium and Holland* hailed it as "possibly the worst beer in the world".

It is an exaggeration to brand **Rochefort 8°** a flop; but this dark and strong Trappist ale – which, with its 9.2 per cent ABV and its overall integrity, would spearhead the line-up of many of a brewery – somehow disillusions me. It is very firm, very rich and somewhat dry, and I have always thought it the most intimidating (for want of a more apposite adjective) of the Trappist beers. In plain language, I find it bloomin' hard work.

My dissatisfaction can probably be traced back to the emotional destruction wreaked by a night's debauchery in Brussels and Bruges, the consequence of which was my bouncing off the walls in a state of grave malady at the latter's railway station in the small hours of the morning. Without aspiring to align myself with those self-pitying individuals who proclaim after a grievous session that "one of those 16 pints must have been iffy", I am positive to this day that I was stitched up by a deviant 8°. It is correct to say that my intake included not only Rochefort but Pauwels Kwak, Orval, Mort Subite Gueuze, a towering bottle of Maredsous, copious amounts of Hoegaarden, a vicious witbier-and-liqueur cocktail and a meal cooked in various mighty ales; yet I am sure the damage was done by the Rochefort at the Mort Subite (which, significantly, my Bro' and I have since debunked as an iniquitous grotto of gueuze-stirring). Honest, guv.

While past misdemeanours have left me wary of tackling Rochefort 8°, I had soaring hopes for **Van Steenberge Augustijn Grand Cru**; but they were, I'm afraid, trampled.

They had been hiked by cosy memories of Van Steenberge Augustijn (less the pretentious "Grand Cru" tag) – among the most vivid of the innumerable abbey beers churned out with profit-hungry audacity by Belgium's brewers – whose sorry absence from the Bottle Store this year has caused me trepidation; if Grand Cru has supplanted it I shall be incensed, for Grand Cru is far from being the beer Van Steenberge, of Ertevelde, East Flanders, reckons it is. It looks like Westmalle Tripel, but there the equivalence ends. It is horribly severe at first and only mildly less grating thereafter; I had just about nurtured a hesitant regard for it when I drained the last mouthful.

Oddly enough, the Scottish frothy ones I most admire are shipped to Belgium and essentially unrenowned in their homeland. Low in hop content, dark, sweet and strong, they are believed to be a throwback to the brewing of such ales for British soldiers in Belgium during the First World War. Although the likes of Gordon's Highland Scotch Ale and Douglas Scotch (both from Scottish & Newcastle) are now re-imported into Britain, I do not prophesy stumbling upon them while reeling around Glasgow or Edinburgh with Eugene; and so it looks as though I shall have to brush up on my sketchy appreciation of "wee heavy" before zooming north.

Draught Bass: see July 22	
Riva Vondel (8.5 per cent ABV):	★★★★
Huyghe Blanche des Neiges (5 per cent ABV):	★★★★
Rochefort 8° (9.2 per cent ABV):	★★★★
Van Steenberge Augustijn Grand Cru (9 per cent ABV):	★★★

November 27

I had planned to dish up my hoard of Rothenburger while Guillo and I, zombie-like, stared at another footie-fest tonight. My scheme was scuppered, though, by a friend in need: Guillo, still smarting from his aberrant XL, yearned to return to the Burton Bridge for a stature-restoring pint, so I generously bowed to his earnest demand.

His respect for the Bridge has plainly been dented to a damaging degree. He is a confused man. He is querying his own taste-buds. He protested that the **Burton Bridge Bridge Bitter** was tart: 'twas not, at least in my opinion, although it was disenchantingly cool and therefore far from flawless.

The dodginess of his assessments is evidently confined to the Bridge's ales, since I could not reproach his withering appraisal of the one Rothenburger lager we managed to sample during the soccer. **Rothenburger Pils** did not signal the revelation of a dynamic Franconian portfolio: it sits somewhere between the maltiness of a Bavarian Pils and the bitterness of a Rhineland Pils – maybe unexpectedly leaning towards the latter – and, although clean and crisp, is not notably well-rounded. I had guessed it would be the weakest of the bunch; and now, having confirmed its pedestrian nature, I pray my instincts were valid.

But this business with Guillo and the BB is a disconcerting affair, make no mistake. How I can extract him from his pit of incertitude is a conundrum to which I will have to devote some thought.

Burton Bridge Bridge Bitter:
see January 16

Rothenburger Pils
(4.9 per cent ABV): ★★★

December 2

December is an invidious month. The streets, almost irrespective of the hour, are jammed with frenzied gift-grabbers. Parents grit their teeth and loosen their wallets. The nation's transitory icons stare out from practically every shop window. Commercialization and greed (the latter in various guises, all of them ugly) run riot. The TV schedules plumb new depths. Some of the poorest compositions in the annals of music clog the airwaves. Party-hatted office-workers hurry to the pubs at 11am, seduced by the siren call of Bud Lite. More bad frothy ones are guzzled than at any other time of the year.

To cap it all, my beer-hunting is slightly hampered by the annual crackdown on drink-driving. Let me stress with all haste that I never consume more than the equivalent of a pint of low-strength British ale prior to getting behind the wheel (and my intake is usually less than that); yet in December motorists are exhorted to touch nary a drop, which gives rise to awkward moral and ethical dilemmas. It is irrefutable that anyone who exceeds the drink-drive limit from January to November and then politely adheres to the legislature when the police are out in force should be locked up without hesitation; but is anyone who habitually relishes a pint, graciously abstains during December and then resumes his or her routine once the festive season is over not guilty of – if nothing else – a contemptible exhibition of hypocrisy?

I have covered more court hearings involving drink-driving than I care to recall and need no lectures on the misery caused and the lives destroyed by the fools who booze and cruise. It does occur to me, though, that to deny myself that infrequent lone pint for the next four or five weeks would be insincere in the extreme: if I think it acceptable and harmless to indulge to a minimal and perfectly legal degree for the vast majority of the year – and I am not sanctimonious enough to pretend that I don't – then I must think it acceptable to do so now, notwithstanding the government's have-none-for-the-road pleadings. Those who modify their behaviour for one month out of 12 surely recognize, if they are fundamentally candid with themselves, that they have only their own interests at heart: they are apprehensive not about flouting the law but about being collared.

Having wrestled with double standards, I wrestled with a double helping of Franconian lager – in my own home, mark you, and with not a vehicle in sight. It is typical of the cellar management I have demonstrated throughout the year that I am hurtling into this chilliest of months with a comprehensive stockpile of bottom-fermented beers and little in the way of warming ales, but – as I have stated before and shall inevitably say again – there is nothing amiss with a cold beer during a cold snap: the mood of the imbiber must invariably take precedence over the mood of the weather, and I pined for something cool while engrossed in Edward G Robinson's fiery performance in *House of Strangers*. It turned out to be a reasonable decision, for **Rothenburger Edel** and **Rothenburger Dunkel** represented a sizeable improvement upon last week's tedious Rothenburger Pilsner.

Although "Edel" is German for "noble", Rothenburger Edel is not a grand beer in any language; but it is a moderately intriguing one and deserves courteous investigation. It is essentially what Bavarians term a "Helles" – an everyday, pale-golden lager – yet it is more bitter than most, with a coarse but entertaining spritziness. Its finish is infinitely more rounded than that of Rothenburger Pilsner, which it soon shows up as a rather gauche and sloppy beer.

The red-brown Rothenburger Dunkel is better again, although not by a massive amount. It has a dense, creamy head; a malty body; and a tremendously dry finish, perhaps underscored by vaguely biscuity notes. A moaner could wail that it is not unlike a slew of other Dunkel beers, and there is no question that such an argument would be depressingly accurate: being a moaner myself, I must whine that genuinely impressive Dunkel has been tough to come by this year – the gorgeous Kaltenberg König Ludwig Dunkel being a prominent exception.

Rothenburger Edel (5 per cent ABV):	★★★★
Rothenburger Dunkel (5.2 per cent ABV):	★★★★

December 5

Oops.

I seem to have made a – ahem – minor miscalculation in my appraisement of **Wallersteiner Classic**, the lager whose sludge content (or should I now say "alleged sludge content"?) earned it a savaging and the stigma of a one-star rating. You see, it transpires that said substance might not have been sludge at all: it was probably sediment. For Classic is unfiltered; and I, to my disgrace, neglected to realize this. The odds are that what I seethingly deemed an offensive micro-organism was nothing more sinister than an immense chunk of yeast deposit which I had artlessly dumped into my glass. And so it elates yet embarrasses me to report that a beer I condemned to the basest echelon, a beer I sentenced to bunk with the utterly evil Asahi Super Dry, can now be unmasked as thoroughly excellent. Sorry.

Shambolically incompetent and horribly imprecise I may have been, but at least I should be afforded credit for my probity. I could have opted not to allude to Classic's Tony-Bennett-like comeback. I could have attributed my faux pas to a dirty glass. I could have blamed El Niño, the much-maligned climatic phenomenon off the west coast of South America (it is, after all, made accountable for everything else at the moment: global warming – El Niño's fault; earthquakes in San Francisco – El Niño's fault; pile-up on the B5012 near Cannock – El Niño's fault; clod incapable of identifying unfiltered lager – El Niño's fault). I could have hidden from the truth or concealed it myself; but no.

And yet, for all my inexcusable ignorance and subsequent magnanimity, I can scarcely conceive that the rudimentary blunder of my having incorrectly disturbed and distributed the sediment in that inaugural Classic can explicate the seismic disparities between it and its successor. I had surmised that the disagreeable perplexities of July's original had been answered when I pulled tonight's from the fridge, held it up against the light − entirely by chance − and saw those tell-tale wisps; but now I'm not convinced. The first was lifeless and distressingly insipid; the second was bright, fruity (lemony?) and hugely refreshing. The contrasts, I feel, are too enormous to ascribe to my ineptitude alone.

Maybe it was an instance of unfortunate coincidence, of two wrongs making a blight. I reckon there *was* something treacherous about that first bottle − exactly what we shall never discover − and my stupidity either exacerbated the problem or, so that justice might be done, merited my exposure to it. The largely affable nature of the Wallersteiner beers I have encountered since that confounding cataclysm, coupled with the suspicious but defensible similarity to Classic of tonight's **Wallersteiner Hochzeits Pils** (it boasts the same fruity tang but less panache; an emasculated rehash?), suggests that the brewery does not draw an abundance of scathing criticism; and so I shall gallantly retract my own vicious attack. Hey, we all make mistakes.

Let history be rewritten.

Wallersteiner Classic
(see July 19 [★]):   ★★★★★

Wallersteiner Hochzeits Pils
(5 per cent ABV):   ★★★★

December 6

With cupboard space at a premium and a cornucopia of kelks, bollekes and flutes clogging up every available surface in the kitchen and dining room, I concluded it would be wise to

urge my benefactors in Germany to laden Mum with beer
rather than glassware at the culmination of her latest trip.
Strictly speaking, what use is an Atlbeker without a bottle of
Uerige? What use is a Berliner Weisse tumbler without a
bottle of Schultheiss? Very few glasses are as tantalizing
when empty as they are when full.

There is a difficulty with this stance, however: 99 per cent
of glasses are desirable, whereas a significant proportion of
frothy ones are not. Every glass I have acquired has been
welcomed – even my Wrexham Lager Krug, which is to be
applauded for its wonderful hideousness – but countless beers
have brought disappointment. And there is a further
complication: as has been illustrated at numerous junctures
this year, a concoction of crushing ordinariness is often
cloaked by a breathtaking bottle and luscious labelling. Even
the cognoscenti are conned from time to time, so what hope
is there for the unwitting?

Which is why Aunt Gudrun, matriarch of Mum's side
of the clan, proudly dispatched to England a **Sailer Franz
Joseph Jübelbier**. She selected it, according to Mum,
because she "liked the bottle": one of those bombastic
crockery efforts, snazzy, swing-topped, complete with
dainty handle and an autumnal portrait of a Bavarian
castle, it must have caught many an untrained eye. What
Gudrun didn't know was that Sailer, of Marktoberdorf,
near Augsburg, in the southern region of Bavaria, knocks
out captivating bottles but somewhat banal lagers.

Jübelbier is a rusty-red Dunkel (which hardly endears it
to me, since the words "rusty" and "red" conjure up
nightmare images of my MG). It has high carbonation, yet
its head – despite an incipient creaminess – proves to be fast-
fading. A stupefying maltiness dominates from start to finish,
although the effect is not objectionable; and a compensatory
hint of coffee gradually emerges from somewhere.

Superior things are expected of Haake-Beck Kräusen,
Mum's more well-advised pick from the supermarkets of
Nienburg. Meanwhile, she informs me that her dedicated chums
are defying my plea for restraint and continuing to accrue

donations to my collection: it is touching to learn as much, of course, but this loyal clique of pensioners is poised to cost me the price of a kitchen extension.

**Sailer Franz Joseph Jübelbier
(5.5 per cent ABV):   ★★★**

December 8

Tonight I was finally reintroduced to the peculiar fascinations of the Yew Tree, the infamously bizarre pub in the disconcertingly desolate corner of Staffordshire that is Cauldon. Although its remote location – its nearest neighbour is a spooky cement-works – imbues it with a perturbing "Slaughtered Lamb" quality (remember the "You made me miss!" scene from *An American Werewolf in London?*), it repeatedly vies for the unofficial title of Greatest Pub in Britain. It is not an establishment upon which folk casually stumble, and – except for the yew tree in the centre of the car-park – there is nothing profoundly attractive about it from the outside even if they should; but inside is arguably the most bedazzling boozer in the country.

The lighting is inadequate, the furnishings are on the dilapidated side of well-worn, and everything could do with a brisk dusting; but all of these ostensible shortcomings are vital ingredients of the Yew Tree's charm. A pub it may be, but it is also a living museum: crammed with antiques (music-boxes, 1950s TVs, penny-farthings, pistols, grandfather clocks, pottery from Stoke-on-Trent [which lies approximately a dozen miles away]), sundry Victoriana (including a pair of Queen Vic's stockings) and pure ephemera (swordfish blades, a gruesome "dog-carrier" [the operation of which should be left shrouded in mystery, methinks]), it is an astonishing testament to the character of landlord Alan East. Each and every dingy nook and cranny houses some sort of relic – midst the myriad heirlooms, to the perverse rapture of beer-lovers who shudder at the thought of the repulsive rubbish foisted upon the public in the '70s, is a Watney's Red Barrel lampshade – and the ramshackle ambience probably disguises an array of artefacts which would amass a small fortune at auction.

When I first visited, circa 1992, a pint was barely more than a quid; that barrier has now been breached, but the deftly-kept **M&B Mild** is still outstanding value. Brewed in Smethwick, Birmingham, M&B Mild is the lesser of the low-gravity ales from Bass's Mitchell and Butler subsidiary (its Highgate cousin is the preferred brand); but it is dark, dry, roasted and gently nutty. What nicer way to spend a blustery December night than to nurse a half of M&B while perched on a pew from St Mary's Church, Stafford, encircled by imposing banks of Polyphons and wooed by Daisy, the Yew Tree's indolent and reprehensibly fickle moggy?

The preceding hours were not so gratifying, alas, with a quest for Yuletide treats providing skimpy dividend. Aside from the predictable glut of seasonally-tagged British ales (of which undignified cash-ins constituted a detestable quota) and a sprinkling of lousy Belgian fare (the saccharine Riva Christmas, the tongue-deadening Bush de Noël), there was bugger all. Amid the multitudinous letdowns, the dearth of German stuff was particularly irksome; yet even that frustration was a mere blip of bother next to the soul-sapping absence of Anchor Our Special Ale, the consequent perpetuation of whose mystical splendour offered horrendously meagre consolation.

M&B Mild
(3.2 per cent ABV): ★★★★

December 10

The ultimate putdown for a beer was revealed to me in queer circumstances today, and I am anxious to share it. And guess what? It was coined by a Robinson.

Enlightenment came while I was watching *A Slight Case of Murder*, a gangster flick which Warner Brothers made in 1938 to quell outraged protests that the genre had spiralled into gluttonous violence. The machine-guns still spat bullets, the hoods still pummelled each other into oblivion, the corpses still mounted up to the ceiling; but it was a comedy – so that was all right, then.

Edward G Robinson (who else?) starred as Remy Marco, a racketeer whose beer is worshipped as ambrosia during Prohibition but renounced as bilge when the authorized brewers return to the fray once the ban is repealed. His prime income vanishes overnight as punters by the thousand appreciate their desperate days of seeking refuge in a Marco's are no more. "We'll never have to drink his beer again!" enthuses one erstwhile customer. Remy, like the drivel-mongers of today, is incredulous: he considers his beer impeccable. Nowadays, I suppose, Whitbread would pay him to contract-brew Budweiser.

Could there possibly be a beer worthy of the "Remy Marco's" cachet? Could any frothy one, even an Asahi Super Dry, satisfy the exigent prerequisites of such a humiliation? Not tonight. A brewing-by-numbers lager like **Rothenburger Vollbier** – the dreary antithesis of its label notes, which impudently and erroneously tout it as "full of taste" – could slip into the role if I were unconscionably bellicose, but I am not; the commendable **Jezek Gold**, from Jihlava in the Czech Republic, is protected by its Budvar-like hue, its chewy hoppiness and its long finish; and the stunning **Haake-Beck Kräusen** is in diametrical opposition to Edward G's ostracized output.

I first enquired after Kräusen when Mum mentioned that my cousin Ortrud was embarking on a shopping expedition to Bremen, where Haake-Beck is based. I couldn't recollect its name and so requested that my dutiful relation simply set off in pursuit of the unfiltered incarnation of Haake-Beck Pils. Ortrud obediently checked out a convenient bar and was assured by the staff that such a beer did not exist – rather like being told by a Burtonian that Pedigree is a figment of your fevered fantasies. It was Mum herself who, responding solely to spotting the Haake-Beck monicker while pushing her trolley, purchased a Kräusen from her sister's local superstore. Haake-Beck's is among the foremost examples of Kräusenbier, a lager which has had a dosage of wort added during conditioning and has then been spared the filtration process. It has a titanic, bright-white head; a delicate, yellowy cloudiness; a soft, yeasty, invigorating body; and a fairly bitter finish, maybe with a dash of vanilla. How sad it is that the stupendously middling creation from another Bremen brewery, Beck's, is extolled in a host of nations while Kräusen, a veritable masterpiece by comparison, is news even to the less astute barmen in its own city; but then in the sphere of beer, where brilliance is seldom rewarded on an appropriate scale, 'twas ever thus.

Cheers, Remy!

Rothenburger Vollbier (4.7 per cent ABV):	★★★
Jezek Gold (5.2 per cent ABV):	★★★★
Haake-Beck Kräusen (4.8 per cent ABV):	★★★★★

December 12

Imagine being a head brewer. Smart job, eh? Now imagine your boss, a munificent bloke, ambling into your office one day and declaring: "Tell you what, mate, you brew whatever you want. Carte blanche. Go crazy." Blimey, how irresistible can a vocation be? Paradise; or is it?

Such is the freedom Marston's has apparently granted under its Head Brewer's Choice scheme. As I have complained before, the project has sporadically thrown up a winner – Oyster Stout is one which springs to mind – but more often than not has delivered a duffer. Upon reflection, although it might strike the layman as a hoot, could churning out 12 or so beers a year be deplored by the professional as a chore? Enviable though the assignment sounds, it cannot permit a deal of scope for refinement: there is a production-line air about the ritual, an inkling that the exercise is a smidgen *too* experimental. Before today's **Marston's Iron Founders Ale** I could sermonize from no real position of expertise, since my experience of the extant range had been restricted to the odiously lame August Wheat and the cloying India Export Pale Ale; but now, after a third "so what?" beer on the bounce, the possibility that the Head Brewer's Choice is too multifarious for its own good cannot be discounted.

Even the notes in the Marston's pamphlets dotted around the Royal Oak, Abbots Bromley, where Stuart and I had a delicious lunch, couldn't get excited about Iron Founders, a distinctly unremarkable addendum to the Head Brewer's Choice portfolio. Perhaps a doting relative at a loss for an expedient Christmas present would like to buy me a hefty batch of Iron Founders' fellows, for provincial prejudice and the curse of sentimentality mean I remain loath to slate Marston's if I can cite a mitigating factor — although I admit that maintaining my support grows increasingly arduous by the month.

A pertinent Head Brewer's Choice for tonight would have been the "rich, dark, mellow" (it sez 'ere) Monk's Habit, because I at last managed to tick off that lingering instalment of *Cadfael;* but, as I made clear in September, only a Trappist ale ranks as a legitimate accompaniment to the escapades of ancient Shrewsbury's most devout detective. To that end I betrayed my own principles, as the pantry's paltry yield constrained me to insult the baddie-bagging Brother by sheepishly sipping **Leffe Radieuse** and **Leffe Tripel** during parts one and two. I dragged out my only **Orval** during parts three and four (well, why rush it?), but prior to that I was compelled to fall back on a clumsy compromise.

Last year I pitched a Leffe Radieuse against a dessert of mocha ice-cream at the Spinnekopke, Brussels, in the wake of coquilles St Jacques à la Rochefort (with Orval) and carbonade flamande (stewed in Liefmans Goudenband and devoured with a bottle of the same). The sweet and warming Radieuse – a brown ale of ample flavour and sturdiness but, absolutely crucially, sparse complexity – was a smashing match for the ice-cream; yet the Orval, much as it did tonight, accentuated without a shred of mercy the gaping chasm separating the Trappist ales from their abbey imitators. It is a very pleasant beer, but – even though "Radieuse" translates as "halo" – it is not holy enough for a *Cadfael* session.

Leffe Tripel has been the De Kluis contribution to Interbrew's ubiquitous family of abbey beers since 1992. It has a vested De Kluis edge, with a nose distantly resembling those of Julius and Grand Cru, but it doesn't possess the sophistication of the bona fide Hoegaarden ales. It is, I'm afraid, no better or worse than a plethora of analogous tripels. Like Radieuse and the third powerful member of the Leffe troupe, the dubbel-ish Vielle Cuvée, it is pivotally deficient in one salient virtue: class.

Which brings me back to Orval; which brings me back to Iron Founders. Orval makes one beer; Marston's makes more than I can endeavour to document. I rest my case.

Marston's Iron Founders Ale (3.8 per cent ABV):	★★★
Leffe Radieuse (8.2 per cent ABV):	★★★★
Leffe Tripel (8.4 per cent ABV):	★★★★
Orval: see February 28	

December 18

I witnessed something extraordinary today. My inherent grimness precluded me from proclaiming as much, but romantics might have interpreted it as a Christmas miracle. It briefly shocked me; then it thrilled me; and then it infused me with a rosy glow and the chirpiest of attitudes. It was a spectacle I never dreamed I would behold, especially in such uninspiring surroundings; but there it was.

I had gone to a bargain-basement wine outlet with our picture editor (who was keen to procure a stack of cheap plonk with which to bribe other media types) and was perusing the mundane merchandise in its beer section when I noticed an elderly gent – nudging his 60s, I would venture – impetuously probing the jumble of Pedigree, Heineken and alcopops. He was manifestly dismayed by the paucity of his favourite tipple, and the snob in me pondered what it might be. Was he scanning for Skol? Craving a Carling? Bursting for a Bud? I could have swooned when, in enlisting his wife's aid, he promptly divulged his beery passion.

"Can you see any of that wheat-beer?"

I raised my eye-brows and loitered, eager to hear more. Ever the cynic, I mused that the root of his hankering lay in one of two explanations: (1) a committed Marston's buff, he had dabbled in August Wheat and somehow developed a bent for it; (2) his grandchildren had charged him with the task of obtaining a heap of Hoegaarden, all of which would be swigged from the bottle by a coven of style-conscious teenagers. He painstakingly examined each disorganized row on each cluttered shelf, snooping behind four-packs on Kronenbourg and ferreting around in a tumult of tinned trash, his impatience intensifying by the second. Exasperated, he eventually summoned an assistant and – to my skittish glee – asked where he would find the wheat-beer from Löwenbräu (he pronounced it "Low-en-brow", naturally, but you can't have everything).

The assistant heaved a boxful of Löwenbräu's filtered Weizen from the bowels of the storeroom; my hero gathered six bottles, jovially telling him: "Aye, it's a lovely beer, that." I yearned to interject, to propose that this uncanny disciple of Weizen track down a crate of Schneiderweisse or Erdinger Pikantus; yet I kept my trap shut, fearing he would dismiss me as an interfering and pretentious prat. It quickly became obvious that he needed no meddling from me, since he crowned his securing of a sextet of Klares Weizenbier with a raid on the hoard of Samuel Adams Boston Lager. All I could do was humbly follow his initiative. A fabulous faith-restorer: it was only right that tonight's **Pete's Wicked Maple Porter** was slurped in his honour.

Limply described as "a robust porter with a smoky maple flavour, coloured with caramel", Maple Porter is one of the triumphs of Pete's recent explosion in invention. To employ the beer-and-cake metaphor advocated by last month's Ipswich Dark Ale, I would say it has the traits of a rich, heavy fruitcake – more so in its bouquet, however, than in its body or finish. It is very dark, a red tinge just about discernible; and it has a dry, prolonged aftertaste. After fatuous tosh like Honey Wheat and Summer Brew, both of which were terribly naff, it is a blessed relief.

Here's to you, old man – whoever you are. Enjoy your Low-en-brow.

**Pete's Wicked Maple Porter
(5.4 per cent ABV): ★★★★**

December 19

A Christmas Day beer bonanza is looking decidedly implausible. If I am to observe my "leave seven days to settle" axiom – and who would want their Chrimbo frothy ones corrupted by agitated sediment? – the hour for mustering many of the world's most illustrious ales has long since expired. I have penned a missive to my Bro' and counselled that he equip himself with a Weizen for the unwrapping of his goodies, a pre-turkey Orval, a Rochefort 8° to chaperon his pudding, a post-meal Hoegaarden Grand Cru and an "Off to bed kids" Westmalle Tripel; yet the preponderance of such delights can now be erased from my own potential menu. Judging by the stragglers in the pantry, I'll be lucky to get a Jezek Premium.

Two more prospective poisons for December 25, both of them Belgian, were dissipated today. **Lefèbvre Floreffe La Meilleure** and **Van Steenberge Piraat** were called into service to mollify my simmering fury after plans for a last-ditch jaunt to the Bottle Store were aborted because of traffic congestion of morale-shattering magnitude. To gorge on them at this premature stage rather than preserve them until the pseudo-festivities was no disaster – laudable though they are, neither is a beer to be saved for a specific occasion – but their removal from the pantry has rendered my puny stash an even gloomier sight.

Lefèbvre's Floreffe ales are among the sublimer abbey beers, and its Abbaye de Bonne Espérance (which doesn't bear the Floreffe alias but is a darker revamp of Floreffe Tripel) is one of the very elite; but whether this qualifies the brewery to christen its flagship product "The Best" is monumentally debatable, since La Meilleure doesn't even eclipse its immediate peers. If the abject daftness and misguided smugness of its name can be disregarded, though, La Meilleure is a pleasing beer: potent (although not as punchy as it was), sweet, a tad creamy and distractingly challenging. The silly Floreffe ballons I bought several years ago are frosted, like the mug for Lefèbvre Barbar, and are therefore proficient in obscuring the beers instead of enhancing them; but this sensory deprivation is proper punishment for my heinous crime of lavishing money upon such absurdities.

Piraat is a curious beer: is it a tripel, a Duvel-like "strong golden" or just a strong ale? As it has some of the nuances of each, the ambiguities of the third classification must be the most fitting. Alarmingly, its awesome clout – 9.7 per cent ABV – is evinced nowhere on the crude label; but anybody who feasts upon Piraat without rapidly fathoming the acute perils of so doing is bereft of the tiniest iota of perception, because its prodigious wallop is conspicuous from the first tentative gulp. It is a floral beer, although Duvel and company are far more flowery; it is warming but less so than Gulden Draak, its Van Steenberge sibling; and it bravely borders on the harsh.

Six days to go, then. Drastic action required. And I really don't know where to begin.

Lefèbvre Floreffe La Meilleure (8 per cent ABV):	★★★★
Van Steenberge Piraat (9.7 per cent ABV):	★★★★

December 20

Pass the JTS Brown.

For roughly 18 months now Gurminder and I have exchanged jocular banter with two venerable chaps who play snooker on the table adjacent to ours at the Spot-On. We respectfully refer to them as the Old Masters. They mess up their pots, bicker, ridicule each other, laugh, have a cuppa and generally amuse themselves. The closest my pool-shooting comrade and I have come to a game with them has been when our cue-ball has taken to the skies and clattered into their table. Until tonight, that is. Tonight we went the whole hog and engaged them in a bout of doubles, Gurminder and I setting out to parade straight pool's patent supremacy by squaring up to the Old Masters at their own sport and subjecting them to a ruthless thrashing. Snooker? Pah. Straight pool is like Anchor Our Special Ale – arcane, elegant, intricate; nine-ball is like Pete's Wicked Lager – dynamic and beguiling but intrinsically brash and graceless; eight-ball is like Miller Lite – moronic, appealing to the lowest common denominator; three-cushion billiards is like Cantillon Kriek – puzzling and malevolent initially, fulfilling and magnificent when understood; and snooker is like a musty bottle of IPA – dull, short of sparkle and to be eschewed.

Quite how assiduously it is to be eschewed only became plain, though, when Gurminder and I were remorselessly trounced. The

Old Masters wiped the floor with us. They bludgeoned us. They massacred us. My highest run was one; Gurminder, unless my excruciating memories of the debacle are specious, rattled in a six or a seven. What would Minnesota Fats, Fast Eddie Felson, Willie Mosconi, George Balabushka et alia have made of our dreadful, mortifying, atrocious capitulation? It was the night straight pool nearly died of shame.

After a doubles pasting, then, a dubbels tasting: **Lefèbvre Floreffe Double** and **Van Steenberge Bornem Dubbel**, both sampled during a contemplative review of *The Hustler*. Given my post-drubbing daze, it was no surprise that they didn't have me leaping from my seat in ecstasy; I was nonetheless a trifle baffled by Bornem Dubbel's sheer triteness. Floreffe Double is somewhat pale but is spicy and smooth; Bornem Dubbel is paler still, with an oak-coloured tint, and is annoyingly dry. My conduct on the green baize did not warrant bounteous spoils, and I did not receive any.

Old Masters, I drink to you. Next week, I swear, you shall be obliterated; and I shall toast straight pool's renaissance in suitably glorious vein.

Lefèbvre Floreffe Double (7 per cent ABV):	★★★★
Van Steenberge Bornem Dubbel (8 per cent ABV):	★★★

December 21

The pantry is now officially devoid of Christmas beer, the solitary aspirant, **Dolle Brouwers Stille Nacht**, having bowed out just three days before the Silent Night from which its appellation is derived. Never have I floundered towards the 25th with such a pathetic arsenal of frothy ones to help me through the ordeal: last year was pretty ghastly, but this year threatens to scrape the bottom of the barrel – and it's not even a barrel of anything decent, damn it. Furthermore, as I have already lamented, it is too late to do anything about my demeaning predicament.

At least the Stille Nacht was not wasted, even though my electing it was very much a knee-jerk reaction to the unforeseen arrival of guests. My cousin David and his brood popped in to convey their season's greetings, and I generously handed David a Gordon's Douglas Scotch – a gesture of altruism I seriously regretted as soon as I gazed upon the alluring combination of the beer itself and the thistle-shaped glass in which such ales are customarily presented. Having bestowed liquid loftiness upon others – even my cousin's 15-year-old son was allocated a tot of Becker's (better his underage carousing be confined to a Rhineland Pilsner than to Hooper's Hooch; and it *is* Christmas) – I was not prepared to refrain from joining in the flamboyance; and so, to a chorus of coos, out came the Stille Nacht and the tall-stemmed Dolle Brouwers goblet.

Stille Nacht, the Mad Brewers' Christmas cracker, is amber-claret, dry and spicy, with a sweet and faintly vinous finish. It seems stronger than it is, although it is in no way forbidding, and I fancy it would be an enthralling beer after but a year's prudent storage (Dolle Brouwers ales mature superbly: I once tried a mid-'80s vintage of Oerbier, the brewery's maiden product, at Kulminator, and it was sensational). Superior to David's Douglas Scotch, more germane than his boy's Becker's: I believe that's 1-0 to me, lads (ah, how the Yuletide spirit flows through me).

The demise of my Christmas cache was trivial compared to the disillusioning, crippling cruddiness of my nightcap. Earlier this week, hailing his eccentric inclination as proof that beer-hunting is not as exclusive a hobby as its detractors might claim, I trumpeted the senior citizen who rocked me on to my heels when he solicited a load of **Löwenbräu Klares Weizenbier**; but that was before I had reminded myself of the "lovely beer" he so cherished, and now I am a broken man. Löwenbräu Klares Weizenbier, to be blunt, is crap.

Yet maybe I am being unfair – not to the Weizen, which is unequivocally dire, but to its wizened fan. He should be praised for his open-mindedness, for the incontrovertible fact is that he dared to

be different. He could have strolled out with a litre of Rolling
Rock under one arm and a trillion tins of Castlemaine XXXX
under the other – this, on the woeful evidence of the activity
at the tills, appeared to be the done thing – but he sought
out a Bavarian wheat-beer; and that it was a Bavarian wheat-
beer of ineffectual calibre is perhaps neither here nor there,
for Löwenbräu Klares Weizenbier may well be a "lovely beer"
in the opinion of someone yet to graduate to Schneiderweisse
or Spaten Franziskaner. My only wish is that one day, either by
fluke or by design, he takes that critical step from his
contemporary fave – bland and unavailing, every bit as feeble as
Kaiserdom Weizenland Kristallklar – to something he will think
even more enchanting; and then next year I'll walk into that
same shop and, grinning broadly, glimpse his frenzied search
for Aventinus.

**Dolle Brouwers Stille Nacht
(8 per cent ABV):** ★★★★★

**Löwenbräu Klares Weizenbier
(5 per cent ABV):** ★★

December 22

An unlikely Santa he might be, but has Eugene rescued
Christmas? He has laid his paws on a pair of relevant ales
which contain no sediment and are thus eligible for
Christmas Day decanting – some feat. Congratulations to
him: he has handsomely out-manoeuvred me. Courtesy
of his benevolence, I can now confront the 25th with the
comfort of two apt beers: Gordon's Xmas, a Yuletide
variation on the Scotch theme; and Bush de Noël, the
skull-splitting palate-grater from Dubuisson, of Pipaix,
Hainaut (okay, so I rejected it at the Bottle Store; but
beggars can't be choosers).
   Tonight was principally a whisky night – 12-year-old
Highland Park, polished off during a *Scrabble* duel which
veered from the turgid to the torrid – but Henderson and I

darted into the Bridge Inn for a swift frothy one in advance of our Leong's. The **Marston's Pedigree**, as ever, was beyond reproach; yet now is the time, with the year in its terminal throes and the last Marston's soaked up, to commence my assessment of whether Pedigree sincerely justifies a top-10 grading.

Back in February I underlined that there could be "no arguments" about Pedigree's prestige, but niggling misgivings have crept in since that audacious avowal. Timothy Taylor Landlord is paramount in my affections for British ales, while Burton Bridge Summer Ale is the runner-up; and it goes without saying that it will be bloody hard for the third-placed beer to squeeze into a top 10 culled from all the premier classics around the globe. It is immaterial, I ought to emphasize, that the ratio of pubs whose Pedigree is scandalous easily outweighs the ratio of pubs whose Pedigree is blissful: negotiating the minefield of reckless landlords and fallacious methods of dispense is part and parcel of tracing an ideal specimen of any beer (although the crusade for an unadulterated Pedi, I must acknowledge, is more tiresome than most). What worries me above anything else is the transformation of Marston's into a "national" concern: it is no longer independent, having been swallowed up by Wolverhampton and Dudley (Banks's), and miscellaneous fingers are in miscellaneous pies — a corporate identity is evolving, empires are being built, pubs are being homogenized and robbed of their charisma. Hoegaarden, Hoegaarden Grand Cru, Julius and Verboden Vrucht were slowly stripped of their herbal subtleties when De Kluis flourished into a giant, and the history of the brewing industry is littered with kindred tragedies; might my protracted allegiance to the Marston's cause be blinding me to Pedigree's decline in a congruous situation?

For now, though bedevilled by dubiety, I will stick to my guns: as I said, tonight's Pedigree was beyond reproach. It retains its stature as a top-10 *contender* (I use the word advisedly); and in nine days I shall rule on whether it is a successful one.

Marston's Pedigree: see February 3

December 25

Two beers? **Young's Luxury Double Chocolate Stout** and **Gordon's Xmas**? Is that the lot? Aye, sometimes your heart isn't in it; and today mine wasn't. If you don't kick off Christmas Day as though you mean business − a Buck's Fizz breakfast or, as I recommended to my Bro', a Weizen with the undressing of the prezzies − the battle is virtually over. Actually, the battle was over weeks ago: the poverty of worthwhile Chrimbo frothy ones (as opposed to normal beers with tweaked recipes and snow-trimmed labels) heralded my downfall, and my remissness in omitting to net an enticing assortment of substitutes (Trappist ales would have been just dandy) sealed my fate. I always had a notion that this would be the outcome. Humbug.

There were fleeting grounds for encouragement when, having scurried into the Wine Rack to wind up my annual fit of frantic aisle-pounding, I hazarded upon a box-set of German beers. "The New Pick of Germany" was daubed across a sepia-toned photograph of a timbered Brauhaus, and I was rummaging around for my last coppers before you could say "rip-off". I recalled that I once invested in "The Pick of Germany" at Small Beer, Lincoln, in '94 or '95 and was quietly impressed with it: Allgäuer St Magnus Heller Bock, Schwanen Schöfferhofer Hefeweizen and Ur-Krostitzer Premium (a pale lager, not to be confused with Köstritzer Schwarzbier) were the most memorable of its constituents.

It did not take long to deduce who had been responsible for this "New Pick": Binding, of Frankfurt, the biggest brewer in Germany. The extent of the stitch-up unfolded before me as I scrutinized each bottle's minutiae. A *real* "Pick of Germany", one bidding to depict regional and stylistic diversity, would feature the likes of Zum Uerige Altbier, Dortmunder Union Export, Becker's Pils, Fürstenberg Pilsener and Schneiderweisse; this inequitable quintet consisted of a Binding-influenced Altbier, a Binding-influenced Export, two Binding-influenced Pilsners and a Binding-influenced Weizen. Even that nostalgic photo was of Binding's bygone HQ. That's what you get for not studying a beer's notes before kissing goodbye to your own.

Of course, there might be a momentously spectacular frothy one nestling in this bunch (although I doubt it), but I have no more ardour for it than I would for a "Pick of Great Britain" which focused only on beers from Scottish & Newcastle. And when it dawned on me that the Weizen I had earmarked for this morning wasn't even cloudy – and what a dismal distortion of Bavarians' wheat-beer predilections that gutless piece of marketing wizardry is going to inflict upon novices – my extant zeal, such it was, evaporated.

And so my bibulating amid the baubles was instigated with a stout at dinner and rounded off with a Scotch ale when the Yule Log was unveiled. No Anchor Our Special Ale; no Kaltenberg Königliche Festtags-Bier; and no *Morecambe & Wise* to assuage my suffering. My Bro' fared just as poorly, having captured not one of the beers I had endorsed in my letter; yet fraternal Schadenfreude could not – and cannot – camouflage my personal failure.

My glumness may have swayed my evaluations, since Young's Luxury Double Chocolate Stout surely cannot be as modest as I thought it. The brewery, of Wandsworth, London, is renowned both for its draught and bottled ales, and a beer of such mediocrity would be a startling anomaly; it happens, though. Young's barley wine, Old Nick, would have brought more Christmas cheer, despite the inauspiciousness of its Satanic connotations. But then no beer can supplant Anchor Our Special Ale when it comes to partnering the year's most revered roast.

Gordon's Xmas, however, is a dessert beer of substantial accomplishment: after all, any ale which can stand up to the sickliness of Yule Log must have some positive properties. In colour it is between the chestnut of Gordon's Highland Scotch and the near-black of Gordon's Douglas Scotch; and it is rich, intense and bitter-sweet. Caké, roaring fire, *Harvey* on the video, a ruminative ale – gosh, it was almost Christmas there for a minute.

Incidentally, why is turkey at the core of the year's most celebrated meal? This is a bird which is universally denounced as irredeemably arid and tasteless, so why should it be used for the mother of all slap-ups? Beware: if this trend were widened to encapsulate beer we would all be commemorating the Lord's birthday with Asahi Super Dry.

Young's Luxury Double Chocolate Stout (5 per cent ABV): ★★★

Gordon's Xmas (8.8 per cent ABV): ★★★★

December 27

As presaged, straight pool's reputation was resurrected tonight with the vanquishing of the Old Masters: our grasp of snooker's petty idiosyncrasies having improved, Gurminder and I salvaged the integrity of Mosconi and his Balabushka-brandishing cohorts by chalking up a 4-0 win. Also as presaged, I saluted our victory with a terrific frothy one: **Guinness Original**, the bottled edition of the most well-known stout – if not the most well-known of all beers – on Earth.

The saga of Arthur Guinness and his brewery rivals – outshines, to be frank – the stories of Pierre Celis and Hoegaarden and Fritz Maytag and Anchor. Guinness began brewing in County Kildare in 1756 before moving to Dublin in 1759, but it was only after more than 40 years that he switched from sweet ale to porter: the beer which was to become instantly recognizable from Belfast to Brussels to Boston was labelled "Porter Stout" back then, although the "Porter" designation was duly jettisoned. By the 1900s, Arthur Guinness II having defined the "dry stout" genre by using unmalted roasted barley (thereby ducking severe taxes levied against malt), Guinness – a brewery established with the princely sum of £100 – was the largest brewer in Europe; and by the 1920s it was the largest on the planet.

There are nearly 20 versions of Guinness, some brewed in such exotic lands as Africa and Malaysia, but its admirers are almost unanimous in their insistence that it is at its finest on draught in Dublin. To dissent is churlish: Pilsner Urquell is at its freshest in Pilsen and De Koninck at its yeastiest in Antwerp, and Guinness is as inextricably linked with its own home city as either. Guinness Original, though, is an aesthetic alternative for the house-bound aficionado: what it lacks in smoothness and creaminess it makes up for in spiciness and dryness, and its elaborately drawn-out finish is restitution for the draught's elaborately drawn-out "slow pour".

A necessarily precious beer with which to acclaim the Old Masters' ruination, then; and, lest anyone should ache for a germ of applicability, let us not forget that it is an Irish expatriate and entrepreneur, Michael Phelan, whom the Billiard Congress of America traditionally dubs "the father of American billiards" (crikey, these beer-and-pool connections get more tenuous by the month). While revenge is a dish best served cold, though, Guinness certainly isn't: contrary even to much of the brewery's own advertizing, it most beneficially expresses itself at cellar temperature rather than in beaded-glass mode. A top-tenner when it was bottle-conditioned and unpasteurized – the hatchetmen swooped in 1993 – and still beautiful now; and very probably the last classic of the year.

Guinness Original
(4.3 per cent ABV): ★★★★★★

December 28

Eugene's Christmas gift of **Dubuisson Bush de Noël**, which I spurned on the 25th after being mortally underwhelmed by the proceedings, was today allowed to flex its muscle on

Belgium's behalf in a contest for the European Heavyweight Championship. Few Belgian beers of gargantuan gusto whoop and holler about their capacity to incapacitate, and – like Dubuisson's year-round ale, the majestic Bush Beer (which, at 12.2 per cent ABV, is the country's mightiest frothy one) – Bush de Noël invites subdued deference rather than the clamorous moronity associated with Carlsberg Special Brew and its loopy-juice clones. It is an unassuming bruiser, a Lennox Lewis of an ale.

In the other corner, beating its chest for Germany, was **EKU 28**, once the undisputed king but now a Tyson-esque figure of forlornness. Its labels still exalt it as "the strongest beer in the world", but this is misleading nonsense: the quoted ABV percentage of 11 – a dejectedly conservative estimate, for once it was vaunted as 13.5 – sends it plummeting down the pecking order, and Samichlaus, from Hürlimann, of Switzerland, was ratified as the most alcoholic of lagers, denying EKU 28 even that dodgy accolade.

Dubuisson ("buisson" is French for "bush") axed its other ales in the early '80s after Bush Beer carved out a quasi-monopoly in sales. This Orval-like concentration on a single product resulted in Bush's being eulogized as one of Belgium's superlative beers. Bush de Noël – launched a decade after Dubuisson reduced its line-up to one – is more strident than its hoppy, dry, chewy stablemate; yet, although rasping, it is strangely moreish and – as would be expected – fantastically warming. Both Bush Beer and Bush de Noël are filtered but unpasteurized; and both are amber-red, with Bush de Noël narrowly the darker of the two.

EKU (whose full title, Erste Kulmbacher Unionbrauerei, harks back to the 1872 merger of two breweries) is one of four breweries in Kulmbach and has a duo of the area's most famous beers in Kulminator, its "standard" Doppelbock, and EKU 28, a perniciously all-out revision of Kulminator (in Germany it is sold as Kulminator 28, the "28" pertaining to its gravity in degrees). There are those who

305

view EKU 28 as nectar, a 'flu-curing sledgehammer to be nipped before bed; and there are those who repudiate it as intolerable syrup; I am somewhere betwixt these diametric schools. EKU 28 is not manufactured with the gormlessness flaunted in the fabrication of some of the canned rocket-fuel venerated by imbeciles (it is lagered for nine months, stretching the brewer's skill to the maximum); then again, tackling a bottom-fermented beer of such colossal maltiness and fruitiness is an unsympathetically stiff test.

So which is the European Heavyweight Champion? Neither. Belgium has a legion of beers more deserving of the laurels (e.g. Rochefort 10°, Westvleteren Abt, Bush Beer), and Germany is not without its own (Kloster Irsee Abtstrunk is a belter in every sense of the word). It would be interesting – and a bundle of fun, too, I'll wager – to survey a crop of candidates en masse; but whether I would be capable of communicating my findings from the ensuing coma is another matter altogether.

Dubuisson Bush de Noël
(12 per cent ABV): ★★★★

EKU 28
(11 per cent ABV): ★★★★

December 31

The year has ended not with a bang but with a whimper: like too many beers, today's frothy ones slotted into that troublesome decent-to-good category. How maddening; but it's at a time like this that I merrily reassure myself, with Lao-tzu-like logic and a deepness liable to strain anybody's brain on New Year's Eve, that if all beers were excellent there would be no excellent beers.

A day of lagers got underway with **Jezek Premium Lager**, an Urquell-ish companion to the Budvar-ish Jezek Gold. Although the latter has haughtier ambitions, Premium is the more agreeable – albeit not by much, and it doesn't impart the marvels implied by its bewitching Bohemian blush. Its chief asset is the ebullience of its label notes, which are crested with a cartoon hedgehog and read so: "Savour the malty flavour and enjoy the distinctive hoppy aftertaste. In Jihlava we say that this beer, like the hedgehog, has prickles but a soft heart." Infectious. A drab duet next: **Erbacher Premium Pils** and **Binding Export**. Erbacher is light in colour and the same in body, although it has a modicum of maltiness; it is brewed with spring-water in the Odenwald National Park, which is all jolly bucolic but doesn't lift it above cipher status. Binding Export is the fuller-bodied of the two, as befits an Export, but is spinelessly one-dimensional: how ludicrous it is that just about the only Export to sneak out of the Ruhr Valley should be an atypically vapid one. Both of these bores are in Binding's "New Pick of Germany", whose misplaced arrogance is comical yet simultaneously enraging.

There was a reason for my selecting **Samuel Adams Boston Lager** as the final beer of the year: I never expect to see it again – not in Britain, anyway. No longer content simply to import Boston Lager and Boston Ale, Whitbread – the genius behind UK-brewed Heineken Export – unleashed in 1997 its despicably ersatz Boston Beer. The Samuel Adams paradigms gave way to fraudulent fizz – flogged in cans, naturellement, and enveloped in hackneyed hype – and Britons were swindled out of a cluster of appetizing frothy ones. I was gobsmacked when I marched into the Bottle Store to be met by a cans-and-glasses display of Whitbread's Boston Beer; amazement ceded to anguish when I confirmed that the genuine articles had been totally usurped.

Boston Beer, for all I know, may since have perished, a victim of a kinkier fad; but the Boston Lager famine prevails. Tonight's bottle came from an out-of-date consignment at the cash-and-carry where I was duped into shelling out for a Löwenbräu Klares Weizenbier (although it should be remembered that the OAP who triggered that idiocy also seized a Samuel Adams), and I don't forecast similar serendipity in the future.

Once hawked door-to-door by Jim Koch, the Harvard-educated executive who abandoned his career to form the Boston Brewing Company in 1985, Boston Lager is a stalwart of the American beer revival. It is darker than a Pilsner but paler than a Märzen, hoppy, soft, malty and then dry. It is not as stirring as its New York adversary, Brooklyn Lager (how I tremble at the concept of a "Brooklyn Beer", but who knows what lunacies could be perpetrated in this avaricious age?); yet I would still mourn its departure from these shores.

Big Ben chimed. I drained my glass. And that was it.

Jezek Premium Lager (4.9 per cent ABV):	★★★★
Erbacher Premium Pils (5 per cent ABV):	★★★
Binding Export (5.3 per cent ABV):	★★★
Samuel Adams Boston Lager (4.8 per cent ABV):	★★★★

LAST ORDERS

A vintage year? To be absolutely blunt, nope. The top 10 will be revealed in due course, but I can assure you at this premature juncture that its predecessor hasn't undergone a radical revision in the past 12 months. I don't wish to imply for an instant that my imbibing during these 365 days has proved unenjoyable; but it would be ridiculous to pretend that I haven't known better years.

I'm about to risk contradicting the brave assertions I made at the start of my latest annual crusade, but I must say this: I simply haven't travelled abroad enough. I remain painfully aware that part of the raison d'être for these scribblings was to illustrate what gratification could be derived from scouring supermarkets, ferreting around in off-licences and investigating pubs; but when you've been engaged in those diversions for a few years, as I have, it is inevitable that the majority of fresh pleasures will be uncovered further afield. I recall declaring in January that I usually manage to snatch an "occasional" junket to Belgium: this year "occasional" has equalled "two", and that's pretty damned hopeless. The fact is that a vast percentage of the foreign frothy ones which fell into my grasp in blighty had already been slurped in previous years; and the only way to avoid that sort of disappointment is to cross the water a little more frequently.

Those jaunts to Belgium – taking in Brussels, Ghent and Antwerp – were unquestionably the highlights of the campaign. I reacquainted myself with a smattering of established favourites – I would never ignore a rare opportunity to sample a De Kluis Benedict (more of which anon) or a Bordeaux bottle of Abbaye des Rocs – and also clocked up an amusing array of first-timers, among them the impressive Bosteels Tripel Karmeliet, the spicy Friart St Feuillien Blond and, somewhat incongruously, the sturdy Löwenbräu Triumphator. Yet everything seemed to conspire against subsequent excursions overseas: obstacles included cash, commitments, work and – supremely gut-wrenchingly – the sheer bad luck which saw my Bro' visit England during a fortnight when it was infuriatingly impossible for us to flee to mainland Europe together.

While it has left me a tad dispirited, however, this state of affairs should not distress anyone else; nor should it deter them from seeking out treats from home and abroad without the need to brandish a passport. As I said even before that account-opening Burton Bridge Top Dog Stout on January 5, beer-hunting is often a matter of compromise: it's just that after all these years of plucking Schneiderweisse from shelves in Sheffield, all these years of loading up with

Liefmans in Leicester, I'm growing a mite tired of compromising. Rorschach, the psychotic anti-hero in the cult comic novel *Watchmen*, advocated never compromising and was promptly vaporized for his obstinate stance: I am more than willing to compromise, for I recognize it is habitually essential, but next year I would dearly like to do so on a less regular basis.

Even without a thrilling itinerary, though, I've succeeded in tasting plenty of beers. I can't put an exact figure on my intake – I'm sad, but I ain't *that* sad – yet it must be comfortably beyond 200 different frothy ones. Encouragingly, the sound 'uns have outnumbered the grim 'uns; and occasionally there has been a genuinely brilliant find (Straffe Hendrik Brune, Brooklyn Lager and Neptune ACME, for example). Moreover, despite repeated trips to the Burton Bridge (hey, give a guy a break: it's a lovely boozer), I certainly haven't toppled into the injurious trap of restricting myself to one pub, one beer or one style; and that's why – irrespective of the sorry absence of jet-setting – I've encountered beers from around the world and in forms ranging from Bock to bitter, Pilsner to porter, Märzen to mild, steam to stout.

Grading those beers has not been easy. Any ranking method has its inherent flaws, and I lumbered myself with a particularly tricky one. It was tempting to employ a "poor, passable, good, great" system, but I couldn't help remembering how Fast Eddie reflected on the death of Minnesota Fats in *The Color of Money*: "There were levels above levels, and Fats was at the top." The line between an excellent beer and a classic beer is a fine one; the line between a classic and a top-10 contender is finer still; and the line between a top-10 contender and actual entry to the top 10 is virtually imperceptible; yet the distinctions have to be made, regardless of how pernickety (and, of course, intensely subjective) the required calculations are.

As it happened, the year witnessed three beers slip out of the elite and threw up four would-be replacements. Those relegated were De Kluis Hoegaarden Wit (plunging to "excellent" status [which is hardly a disgrace, I suppose]), Pilsner

Urquell (demoted to "classic") and – aye, I'm afraid it had to be – Marston's Pedigree (which stayed a top-10 contender but ultimately failed to secure one of those precious slots on the A-list). The prospective substitutes were Anchor Liberty Ale, Burton Bridge Summer Ale, Richmodis Kölsch and Aecht Schlenkerla Rauchbier; and, having agonized over their relative merits, I have decided Schlenkerla is the unfortunate candidate which should loiter on the fringe for at least another year. Not a dramatic amount of movement to show for 12 months' quaffing, then; but I never expected extravagant modification, to tell the truth.

And so the top 10, in the wake of 200-odd frothy ones and at a cost upon which I don't really care to dwell, is – in the traditional no-order-whatsoever format – as follows:

Orval	**Schneiderweisse**
Abbaye des Rocs	**Burton Bridge Summer Ale**
Anchor Our Special Ale	**Westmalle Tripel**
Anchor Liberty Ale	**Richmodis Kölsch**
Timothy Taylor Landlord	**De Kluis Benedict**

Should these be universally hailed as the 10 sublimest beers on the planet? I think not. They are without doubt *some* of the sublimest beers on the planet, and I might even go so far as to suggest that two or three of them should grace anybody's pick; but I am not sufficiently pious to insist that the entire selection is incontestable. Each to his own; yet I would have no hesitation in wagering that a beer buff who equipped himself with every one of the above would struggle to complain (and he would be ceremoniously chinned if he did dare to dissent, obviously).

There is no enormous worth in detailing the reasons behind my choices – the answer, quite frankly, could be boiled down to a fundamental "I love 'em" and merely left at that – but there are a couple of issues which I would like to raise before signing off.

The first concerns a topic I have mentioned before: how memories of a beer can manipulate one's affections for it.

311

Almost exactly 12 months ago, in introducing "the beers to beat", I admitted that Westmalle Tripel was finally – and rightly – elevated to the loftiest echelon only after my Bro' and I were beguiled by the monastery at which it is devotedly fashioned; now Richmodis has joined the premier pack on the strength of similar influences. I candidly concede that Richmodis might not have attained a "classic" stamp, let alone hurtled into the top 10 like an exploding cork, had it not been for my rose-tinted recollections of reclining on Uncle Henny's patio and my consequent fondness for the lone Richmodis in which I revelled this year. I can make no excuses for such inequities: this is a purely subjective exercise, as I stressed earlier, and my heart has a big a say as my taste-buds when it comes to compiling the roll of honour (besides, it *is* a beautifully delicate ale; and I don't envisage boasting cherished memories of Skol or Miller Lite, so a lousy beer should never profit via this reminiscent route).

Secondly, a brief word about De Kluis Benedict. I have to wonder whether it is fair to incorporate in the top 10 a beer whose production has long since ceased: on balance, it probably isn't. To urge people to rush out and attempt to procure an ale which isn't even made any more is a trifle silly; and so, although it will maintain its standing as top-10 material until Kulminator's stocks are exhausted, Benedict – an exquisite beer whose demise typifies all that is wretched about the brewing industry – will be removed from its berth with the utmost discretion when the ensuing quest draws to a close.

That tragic but sensible act is another year of beer away; and I shall carry on supping all-comers throughout that period, because the pursuit of the perfect frothy is never over. Robert Trent Jones, the most prolific creator of golf courses there has ever been, had a stock response when asked to name his crowning lay-out: "Why, I haven't designed it yet." It would be a foolish and rather unromantic man who felt able to proclaim that he had drunk a beer which would never be bettered; and that's why the search continues. Cheers.